There's a ship to sail tomorrow
On God's waters wide and deep.
There's a guide that will go with her
That will never slv

He watches ove
The Commandei
And He'll not foi
And the Old Red,

Lewis E. Seeley, May 1941

I am thinking of you, Mother
Though I would not cause you pain.
We are going out to battle
And we may not meet again.

God knows the hidden dangers
As we enter the bitter fight.
We are under His protection
And He always does the right.

But while I am in His keeping
What so e'er He wills to do,
I have ever found Him faithful
(He reminds me so of you.)

Now I reach by faith to touch Him,
As you have taught me to,
While you pray, I'll fight! Defending
Our dear Red, White and Blue.

After the conflict is ended,
Should a gold star replace your blue,
Be brave and courageous dear Mother,
'Twas for my country and you.

Lewis E. Seeley, September 10, 1942

A Personal Journal
Aboard a World War II Destroyer
(U.S.S. Rowan DD 405)

Lewis E. Seeley

and

Lorraine Seeley Buell

ISBN: 1-882127-02-1
www.ussrowan.com

Published by
MagicImage Publishing
740 South Sixth Avenue, Absecon, NJ 08201
Phone: (609) 652- 6500
Fax: (609) 748-9776
www.magicimage.com
sales@magicimage.com

President
Michael D. Stein

Layout & Production
John Conforti

Manufactured in the United States of America
Printed and Bound by McNaughton & Gunn Lithographers

Table of Contents

Dedication

In memory of those who died on September 11, 1943...

ALLARD, John E., F2c
ANTONNELLI, Rocco, S1c
ARCHIE, Mathis A., CMM
ARMSTRONG, James, StM2c
ATTINGER, Frank E., B1c
ATWELL, Charles E., S1c
BASS, Wallace E., MM2c
BENT, George G., SF3c
BERNARD, Neldor P., S1c
BERG, Edmund L., S2c
BERRIGAN, Walter A, F2c
BESSELL, Lester R., S2c
BLAIR, James W. Jr., S1c
BLOOMER, Frank J., RM3c
BOUTIN, Ernest J., S1c
BOWEN, Donald V., GM1c
BOWMAN, Merle A., FC(M)3c
BREITKREUTZ, Julius A., 1c
BROWNING, Leslie E., S1c
BRUCE, Robert V., ENS
BRYAN, Melville A., S1c
BURKE, James F. II, SM2c
BURKE, John W., S1c
BURTON, Lorene L., F2c
BURY, John L., S2c
BUSHTA, Frank A., F3c
CABLE, Stanley R., S1c
CANTRELL, LeRoy, 1c
CASH, Paul H., GM3c
CECIL, James R. Jr., S1c
* CHASZAR, Joseph W., CSP(A)(AA)
CHRISTENSEN, Earl E., EM2c
CHURCHILL, Thiel C., S2c
CLONINGER, Marl J., WT1c
COLE, Ray E., BM2c

COLLINS, Fred F., MM1c
COLLINS, Clarence E., Ck2c
COLLINS, Rudolph, S1c
CONROY, James A. Jr., S2c
COX, Donald J., S2c
CROGAN, Henry E., RM3c
CURTIS, Ralph M., FC(R)2c
CWIECK, Waclaw, S2c
DEBRUYN, Gustav C., SoM3c
DENNISON, Marvin H., TM3c
DILL, Robert A., CEM(AA)
DILLON, John B., EM1c
ELLIS, Homer H. Jr., TM3c
ENGLEHUTT, Walter L., MM2c
ERICSSON, Warren C., S1c
ERNST, Raymond, CMM(AA)
ESTABROOK, Albert E., CPhM(PA)
FAHNESTALK, Harvey C., 2c
FERGUSON, Azra H., CMM
FERGUSON, Lewis H., EM3c
FIETZ, John E., LT(jg)
FIGHTMASTER, William H., S1c
FOX, William H., FC(M)1c
FRENCH, Clayton F., S1c
FRETWELL, Billy C., TM1c
FURLOW, Talmage R., EM2c
GELINA, Jose, St1c
GEORGE, Tony G., F1c
GIALOMBARDO, John, S2c
GOLDMAN, John L., EM2c
GRONEK, Alexander F., Cox
GREEN, John J., LT(jg)
GRUEHL, George R., SoM2c
GRUEL, Clifford L., WT2c
GUESS, Delbert E., MoMM2c

COLLIER, Willis O., F2c
GUTHRIE, Harry O., S2c
HAMER, John C., S1c
HANNA, Frederick K. Jr., F2c
HARDEE, Wilber J., S2c
HARKEY, Robert J., S2c
HARRELL, Eugene, F2c
HARRISON, Hosla C. Jr., S1c
HARTER, James W., MM2c
HEDGES, Marion F., MM2c
HOFFMAN, Edward G. Jr., S1c
HOOVER, Francis H., EM2c
HOWELL, James H., F2c
HUFFMAN, Warren M., S1c
HUGUENIN, Harry J., RM3c
HULL, Harold H., F2c
HUNTER, Carroll E., GM3c
HUTCHENS, Delbert, S1c
INGERSOLL, David W., WT2c
ISMAEL, Carl A., RT2c
IVANS, Peter, WT1c
JAGLO, Frank M. S1c
JAMES, Joseph H., S1c
JENKINS, William F. S1c
JOHNIDES, John A., MM2c
JOHNSON, Lewis A., MM2c
JONES, Vincent C., S1c
KANE, Thomas, F1c
KASTLER, Calvin O, S2c
KELLEY, Willis D., MM1c
KENDRA, Theodore J., MM 2c
KENNEDY, Olin S. TM1c
KERR, Mervin W., TM2c
KING, Joseph W., QM2c
KISTLER, Robert S., S2c
KLINCK, John, MM2c
KRAL, Jack J., S2c
KRISSAK, Albert F., MM2c
KUBRAK, Louis F., MM 2c
LAAKMAN, Henry F. Y2c
LABORDE, Joseph, BM2c
LACOMBE, Donald J., s2C
* LANE, Roy J., TM3c
LANKFORD, James R., TM3c

GUNNOE, Willie, S2c
LEA, William T., Jr., SF2c
LEE, Simon, GM2c
LOE, Ethan E., Jr., RM2c
LOE, Shirley O., SK3c
MACKIE, Wiley T., LT(jg)
MARTIN, Robert A., F1c
MASTERS, Willard E., S1c
MATTHES, Glenn E., MM1c
MAYBERRY, Vernon. S., Jr. MM1c
McCAULEY, William B., TM3c
METZLER, Albert C., MoMM1c
MICIOTTO, Camile A., SC2c
MILTON, Edward J., Jr., GM2c
MOFFETT, Charles E., GM3c
MOODY, Ernest G., Jr., Ck3c
MOORE, Clyde L, B1c
MOORE:Grover K., MM1c
MURPHY, Ben W., F1c
MURPHY, Burl R., SoM3c
MYERS, Glenn D., EM3c
NEIL, William E., F1c
* NIETO, Antonio M. , Jr., S2c
NIMMONS, John T., Jr.S2c
NOURSE, Stephen H., GM3c
NOVAK, Robert J., F2c
NOWOSIELSKI, Andrew F. Jr., S1c
O'DONNELL, Claude J., EM2c
O'MALLEY, James R., S2c
O'REILLY, Edward J. Jr., TM2c
PADREZAS, William B., S1c
PAPINI, Setmo J., S2c
PAPPAS, Leo L., EM3c
PARK, Thomas P., S2c
PAROLISI, Douglas E., S2c
PERRELLI, John A., S2c
PITZER, Richard E., SC2c
POWER, Joseph, CWT(PA)
PRUETT, Russell R., S1c
RETALLACK, Herbert S., F2c
RIDENOUR, Henry E., S2c
RIVERS, Harris A., RM3c
ROBB, William G., MM2c
RODGERS, Garthia D., SF2c

ROSE, George R., RM3c
RUEL, Rene J., SoM3c
RUNG, Frank H., CMM(AA)
RUSSELL, Frank M., TM3c
SANDERFORD, Herbert H., S1c
SANDI, John, S1c
SHAFFOLD, Francis M., SC3c
SCHECTER, Louis, PhM3c
SCHULTZ, William O., SC3c
SEDGELEY, Norman E., F1c
SEELEY, Francis K., SC1c
SEMO, Charles J., F2c
SHANK, Leonard R., BM2c
SHELDON, Leslie R., F1c
SIDES, William A., S1c
SJOSTROM, Harold G., CMM
SMITH, Donald, EM3c
SMITH, Donald W., S2c
SMITH, Harold D., S1c
SMITH, Silas W., TM3c
* SNYDER, Richard H., F2c
STERN, Arthur, ENS
SOWDER, John G., MM1c

STOCKER, Winfield C., TM3c
STORTI, Carmine A., M1c
SUPERNOIS, Donald W., CMM(AA)
TAYLOR, Paul L., StM2c
TAYLOR, Walter B. Jr., MM1c
VANEK, Donald W., S2c
VENTERS, George J., SoM3c
VIETH, Arlington W., CSP(A)(AA)
VRTIAK, Joseph, S2c
VUNCANNON, Junior, S1c
WADE, Alwin G., MoMM2c
WALL, Frank A., Gunner
WARNKE, Walter W., F2c
WELCH, Albert Jr., F3c
WELLS, Robert D., MM2c
WHITE, William R., QM3c
WITLOCK, Ashby A. Jr., MM2c
WILSON, James G., S2c
WISE, Robert L., MM1c
WOOD, Lewis S., MM2c
WORTHINGTON, Floyd E., RM3c
YATES, Raymond H., TM2c
ZILKE, Samuel G., Jr., GM2c

*Indicates Passenger from the *Rhind.*

...And of those who survived

ABBOTT, Robert F., F2c
BARRALE, Anthony F., RM1c
BARRY, David J. Jr., RM1c
BROWN, Leo F., LT(jg)
BULLINGTON, Walter R., RT1c
BYXBE, LeRoy, S2c
CLAY, Malcolm A., S1c
COLE, John D., Cox
CROWDER, Norman M., CSK(A)
DANIELSEN, Roy P., WT2c
DAVIS, Lloyd J., FC3c
DAVIS, Bertice F., GM3c
DePRIEST, Billy, CFC(AA)
DESCH, Bernard H., SoM2c
EGAN, James I., SoM3c
EASTERLING, Wayne H., S2c
* ECKSTEIN, John R., S1c
FINNELL, James E., S1c
FORD, Robert S., LCDR
GAGNON, James S., SoM2c
GARRIGUS, Walter F., TM2c
GLENN, Everett M., LT
GRAY, Festus P., S1c
HAGEN, William H., S1c
HAGGERTY, Edward J., Y2c
HAINES, Martin L., ENS
HARVEY, Ernest C. Jr., SM2c
HENNESSY, Richard J., S1c
HENRY, Ned, S1c
HILL, Robert B., S1c
HIRSCHHORN, Fred Jr., LT(jg)
HUNTER, Gerald D., S1c
ICENOGLE, Leonard R., S1c
JILCOTT, John H., SM1c
JONES, Murry M., F2c

KESS, Stephen F., TM1c
KEY, Frank, FC(R)2c
KOZLOWSKI, John, FC(M)1c
LANOUE, Russell V., ENS
LARSEN, Robert E., S2c
LAUGHLIN, William A., S2c
LAYNE, Ralph Jr., S2c
LEECH, James B. Jr., S2c
MAZAITIS, William J., S1c
McCALL, Rupert C., RM3c
McCARDIE, Harold J., Cox
McROBERTS, John D., S2c
MERKER, John G., S2c
MIKLOSI, Albert A., S1c
MILLSPAUGH, John D., S2c
MOORE, Robert C., S2c
NEAL, Allen W., S1c
O'CONNER, Joseph V., S2c
OSTOPOWICZ, Leonard L., S2c
PAEZ, Rudolph, SoM2c
REA, Howard W., LT(jg)
*RICHARDSON, John, ENS
RILEY, James G., F1c
SARVER, James F., S1c
SCHWANN, Robert W., SoM2c
SEELEY, Lewis E., SC1c
SENTER, William C., F3c
SPIECHER, John S., LT(jg)
STODDARD, Spotswood D., LT(MC)
TEFFT, LeRoy H., S2c
THOMAS, Meryn E., S2c
ULIANO, Richard T., CCS(AA)
VOGEL, Louis W. Jr., Cox
WHONUS, William H., CBM(AA)
WYATT, John, LT

* Indicates Passenger from the Rhind.

Acknowledgments

Many people helped make this book possible. The list would probably be longer than the book, itself. Still, I would be remiss if I did not take this opportunity to thank:

Lewis E. Seeley, my dad, who put up with endless cross-examination while I waded hip-deep through his memory.

Helen J. Seeley, my mom, who taught me the finer points of language from the time I was little and who edited with a VERY sharp pencil.

Chris Harvey and his amazing memory for details, who patiently reviewed sections with me over and over until I got the picture; and who introduced my parents.

Bill Ward, who put this story in perspective.

Stephen F. Kess, for his carefully maintained diary, which helped me so much.

June Rouse, editor and friend without equal.

Linda Anderson, publicist, who helped me navigate the dark waters of self-promotion.

Michael D. Stein and John Conforti of MagicImage Publishing.

"Woody" Woodward of the *Bristol* crew.

The crew of the *Rowan*, who thoughtfully answered all my questions.

The families of the *Rowan* crew, who were so supportive.
Relatives and friends who read the manuscript, commented on it, and lovingly remembered missing details.

And finally, Ken Buell, my wonderful husband. Without his love and encouragement, I never could have gotten this far. Thanks to him, there is a last chapter!

Foreword

On a stormy night in December 1982, Mom and Dad came out to Chicago to visit my sister and me. Dad told us about the nightmares he had been having; flashbacks to the night when the ship he had served aboard in World War II was sunk.

His sister, he told me, had suggested he write his story down but since he didn't have much skill as a writer, the task seemed impossible. "I can write it for you," I offered without hesitation. "In fact, I would love to do it. Tell me the story and I'll write it for you." I was envisioning a few interviews, a month or two of work and that would be that. I didn't realize I was embarking on the journey of a lifetime.

When I sat down with Dad and a tape recorder, I asked him to tell me what happened, in his own words. "Well," he replied, "The ship was torpedoed and sunk in forty seconds."

I waited for him to go on. When he said nothing more, I joked, "Dad, this is going to be a short book if that's all you have to say."

He apologized but after so long, he said, it was hard to remember. And his general quarters station didn't put him in line to see much of the ship's action. If only we could track down other survivors, they could help. Dad felt that one person in particular would be key - his best friend aboard the ship, Ernie Harvey. He had been a signalman on the bridge, up where the action was. But what were the chances of finding him after forty years?

For my father, beginning this project was just what he needed to breathe new life into his retirement years. He and I began putting the pieces of the story together, each for our own reasons. He saw the book as an opportunity to record the past for future generations. Initially, I saw it as a project to which I could apply my writing skills with the goal of publishing it one day. The differences in our motivation didn't matter. We worked well together. When I asked him questions, he would answer me as thoughtfully and honestly as he could, and I was often surprised by his candor. He allowed me to get to know him, sharing with me his fears and doubts, his joys and triumphs in a way rarely experienced in parent/child relationships. This alone made all the effort worthwhile.

As we worked, I discovered too many holes in Dad's memories and it soon became obvious that his initial observation that we needed to find Ernie was correct. I determined to find him, although I had no idea how to go about it. Worse yet, I didn't have much to go on. All I knew about Ernie Harvey was that he came from Georgia originally, and had been blinded by shrapnel when the ship exploded. He married his Philadelphia-born nurse and later, with her assistance, became an attorney. But where would they be living after all this time?

I decided to start my search in my hometown at the Skokie, Illinois library in the out-of-state telephone book section. I looked up E. Harvey in every Georgia telephone directory. I wrote to each of them. In March 1983, on the day that I was going to California to meet my parents at my uncle's house for a family reunion, I received a letter from a Decatur attorney - Mr. E. Christopher Harvey. Even before I opened the envelope, I knew this was the one. In his letter, he said that when he saw "L.E. Seeley" (my initials are the same as my father's) on the correspondence from me, he thought he "was getting a letter from a ghost."

With Chris's help, the project began to take on a new dimension. Not only was his memory sharp and clear, he also had some addresses of other survivors. Through his contacts, I got the address of *Rowan*'s captain, Robert S. Ford. I wrote to Captain Ford and made an appointment to visit him on my next trip to the West Coast. During that visit, I sat with the captain and his wife for many hours and explored his memory. I was struck by the depth of his grief and guilt, even after all these years. I knew from the other men of the crew that I had spoken to that Captain (retired Admiral) Ford was not well liked. I wondered what would happen if they could see him the way I saw him during that visit.

Over the next year, we located a good number of survivors and former crew. From there, it didn't take long for talk to begin of a *Rowan* reunion. The first reunion, held in September 1985, was really where we began pulling together all the pieces of *Rowan's* human history. Armed with a tape recorder, a box of blank tapes and note pad, I spent four full days asking questions and listening to answers. Because I knew so little, I wasn't ashamed to ask questions and no one seemed to mind answering. All that research, however, left me with the monumental task of organization. It was like trying to put together a giant jig saw puzzle without the photo to go by.

Once I had a transcript of the tapes (Dad undertook that Herculean task), I had to put the text in a logical order. I wanted to make it something that anyone could understand, even someone who had never been on a ship before. June Rouse, my first editor, helped me immeasurably. She had no Navy background and didn't know a fo'c's'le from a fantail. If she didn't understand a term, I would take the time to work an explanation into the text.

After I had the personal stories straight, I had to put them in an historical framework. There were times when every surface in my office was covered with books, maps, action diaries, interview transcripts, and earlier edited versions. My objective was, to the best of my ability, to write a story that was not only entertaining but also accurate.

In the face of this lofty goal is the indisputable fact that oral (and even written) history is an inexact science, and sometimes even so-called expert sources disagree on certain points. This telling is not perfect nor does it include all the wonderful anecdotes that were shared with me, and I would like to apologize now to any of the former crew of the *Rowan* or other historical experts for any inaccuracies they might discover. Oversights are unintentional. Sometimes I had to improvise because I just couldn't make sense of a story with the information I had available. While most of the dialogue is fictitious, it's "plausible." A few things were fabricated solely for the sake of the tale.

In spite of all this, *Shipmates* is a labor of love and I have given it the very best I knew how.

Lorraine

I am weary of my journey
For my sea is dark and rough.
I can not think. I can not see
But Jesus knows and that's enough.

When I am lonely and forsaken,
Foes annoy and friends rebuff,
My heart is stone, I walk along,
But Jesus knows and that's enough.

When my eyes are closed forever
No temptations can ensnare
Oh, may I hear the gentle whisper
"Weary one, I know, I care."

When I am living in His presence
In that city four square
Thrilled with joy and sweet remembrance
When He said, "I know, I care."

In a vision I was standing
Beneath the harbor lights
Gazing out over the ocean
When a ship came into sight.

Hark! I hear some calling.
I raise my hand to my brow.
"Mother! Look! See! Here we are
In the lookout on the prow.

Suddenly I awoke to find
I had fallen asleep and dreamed
But my heroes had called and waved to me
It was all so real, it seemed.

But I cannot dream on longer
They are in danger, 'tis true.
But the mighty Rowan sails gracefully on,
Bearing the Red, White and Blue.

Lewis E. Seeley, July 23, 1942

11 September 1943

A thunderous explosion tore through *Rowan* and pitched me forward against the bulkhead. Another, even louder, rocked us to port.

"Control! Control!" I shouted through the telephone hanging around my neck. "What's going on?" I could hear nothing on my headset. Just dead silence. At first I thought a gun had exploded but in a blink of an eye, the lights went out in #2 upper handling room and all the familiar sounds of the ship stopped. I was scared. In the eerie silence, I could hear a sizzling, like cold water dripping onto hot metal.

Rowan heeled violently to starboard, then back to port tilting ever deeper astern. She was going down! I was numb with disbelief and fear. How could this be happening? I wasn't prepared. I didn't know what to do.

Instinct took over where reason failed. Through the darkness, I groped to find the dogs on the right side of the handling room door. I found them and tried to pound them open, but it was going too slow and I was sure I'd never make it in time. Someone started working on the left side of the door and with the extra help, the last fastener gave way. As the ship's list deepened, the door swung wide and I could see that it was Bill Hagen who had assisted me in opening the door.

I stuck my head out to see what was happening. *Rowan* was rolling to starboard, her bow now lifting all the way out of the water. The pitch of the deck was a good forty-five degrees and in the fire's light, I could see powder cans and rafts that had been torn loose by the explosion tumbling across the deck and into the sea. Many of my shipmates were tumbling, too, desperately clinging to railings as they fought against the pull of gravity.

The air, thick with the pungent combination of vapors from spilled fuel oil and spent munitions, stung my eyes. The angry hiss of steam grew louder as the Mediterranean engulfed the twisted wreckage of *Rowan*'s stern. Looking aft through the midnight gloom, I saw the nightmarish stare of the windowless bridge backlighted by fires and the shocking sight spurred me on. No order was given to abandon ship, but everyone knew we had to get off fast.

I was pretty sure Camille Miciotto, Pappy Cole and Jim Gagnon were right behind me, pressing to get out, but I didn't look back. I took one step over the coaming preparing to hit the water, but was instantly stopped cold, garroted by the telephone headset still hanging around my neck. Hagen maneuvered around me and dove headfirst into the inky black water. Through the smoke, I could barely make out the phosphorescence of his splash as he disappeared beneath the waves.

I ripped off the headset, put one foot on the lifeline and dropped about ten feet into the water. I plunged several feet below the surface. Struggling back up again as quickly as I could, I gasped for air and looked behind me to see where I was. Right over my head was the immense hulk of the ship's anchor. A sudden burst of adrenaline shot through my veins. I was sure there was no way I could get out of this alive but I wasn't going to go without a fight. I took one stroke with my right arm, another with my left. Lifting my head for a gulp of air, I glanced over my shoulder again to see how much time I had left. To my astonishment, *Rowan*'s dying form was about a hundred feet away. With nearly everything aft of the bridge blown off, she was slipping straight down by the stern, pulling away from me. Only ten feet of her bow remained above the surface, pointing toward the sky. Seconds later, she was swallowed up by the sea.

My actions were instinctive. I kicked off my shoes and unhooked my life belt from around my waist, snapping it into a belt keeper on my dungarees. Then I started swimming away from the ship. With my pulse pounding in my head, I pulled my way through the oil-coated waters. I didn't swim far because I might need to conserve my strength until help arrived...if it arrived...before the Germans returned to strafe us. Feeling profoundly weak, I moved to where I felt I was safe from the threat of undertow. I inflated my life belt and secured it around my waist.

The silence roared in my ears. I couldn't see or hear anyone else. As far as I knew, I was the only survivor. I swam back to the point where the ship had disappeared, hoping to find other survivors. But I knew I wouldn't find my brother, Francis Kirwin - "Bob." Although the part of the ship he was in had not been damaged by the explosions, he would have been too far below deck to have escaped. I treaded water and tried not to think.

Just then, I heard something. In the distance, there were voices and cries for help. I held my breath so I could identify the direction from which they came. Through the smoke that still obscured the night sky, I could just make out a glow off to my left. I swam toward it and saw it was a raft that had caught fire in the explosion.

Out of the dark rim just beyond the burning fragment was another raft. In the faint light of the fires, I saw the shapes of men hanging on its sides. McCardie, Byxbe, Miklosi and Tefft were nearby. Several more were sitting in the raft. One of them, I recognized right away. It was the captain, Lt. Comdr. Robert S. Ford, who appeared to be seriously injured. He was propped up against the side, cradling his left hand. Next to him, on the side opposite me, was a face I almost didn't recognize for the oil that covered it. With a stab of shock, I realized it was my best friend, Ernie Harvey.

I quickly swam around to where I could speak to him and asked, "Are you hurt?"

Ernie didn't look at me. Staring into the darkness he replied quietly, "Yes. I have a cut across my throat that hurts like thunder." Then, as if talking to himself, he added, "I must have oil in my eyes because I can't see."

I grabbed hold of the rope on the raft and held on. I wasn't sure if I should tell him about my brother. But then, maybe he should know. "They got Bob," I said in a voice that was hardly a whisper. The words hurt so badly inside me that I was sure I had made a mistake telling him. I knew if he offered his sympathy, I wouldn't be able to hold myself together. I pushed off from the raft and swam away, looking to help other survivors whose cries I could hear close by. I had to keep moving, to keep busy.

I don't know how long we had been in the water, an hour, maybe more. I was too numb to tell. Although the water was not terribly cold, I was getting chilled. Some of the men were pretty badly injured. Would help get to us in time to save them? The Germans had already made one pass of the area. Would they return? It was deathly quiet except for some men who were moaning in pain. Others were swimming around, quietly asking if anyone had seen a buddy who was unaccounted for.

Although I was aware of those sounds, I really didn't pay attention to them until I realized that a voice I was hearing was somehow different. I held still and listened more intently. It was coming over a loudspeaker. Others heard it, too, and called for quiet. If it were the Germans coming back, we would have to dive under the water or risk being strafed. Even the injured muffled their cries.

"Stand by to pick up survivors," it said in English.

Suddenly, out of the darkness, the destroyer *Bristol* (DD 453), loomed over me. She was no more than twenty-five feet away. From my position in the water, she looked enormous. With all the strength I had left, I swam to her and started climbing up one of the cargo nets that had been thrown down the side. The going was tough because I had no shoes on and the ropes bit into my feet. The sailors on deck kept urging us to hurry but try as I might, I was too waterlogged and weary to move any faster.

A few feet from the top, my energy ran out. When I was sure I couldn't go any farther, strong arms reached out and pulled me up the rest of the way. A sailor named Woodward wrapped a blanket around me and led me down to the mess hall where I sat, dazed and disoriented. He must have handed me a mug of coffee

4

because I found myself sipping the hot black liquid without any memory of how I got it.

Once the *Bristol* was underway, the survivors, now gathered in the mess hall, were counted. Sixty-eight *Rowan* men had made it, plus two passengers from the *Rhind*, Eckstein and Richardson. We were issued some basic necessities, like soap and a razor, some paper slippers and cigarettes. I didn't need the last item, but the others were much appreciated. A crewman guided me down to the shower room so I could remove some of the fuel oil and seawater that clung to my skin. The fresh water beating down on me helped revive me but it had a down side - the numbness began to wear off and questions raced through my mind. I needed to find out what was going on.

I headed back to the mess hall and arrived just in time to see Ernie being led aft toward a berthing area in the crew quarters. I followed to see how he was. A corpsman helped him into a bunk, gave him a shot of morphine, and left.

I went over to my friend and sat on the deck next to him. His eye was badly injured and there was concern that he would lose his sight. I wanted to help him with the pain and fear he felt but instead, I wound up unburdening myself of the grief I was carrying. Like the good friend he was, Ernie tried to comfort me. He sat up, wrapped an arm around me and cried with me. But slowly, the morphine began to take effect and sleep overtook him. I laid him back in his bunk, pulled his blanket over him and left him to sleep.

If only I could have found some drug to numb my pain. With no one to talk to, the terrible agony inside me began to grow, threatening to consume me. I made my way out on deck, hoping that in the night air, I would find some relief. I roamed the ship restlessly. If I could wear myself out, maybe I could fall asleep and forget. I paced for an hour, maybe longer, struggling to force back the tears that burned my throat. Finally, as the first hint of dawn was turning the eastern sky a pale blue, weariness won out. I propped myself up behind the #4 gun near the after depth charge racks and fell into a dreamless sleep.

I don't know how long I slept, but I awoke with a jolt, startled by what sounded like the call of a bugle. It was a mournful sound, one full of pain and fear. As my head cleared, I realized that it was just the wind in the rigging. Still, it evoked deep and painful memories of my brother.

When we were young, we inherited my grandfather's old family trunk. Among the relics it contained was a bugle we boys thought came from the Revolutionary War when Abner Seeley served with the Green Mountain Boys. It was pretty banged up but Bob loved it. He carried it around with him almost everywhere he went. Although he never took lessons, he had a way of expressing himself through that horn. He could make the bugle sound happy or sad or even make it cry out in case of danger.

As I came fully awake, and the memories of the nightmare I had survived returned, I wished with all my heart that what I had heard was not the wind, but Bob calling for help, for my help, for help I would have given anything to offer. But Bob was dead.

Pain tore through my heart as I could imagine exactly how he had died, as if I had been there myself. Bob was down in the cramped quarters of the #1 magazine, down in the lowest level of the ship. When the torpedo struck, the lights went out, plunging him into the blackest darkness. The steep pitch of the deck caused confusion and vertigo. Within seconds, the Mediterranean surged through the companion-ways and corridors. Even if Bob had not been rendered immediately unconscious by the concussion of the explosions, the sea would have claimed him instantly if he had undogged the hatch. The water pressure would have pinned him into his metal grave. There would have been no escape. No way out. His had unquestionably been a violent, suffocating death.

Only the day before, my duty station had been aft of Bob's location, in the #2 magazine. During a night action in Salerno, the man in the upper handling room had passed the wrong ammunition. I was ordered to leave the #2 magazine and take over for him. He took my place below deck. That mistake doomed him and saved me. If that change had not been made, I would have been killed along with the others.

Did I deserve to live any more than they did? They were dead. I was still alive. Why? I had no answers, only unanswerable questions. I tried to fight back the thoughts but they tormented me over and over again, like a record stuck in a groove. I felt helpless, empty inside. Overcome by my sorrow, I put my head into my hands and sobbed. In convulsive waves, grief swept over me again and again like the waves that rushed over the fantail of the *Bristol*.

Exhausted but unable to fall back to sleep, I stood up and found a spot where I could sit a little closer to the lifeline and watch the wake of the ship. I tugged the woolen blanket tighter around me and shivered in the early morning air. I tried to block out my thoughts but the harder I tried the more violently the images of the night exploded in my imagination. I began to fear that I was going insane. From somewhere within me, a voice of reason emerged to tell me that if I kept torturing myself with those dreadful scenes of destruction, I would surely drive myself mad.

Bristol rolled deep into a swell and a wave washed over the deck where I was sitting. To avoid it, I had to lift my feet to let the water pass under them. As I watched the water recede, I thought how much like the ocean waves were the waves of my emotions and I wondered if I could handle the overwhelming feelings of shock and isolation the way I did the waves, by lifting up over them. I had to find some way to endure the agony. It was worth a try.

A few moments later, grief came crashing upon me again, but this time I closed my eyes and lifted my heart up away from the onrush and allowed it to pass under me. It helped. The stabbing torment was less painful. As I got better at this I found a measure of peace. I moved my mind away from the memories, farther and farther away.

Much of that time immediately following the sinking is a blur of monotone memories and deep emotional pain. The only tangible memento I brought back was an Italian Lira note, which many of the survivors signed. It would prove to be a link to my past and my brother, an invisible bond those of us who remained formed with each other.

When we returned stateside in October 1943, we all went our separate ways. I made no plans to see any of the others again. I just wanted to get back to living life. I left the ghosts of the dead behind me, gone forever...or so I thought. I didn't know those ghosts would be back again one day and that I would need to seek out the company of my shipmates to help me put them to rest.

A Time to Remember

Time may heal all wounds, but it sometimes takes more than you think you can spare. Meanwhile, your constant companion is suffering and self-doubt. You do almost anything to avoid facing the misery, but facing it is the only way to put it behind you.

When the *Rowan* sank, I suffered no broken bones, no severed limbs, not even a scratch. But an even bigger part of me was destroyed, as mangled as the wreckage of the ship. No one could see my injuries, yet they were as real as any suffered by others of the crew. I was lucky to have my new bride, Helen, waiting for me upon my return. She was my shoulder to sob on and, in the dead of night when the sound of an airplane flying low over the house made me jump under the bed, she was there to calm and soothe me. She was my Rock of Gibraltar. Her love probably saved my life, but she could not help me with one duty I found too painful to face - telling my family about how Bob had died.

October 1943

I went home to Illinois on survivor's leave. Helen was with me. It was the first time my folks would meet her in person. They were still grieving Bob's loss and although they greeted her warmly, the mood in the house was somber. Mom showed me the telegram they had received after the ship was sunk.

It read:

> *The Navy Department deeply regrets to inform you that your son Francis Kirwin Seeley, ship's cook first class, U.S. Navy, is missing following action in performance of his duty and in the service of his country. The department appreciates your great anxiety, but details not now available and delay in receipt thereof must necessarily be expected. There has been no casualty report concerning your other son, Lewis Everett, ship's cook first class, U.S. Navy.*
>
> Rear Admiral Randall Jacobs,
> Chief of Naval Personnel
> Arlington, Vir. 4:14 p.m.

It had taken a week before they heard I was alive and that time had been almost unbearable for them. Now that I was home, everyone wanted to know what happened, and I owed it to the family to tell them. But I was not ready to talk about it. Just reading the telegram had started the nightmares all over again. Out of respect for my feelings, they never pressed me, sacrificing their own peace of mind for mine.

During the two weeks we spent in Macomb, I tried to talk about it several times but bitter emotions would well up in my throat, choking off my words and overwhelming me with grief. For days after each attempt, I would withdraw. To stop the hurt inside, I got in the habit of lifting up over the pain. Avoidance became a way of life. It was a poor way to treat what ailed me, but it was the only way I knew.

In spite of the sorrow I held inside me, I led a full life. After the sinking, I went on to serve nearly thirty good years in the Navy. I had a wonderful wife and three healthy children, Mary, Julia, and Lorraine. When I retired from the Navy, I spent another fifteen years as food service manager at Dartmouth College. I worked hard, taking advantage of every opportunity to advance. The more pressure I put on myself, the easier it was to keep the memories walled off. In all that time, I never openly grieved the loss of my brother and shipmates. Those powerful emotions remained buried within me. It was inevitable that they would eventually find other ways to make themselves felt.

Poor health forced me to look at the emotions I had suppressed for so long. About the time I was to retire from Dartmouth, I started feeling worse than usual. I went to see the doctor at the veteran's hospital for a checkup. Diabetes, I was told. It wasn't severe and could be treated with diet and exercise. But I felt like I was dying and I was starting to wonder whether I even wanted to live.

I wasn't afraid of death, but contemplating my mortality seemed to rouse my brother's ghost. No matter how hard I tried to block it out, his memory kept intruding on my thoughts. Sometimes I would go for a walk through our town of Hanover, New Hampshire, and my mind would drift to the time when I was a boy in Macomb, Illinois. I'd think about Mom and Dad and how we weathered the Great Depression out on the farm. The five of us kids didn't especially love those days of hard work, freezing winters and sizzling summers but now, with the bad times forgotten, those days seemed so sweet.

And then I'd remember Bob. Suddenly, it was September 11, 1943. My stomach would churn. The recollections were as vivid and horrifying as ever. The explosion. The anchor hanging over my head. The bow disappearing beneath the waves. Bob locked down in the #1 magazine. As always, I would pull away from the dark coldness that surrounded those memories, just as I had aboard the *Bristol*. Forgetting was a conditioned response, a habit I couldn't easily break. But the feelings concealed behind my wall had been awakened. They refused to be still anymore.

I began to realize that the only way to get rid of the nightmares was to talk about them. But who would I tell? And what would I tell them? It occurred to me that I should start with those who most wanted to know about those dark days - my brother and sister.

I finally worked up enough courage to tell Myron and Mildred. By the time we were finished talking, I found a tremendous sense of relief. At last, Mildred said, "I think I know why you were spared. So that you can write this story. I want my children to read it. They should know about their uncles. And that way, none of us will ever forget."

I was spared to write about the sinking? The idea was crazy. Was that a good enough reason to live when so many others died? Besides, what more could I offer other than the painful release of emotions I had just shared with them? I was a cook. I knew nothing of any of the command decisions made on the bridge. I saw little, if any, of the action isolated as I was inside the handling room. Any memories I did have were buried so deep, how could I ever pull them back? Did I really want to remember everything? And my writing skills were certainly not equal to this task.

In spite of my initial rejection of the idea, Mildred had planted a seed in my mind. Maybe I should write the story. It would be something I could leave to my children and grandchildren so they would know more about me than I knew about my own grandparents. I knew I couldn't do it alone. I began to think about how to begin. I would need help. The faces of all the people I had known from the ship drifted into my imagination. Absently, I wondered if any of them were still around. After forty years, finding them would be nearly impossible. But I would try.

For the first time in years, I felt light. I was beginning to believe that it was not yet time for me to die; it was time to remember.

Francis Kirwin
"Bob" Seeley

Summer 1940

J uly 1940. It was hot in Macomb, Illinois, typical for this time of year. My mother had a favorite little song she would sing that described the season perfectly. It went,

When it gets too hot for comfort
And you can't eat ice cream cones,
'Tain't no sin to take off your skin
And dance around in your bones.

All that summer, I sat out on the front porch of our house on Carroll Street and wondered about my life. There was so much world out there but I felt stuck on the sidelines. The Great Depression was ending. Many people were able to find work but not me. I did all I could to support the family, especially since Dad's stroke in 1936. I worked part time as a cab driver, and sometimes hauled coal from the mines to homes for heating furnaces. I had applied for work at Caterpillar Tractor in Peoria, even went up to Moline and Galesburg looking for work, but no one was hiring unskilled labor.

I kept myself busy reading adventures, like Nordoff and Hall's books. *Mutiny On the Bounty* and *Pitcairn Island* were two of my favorites. Those stories filled my mind with images of exotic South Sea Island ports, and I dreamed of going to some far-off tropical paradise. Macomb was closing in on me. Now, almost twenty-two, I was hungry to experience the world. There was adventure ahead and I wanted a ringside seat!

There was a subtle push for young men to join the military, although I believe it had more to do with the lack of employment than it did with the prospects of war in Europe. I didn't think much about the world situation. As long as the United States was not involved, neither was I. Occasionally, veterans of the "Great War" warned that we'd be in it over there soon. "If it were me, I'd enlist rather than be drafted," they advised. "At least that way, you choose what service you go into."

The move toward the military caught up with me in March 1940, when some of my friends started urging me to join the National Guard. It was a source of income and the armory gave me a place to go and socialize with my friends. It was then that discovered I enjoyed the discipline of military life and after a few months in the Guard, I decided that this might be the career I was looking for. Even with my tenth grade education, I could find real adventure, a steady job, and a good income.

By the end of July, I took a bus over to Peoria to check out the services. I dropped into the Army recruiter's office, but dismissed that possibility immediately. Not enough glamour. The Marine Corps and the Army Air Corps were very tempting. In fact, I almost decided on the Air Corps.

Then, the Navy recruiter started coming to Macomb. As soon as I saw the chief's crisp white uniform, I decided that the U.S. Navy was for me. He filled out the enlistment forms and as I was about to sign my name, he said, "You realize you're signing up for six years, don't you?"

"It would suit me if it were for twenty!" I replied confidently. How prophetic my statement proved to be!

9 October

I was discharged from the Illinois National Guard and officially joined the U.S. Navy. At Great Lakes Naval Training Center, I was assigned to Company 89. Shortly after we arrived, my squad was marched double time to the barbershop where each of us received the thirty-second, six-pass haircut special. We got our uniforms and from then on, our attire was to be undress blues, leggings and white hat.

About a week after I arrived, out of the blue, my brother Bob showed up. He had joined a week after I did, claiming I was his inspiration. "And I look great in navy blue," he said. Whatever his reasons, I was happy to see him. From then on, we spent as much time together as we could, and often discussed how great it would be if we wound up at the same duty station. I would graduate a week before Bob and our chances of that happening were slim. Still, it gave us something to dream about.

L.E. Seeley
Boot Camp
1940

When I was assigned to the Out Going Unit (OGU), available for assignment, I was given routine dental and medical examinations. The doctor poked me in the groin and without a word of explanation, scrawled across my chart, "Hernia. Medical Hold."

I couldn't believe it. I felt fine. How could this happen? I went back to the barracks and brooded. The next morning and each morning thereafter, I went back to sick bay and asked to be reexamined and released. No one would even look at me. When Bob reported back from boot leave, he passed his physical with flying colors, which left me in a stew. I immediately stepped up my efforts, badgering the doctors to turn me loose. I must have made enough noise because after a week, I finally got a doctor to say I was fine and pronounce me fit for active duty.

The delay put Bob and me in the same OGU. Right before Thanksgiving, we got our assignments. I found my name in the draft going to the USS *Enterprise*, a carrier. Bob was headed for the destroyer, USS *Rowan*. Although we hadn't really expected to wind up with the same duty, we had held out some hope. A sailor who overheard us suggested we trade assignments with someone from one ship or the other.

Noting the names of the men in each draft, we wasted no time in looking for someone who would agree to the change. No one wanted to give up an aircraft carrier for a "tin can." But Bob found a taker from the *Rowan* draft who jumped at the chance to go to the *Enterprise*. I knew what I was giving up, but making the sacrifice to be with my brother was worth it. That decision would forever change my future.

We had one more duty before we shoved off. The Navy required us to fill out emergency information records, like next of kin, and dependents. They offered us up to $10,000 life insurance benefits, which we both accepted, naming our parents as dependents and beneficiaries. At graduation, our recruit pay of $21.00 a month increased to $36.00 a month. Of that, an allotment of $25.00 went home and a small amount paid the insurance premium. That left us less than $10.00 for spending money. It wasn't much but with room and board paid for, it was adequate for our needs. Supporting our family was important to us and we did whatever we could to help.

4 December

The seven NTC graduates bound for the *Rowan*, Bob Rettig, Ray Schnitzler, Shorty Shay, Fred Quinn, Russell Pruett, Bob and I boarded a train to Chicago. At Union Station, we transferred to a transcontinental train that would take us to Los Angeles, then to San Diego to meet our ship.

Fred Quinn

After boot camp, that cross-country trip was a real luxury experience. The food was good, we could pretty much sleep all day if we wanted to, and no one was yelling orders at us. Bob and I soaked it all up. We talked a lot and watched the countryside pass by. I think that was the first time I ever really got to get to know my little brother as an adult. You couldn't help but like Bob. He had a good sense of humor and a strong sense of honor and loyalty.

Even though I could see Bob as my peer, he was still my little brother. Although I wouldn't have admitted it to him, I was always protective of him, even when he was little and a tag-along pest. Now, as a nineteen-year-old, he may not have either needed or wanted my protection, but it was always available to him. Being on the same ship, I felt we would always be there for each other in case of trouble.

If only it had turned out that way.

Rowan (DD 405)

9 December 1940. It was just before noon when our train pulled into the San Diego station. The new *Rowan* draft left the shade of the terminal and all of us squinted under the glare of the cloudless sky. We crossed the street and took a trolley down to the docks. From there, we shouldered our heavy sea bags and trudged, two-by-two, down to the Navy landing.

When we neared the docks, Quinn pointed out a small navy gray boat approaching. Pausing to catch our breath, we watched as the boat crew tied up. The coxswain came ashore and handed a parcel to the shore patrolman standing at the landing guard station. It seemed to us that the SP might be able to help us find where we belonged and we headed over to ask him if we were in the right place to pick up the *Rowan*.

"*Rowan*?" he repeated as if trying to place the name. "Yeah," he said glancing over his shoulder toward the bay, "she's moored to a buoy out in the harbor. The next guard mail boat's due here in about thirty minutes." He pointed to the spot where the boats tied up and said, "You can catch it over there." As a unit, we turned to the right to find the location. "But don't drift off," he cautioned, "'cause it won't wait for you."

Fat chance of our leaving the area. It was noon, it was hot and I, for one, was ready for dinner. We dragged our bulky loads to a point nearby and sandwiched ourselves together in the only shady spot we could find. And we waited.

Before long, we heard the approach of a small craft. Schnitzler and Quinn jumped up to get a better look. When they spotted the numbers '405' painted on the bow, Schnitzler yelled, "That's ours, guys. Let's move." All of us jumped to our feet and shoved our sea bags a little closer to the end of the landing. The small craft didn't look big enough to accommodate our gear and all of us.

When the boat was about two feet from the dock, the bowhook jumped ashore and secured the bowline to the cleat. Moving aft, he positioned boat's white fenders to avoid damage to vessel or dock, and pulled on the stern lines to bring the boat alongside the pier. With the boat snugly in place, he hitched the line around the stern cleat. The whole process took less than a minute.

With the boat secure, the coxswain pulled the lanyard on the brass bell in front of him three times to inform the engineer to shut down the motor. Everything suddenly became quiet. The only sound was the disturbed water licking up underneath the landing.

The coxswain picked up the mail pouch behind him, stepped onto the dock and handed the bag to the shore patrol. After a brief conversation with the SP, he turned to us and asked, "You the new draft for the *Rowan?*" In unison, we replied in the affirmative. "Okay," he said without paying us much attention, "climb aboard."

The craft took off and proceeded at a sedate speed until we entered the bay. Four rings, 'ahead full,' and the pitch of the boat's engines swelled to a deep, powerful, churning sound. The bow raised up as the speed increased to full throttle. The water whooshed beneath us, kicking a fine spray into our faces. Conversation was nearly impossible but I wasn't interested in talking. I was too busy scanning for the escutcheon that would identify the *Rowan*.

After about ten minutes, I caught sight of her. Even before I saw the name plate, my eye was drawn to her form. She was sleek and trim and built for action. Though not exactly voluptuous, for most of her lines were angular, she had all the right accessories in all the right places. Her proud, erect bearing gave the impression she might be fast, and her competent, cocky air inspired in me a feeling of confidence. With her signal flags two-blocked at the yardarm, she was dressed rather flashily in bright, gaudy colors that were very becoming on her.

I didn't know, nor would I have cared, that the flags had been hoisted simply to allow them to dry. For me, those banners were a sign welcoming me home. It was love at first sight. With her six foot high, white drop shadow numerals boldly identifying her as DD 405, USS *Rowan* was like a new bride and I felt possessively that she was all mine.

I had memorized her specifications. Three hundred forty-one feet in length, thirty-six feet at the beam, and a fifteen hundred ton displacement, she was the third fighting ship named in honor of Vice Admiral Stephen C. Rowan. Built in the Norfolk Navy Yard and put into commission on 23 September 1939, she was a single stack Benham Class destroyer, capable of doing thirty-seven knots or more, in a pinch. With the union jack at the bow and ensign at the stern fluttering in the breeze, she was a thrilling sight, truly one the U.S. Navy's greyhounds of the sea.

The helmsman gave the tiller a sharp reverse angle and swung the boat alongside the gangway. Three bells to stop. "This is it," he said. "It's not the Ritz, but it's home."

When my turn came to debark, I tossed my gear up to the deck and climbed the ladder. As I stepped aboard, I faced aft and saluted the colors. Then I turned and saluted the officer of the deck and said crisply, "Request permission to come aboard, sir." I stood at attention and waited for him to return my salute.

"Permission granted," he answered.

The first man aboard had given him our orders, so there was nothing more for us to do except wait while our names were entered in the log. I retrieved my gear and stood at rest along with the other new men. I was already familiar with the routine of hurry-up-and-wait, which I learned in boot camp. I didn't mind. I passed the time by looking around my new ship. The bonds of love between us were forming quickly.

A seaman first class dressed in dungarees came up to us and said tersely, "I'm Whonus. Pick up your gear and follow me." He didn't turn around to see if we were following as he quickly headed forward with that peculiar, rolling gate of a long-time sailor. He brought us to a storeroom and instructed us to leave our gear there. He stood aside to let us stuff all our belongings inside. Then he led us to the mess deck, one level below the main deck, where they were holding some food for us. It was well past dinner and with great gusto, I hungrily fell upon the meal.

After our quick dinner, Whonus came back to give us a cursory tour of the ship. "I'll show you the places you need to know about. We'll start right here in the mess hall," he said. "See those hooks?" He indicated sets of hooks fastened to the overhead. "That's where you swing your hammocks when the mess deck is cleaned after supper."

He led us forward past the #1 upper handling room, the chief petty officer's quarters and up the ladder to the forecastle, "pronounced 'fo'c's'le'," he emphasized. He took us forward to the bow, then turning aft, pointed out the #1 gun turret, the #2 turret and above it, the bridge. The last stop was the head. "All the comforts of home," he commented dryly as we peeked into the compact privy. "Quarters on the fo'c's'le at 0800." With that, he left us on our own.

Bob and I made a complete turn around the ship. The odors of fuel oil and seawater permeated the air, and we could hear the constant and steady hum of the blowers that circulated fresh air to the innermost parts of the ship. We would get used to those smells and sounds, even grow to like them, in a way, as we learned to associate them with the feeling of home.

We were heading back toward the mess hall to pin down the location of food and sleep when we heard someone call, "Hey! You two sailors!"

Both of us turned. "Seeley, aye!" Our unison response was a conditioned reflex.

"Two Seeleys, huh?" the sailor said with a chuckle. "I have to have some way of separatin' you two." In the slowest Southern drawl we had ever heard, he said to me, "I'll call you Big Seeley," and to Bob, "you'll be Little Seeley. Y'all are in 'X' Division until you get assigned to a reg'lar division. I'm Waters, your section leader. Report to me tomorrow at quarters. Be there before 0800. I'll muster you and then get y'all started."

22

When the mess deck was cleaned after supper that first day, it was time to swing our hammocks and turn in. At taps at 2200 (or 10:00 p.m.), we were still excited but after our long day, we were ready to turn in. I was starting to adjust to my new home but soon, I would face my first test of initiation to life aboard ship.

USS Rowan Commissioning Photo, September, 1939

First Day

I awoke the next morning to of some of my favorite smells - the aroma of coffee brewing and bacon cooking. It took me a few seconds to identify my strange surroundings but as soon as I did, I jumped to my feet, fully alert. I gave Bob, who was sleeping nearby, a shake and said, "It's time to get up."

0500. Reveille wouldn't be for another half-hour but because our sleeping quarters doubled as the mess hall, we had to vacate early. I was ready to chow down but on a ship, you work before you eat. After we unhooked our hammocks, trussed them neatly and carried them to the designated storage place, our duty was to sweep and "clamp down," that is, swab the main deck and passageways with clear water. As I wrung out the mop, I joked with my brother that this early morning activity would not only help us work up an appetite, but also put us first in the chow line, which I considered a benefit.

At quarters for muster, Bob and I were logged in present and accounted for, and dismissed for duty. As we had been instructed the afternoon before, we headed to the fo'c's'le and reported to Waters for assignment. "First," he drawled out his instructions, "y'all get some rags and scrub some paint work." Almost as an afterthought, he added, "Y'all keep on your toes. Some of the old timers like to have a little fun with you kids." A leathery smile creased the corners of his eyes as he hurried us off to get started.

As we went forward to the locker to get our equipment, another crewman warned us to step lively and not be fooled by Waters' laid-back style. Not even he was above a little tomfoolery.

The next day, Waters put us to work painting all the surfaces we had prepared the day before. Waters detained me for a moment. "I have a special assignment for you," he said in a serious voice. "I want you to go to the paint locker and get a pot of green and red striped paint."

Even though the request was coming from the man who had warned us about pranks, I was suspicious. The problem was that I was learning so many new phrases and new meanings to old words that it just might be possible that there was some special navy paint. Rather than risk a charge of failing to follow an order, I played along.

I went to the paint locker. "My section leader sent me here for a pot of green and red striped paint," I said to the sailor in charge. I looked for a smile or a hint of some kind that might clue me in that this was a joke.

Without batting an eye, he told me, "The striped paint is kept in a storeroom on the fantail." He turned away and went back to his work.

I followed instructions. Continuing aft past the stack, past #3 and #4 gun mounts to the fantail, I found a sailor who looked as if he had some time in the Navy and asked him if he knew where I could get a pot of green and red striped paint.

"Oh, sure," he said helpfully, "but not here. The only pot of striped paint is on the signal bridge." He pointed forward with one hand while shading his eyes with the other.

As I headed back the way I came, I heard some snickering behind me. That did it for me. They had had enough to laugh about at my expense. Instead of going to the bridge where I knew I would only find another jokester, I returned to Waters. "The green and red striped paint is out of stock. You'll have to put in a requisition for more."

The joke was over but Waters had had his fun. He handed me a pot of navy gray paint and a brush. "All right," he said. "This will have to do. Cover up those red spots y'all made yesterday." His approving glance told me I had passed my first test of initiation. I was just as glad to get back to work, and there was plenty of it. The rule was "If it moves, salute it. If it doesn't, paint it or shine it." Life aboard ship settled into a comfortable routine. Up at 0500. Sweep and clamp down from 0530 to 0630. Clean up and breakfast from 0630 to 0700. Quarters for muster at 0800. After quarters, turn to ship's work. Until 1100, there was paint work to scrub and repaint, and bright work, like brass nameplates, turnbuckles, etc., to shine. At 1115, we broke for dinner. At 1300, daily routine resumed.

At 1600, a boatswain's mate would pass the word, "Sweepers, start your brooms. Give a clean sweep-down fore and aft." All other work would cease while the microscopic quantities of dust that had accumulated from the day before were swept from the deck and deposited into the sea. We never questioned the need. We just did it.

1615 hours, word would be passed to "knock off ship's work," letting us know that we were finished for the day. For a third of the crew, that meant we would eat supper and report to our duty station for the evening. For the other two sections that rated liberty, there would be a stampede to the showers to get cleaned up and ready to go ashore.

The first liberty boat left at 1630, but Bob and I, far too accustomed to having no extra money to spend, never made that one. We stayed aboard for our meals. We didn't squander our meager seaman's pay by eating ashore. Meals aboard the ship were free - and good.

Once, Bob and I were going on liberty just as Captain Harrison was getting into his gig to go ashore. We had heard that whenever space was available, he would invite his men to ride with him. The captain used those opportunities to get to know the crew better. When he asked us to come along, we were happy to accept. The captain put us at ease, asking us about where we were from and how things were going for us aboard the *Rowan*. By the time we reached the docks, I had a new respect for our skipper. Although he was strict when he had to be, Captain Harrison was

Captain Harrison

more than gold bars. He was a man who, like my ship, I was proud to serve.

For Bob and me, liberty didn't mean drinking. Our early training in Macomb had taught us how to entertain ourselves royally without a nickel between us. The thing we liked best was to go into town to look in store windows. Once in a while, we would buy some trinket or maybe just a postcard to send back to family and friends.

Our frugality made us targets for those who were less conscientious, and early on, we learned the wisdom of Shakespeare's advice, "Neither a borrower nor a lender be." The best way to hold onto your money was never to have any in your possession. With most of our pay allotted to our parents and insurance, we drew only enough to purchase soap, toothpaste, etc. This helped us to maintain good relations with our shipmates. Word soon spread. "Seeley boys are always broke."

Pity the poor seaman with money in his pocket that intended to remain aboard for the evening. If word got out, he would be hounded by favor-seekers promising huge returns. "If you let me have $5.00," they'd say, "I'll pay you $10.00 next payday." The borrower paid up if you got to him before all the others who wanted to collect. There was always a long line of collectors waiting at the other side of the pay table so the debtor could not escape. There were usually a few disappointed collectors as the money ran out before all the debts could be satisfied.

I was beginning to feel at home aboard the ship, learning the ropes, making new friends. Even with everything going so well, I felt I was sliding into a comfortable rut. The same force that pushed me out of my doldrums back in Macomb was starting to nag at me again, driving me to get into something with more of a future. Others might have found deck work satisfying, but it was not the career I cared for. I didn't want to be chipping paint any longer than I had to.

17 December

As my first week aboard the *Rowan* was drawing to a close, I started checking the various departments to see if I could strike for a rate, the Navy version of on-the-job-training. You applied then waited until there was room for you as an apprentice. I applied all over - from the black gang to the radio shack - but nothing was available. Eager to advance, I was determined to take the first opportunity that came along.

I didn't know then that I would live with that decision for the rest of my life.

Striking for Cook

Monday, 16 December. 1240. Bob and I were on a stage hanging over the side of the ship applying another coat of navy gray paint to the red leaded spots. I was dipping my brush into the pot, silently hoping a job would open up soon, when someone called down to us.

"Hey, Seeley, you still looking to strike for a rate?"

"Sure thing!" I replied. I didn't even give my brother a chance to speak, even though "Seeley" could have as easily meant him. I was halfway up to the deck before I even asked what the job was. That's when I found out I was striking for cook. While cooking wouldn't have been my first choice, it was the only one available. True to my word, I took the first opportunity that came along.

As would become my custom before reporting for duty, I went aft to the shower room, bathed and changed into my whites. I put on my apron and hat and just before 1300, reported for duty to the leading cook, First Class Petty Officer Sam Burroughs. The noon meal was over and clean up had just started.

I glanced around to acquaint myself with the ten by twenty-foot galley. Along the forward bulkhead, there was a stainless steel worktable and a sink piled high with dirty pots and pans. Above the sink was a serving window where stewards and mess cooks picked up and returned food serving equipment. On the starboard bulkhead were four thirty-gallon steam kettles in which food was prepared. Along the aft bulkhead were two three-foot electric griddles. Next to them was a stack of three electric ovens and a range, which was used mostly by the officer's cook but occasionally, by the ship's cooks for deep-frying.

Burroughs was one of the four cooks aboard *Rowan* who would teach me my trade. A big red headed thirty-year old, Sam was a likable man with a devil-may-care attitude. Thanks to his fondness for beer, his belly bulged out over his trousers. Although he was known to drink prodigiously while on liberty, he was never under the influence aboard ship. He looked up from his work when he saw me come in. "Here," he said without ceremony. Handing me an empty black pan that was greasy and encrusted with burned on food, he said, "Take this to the sink and make up a pot of soapy water."

I knew what that meant. While this was almost as bad as chipping paint, at least here I could look forward to a future. I didn't wait for further instructions. I added the pan he handed me to the collection of pots, pans and dishes that were stacked in the sink, and got to work with my typical zeal. Elbow deep in hot sudsy water, I scoured everything I could lay my hands on. In half an hour, I had finished. By the grunt of approval I received from Burroughs, I could tell I was making a good impression.

Sam did a lot of grunting. It was his most common mode of communication. He grunted disapproval, too. He grunted when he was pleased or displeased. He could get a lot across with that one sound. Oh, he could talk, but he didn't like to and even when he did, it was almost inaudible.

Sam put me to work emptying out one of the thirty-gallon steam kettles for cleaning. I knew his instructions had to be important. "Careful when you empty the water out of those things," he told me clearly and slowly, looking straight at me to make certain I understood. "They're heated by steam piped directly into 'em from the boiler down in the engine room." I nodded as I opened the drain spigot on the underside of the kettle, about fourteen inches above the deck. Billows of steam rose from the scalding water.

Burroughs added another warning. "Keep that empty coffee can under the spout or the water will slosh all over the place. Makes the deck slippery." There was a ridge on the deck around the kettles that was supposed to channel the water into the floor drains at the corners of the galley but I could see that if we were underway, it would be useless. Once water started splashing around, if you weren't careful, you could wind up on your behind.

I was lucky to learn as much as I could about cooking while we were still securely tied up in San Diego harbor because in the galley, potential danger lurked everywhere. There were hot ovens, a range top which often held black pans full of hot cooking fat, and steam kettles more than half full of boiling water. If your feet came out from under you when you were rolling around at sea, you could be in real trouble.

A few days later, I worked with another of *Rowan*'s cooks, Clarence Hatchell, a second class petty officer. He was a heavy, solidly built man with huge forearms. Much more serious about everything than Burroughs, he was always talking about getting out of the Navy. His enlistment was nearly over and he would say, "As soon as I get my discharge, I'm going to put an oar over my shoulder and walk inland. As soon as someone asks me what it is, that's where I'll settle." I don't know if he was really as unhappy as he sounded, but he didn't have nearly the enthusiasm for the Navy that I did. Nevertheless, he was a hard worker who encouraged and assisted me whenever he could.

Hatchell and I had the first watch of the day in the galley from 0400 until 1200. The night before, I left word with the boatswain's mate-of-the-watch to wake me up at 0345. I awoke just before he reached out to shake me. "I'm up," I whispered. I rolled out of the sack, showered, dressed in my whites and headed forward to the galley.

This was the part of the day I liked best. The air outside was crisp and clean, and I paused for a few moments at the break of the fo'c's'le to fill my lungs with that fresh air before going into the galley.

I didn't linger, however, because I was motivated to get to work. Just the thought of brewing coffee and sizzling breakfast meats made my mouth water. As I headed toward the galley, I was looking forward to a good meal. I didn't think about the fact that I was reporting to duty to prepare breakfast, not eat it.

I went right over to the steam kettle to pour myself a cup of coffee. To my surprise, the urn was empty. "Where's the coffee?" I asked Hatchell. The cook picked up an empty sugar bag and handed it to me, pointing toward the issue room without saying a word. He turned away to continue preparing biscuit dough. I looked down at the cloth bag in my left hand, then back at Hatchell.

He glanced in my direction and noticed my blank expression. While pulling out a baking sheet, he said, "Break out the coffee in the issue room and put three scoops of ground coffee in that bag. Tie a knot in the open end leaving plenty of room for the grounds to expand. When the water in the kettle starts boiling," he said, nodding in the direction of the urn nearest the galley door, "drop it in and shut off the steam. Let it steep for about ten minutes."

I wanted to follow his instructions to the letter, but I wasn't sure even where to look for the coffee. After a brief search of the issue room located across from the galley passageway, I found an open forty-pound vacuum-packed tin. As directed, I scooped out the coffee, tied off the bag and dropped it gently into the boiling water.

Soon, the enticing aroma of brewing coffee began to mingle with those of sausages frying and the biscuits Hatchell had slid into the oven. My stomach was beginning to remind me that it had been a while since my last meal. I waited the required ten minutes for the coffee to brew, then helped myself to a cup. As I did, I asked Hatchell, "When do we eat?"

He gave me a look that reminded me a little of Waters when he sent me off looking for the red and green striped paint. "Oh, maybe around 1000, if you're lucky." I couldn't be sure if he was on the level. "You might as well learn right off," he said, his ruddy face dead serious, "cooks eat when they get the chance. Sometimes you don't get a chance and you miss out altogether. Most of the time, you eat while you work." He crossed his arms over his ample belly. He made it sound like being a cook was the perfect job for anyone looking forward to starving to death. I should have known I didn't have anything to worry about.

Judging by his profile, he hadn't missed many trips through the chow line.

Richard Uliano, *Rowan*'s third cook was probably the best of the lot. Because of his Italian ancestry, everyone called him "Wop", a nickname he accepted without complaint. Uliano had a medium stocky build, a dark complexion and a full head of thick black hair. With an easy-going attitude and a keen sense of humor, Uliano always had a good word for everyone. I didn't know anyone who didn't like and respect him.

I noticed early on that he was always exceptionally neat. Unlike everyone else's uniform, my own in particular, his was as clean at the end of his watch as it was at the beginning. "Say, Uliano, how do you keep from getting dirty?" I asked. "I wind up covered in everything we serve."

The Italian, who was expertly slicing the meat loaf we were serving for supper, finished his work and carefully placed the meat in a serving platter. He turned toward me and glanced at my soiled apron. "You know why you get dirty?" he began. Using the knife in his hand to point to the pan I was carrying, he said, "See what you do? When you move a heavy pan from place to place, you use your stomach to assist your arms. I never do that." Picking up the large platter of meat loaf in front of him to illustrate his technique, he said, "I hold the pan like this, well away from my body. That's how my clothes stay clean." I could also see why he had such strong arms. With that one tip, Uliano saved me hours of scrubbing my duty whites.

Of all the cooks, I spent the most time with Third Class Petty Officer Cicero Decker. Tall and lanky from the hills of Tennessee he had a penchant for alcohol and trouble. He had been court marshaled a number of times and was up and down in rate more often than anyone I have ever known before or since. He was a free spirit who, when sober, was hard working and dedicated. But when anyone popped a cork within earshot of him, he was bound for rough waters.

In the galley, Decker was at his best. He had a smooth, relaxed style and I learned a lot, especially about frying foods, just by watching him. We had no thermometers and had to estimate the temperature of the cooking fat by flipping a small amount of water into the hot grease. When it sizzled just right, it was ready.

Cicero had developed an easy wrist action for flipping water that I admired and tried to copy. But style counted for little. Deep fat frying was dangerous if you didn't know what you were doing and at first, I didn't. Every time I put a piece of raw meat into the fat, the hot liquid would spatter and sting my arms, neck and face like hundreds of angry bees. Cicero had mastered a technique of carefully slipping the meat into the fat at arm's length and rarely was he stung by the spatters. I watched him and learned.

Decker showed me another useful skill. When he was frying food, he would grab a handful of salt out of the tall can that always remained on the range. Whenever fat would spill onto the cooking surface and ignite, as it often did while we were underway, he'd apply the salt liberally to the flame with the same fluid motion he used to flip water into the fat to test the temperature. His aim was always accurate, never getting any salt in the food as he doused the fire and soaked up the excess fat. Although I could never copy his technique exactly, I had the chance to practice often and soon became expert in my own right at quickly putting out range fires.

Decker had a way of combining Navy regulations with down home philosophy. Once I asked him how he could tell when something was cooked. He grinned and said, "If it's a-smokin', it's a-cookin', if it's black, it's done." I never followed that advice, but I always remembered it. In spite of Decker's service record and everything that would happen between him and me, he was a good teacher. He took the time to answer my questions and never minded my watching his cooking technique. He taught me a lot.

In reality, though, learning was the responsibility of the individual. I would ask questions when I needed to but with only two of us on duty, there was no time for long explanations. I learned by watching what the others did, following instructions found in the Navy cook book and working extra hours on my own when I needed to. Most of the technical information would come from the courses taken in preparation for advancement. It was simple: If you wanted to learn, you learned. If you didn't, you found yourself back on the deck force chipping paint, a fate I wasn't about to let befall me.

On Thursday at noon as I was getting off duty, Bob showed up in the galley in his whites and apron, telling me what an inspiration I was. It turns out, he was striking for cook, too. I couldn't have been happier. At last, both of us were on our way to building our future in the Navy.

20 December

Sunset. As soon as ship's work knocked off for the day, Carpenter's Mate Frankie Rung and a couple of electricians hoisted a huge star up onto the mast and strung it with colored lights. When the sun went down, you could see those lights from almost anywhere in the harbor.

As Bob and I stood on deck under *Rowan*'s star, we remembered the hard times of the Depression all too well. This Christmas, we were deeply grateful to our country and to the United States Navy for giving us a home, food, and a shining star to light our way.

Christmas fell on a Wednesday, which meant we got a break in our daily routine. While we had to be up at 0700, those not on duty were allowed liberty. Bob and I didn't go because the cooks were putting together a huge holiday dinner with turkey and all the trimmings. There was even pumpkin pie with whipped cream. Since we were striking for cook, we worked almost all day, but the delicious smells made the job more enjoyable. It wasn't home, but it was a mighty good substitute.

26 December

Word was passed to make preparations to get underway. The Christmas star and lights came down and the pace aboard the *Rowan* picked up. Up till now *Rowan* had not left her mooring in the secure confines of San Diego harbor, but adventure beckoned beyond the breakwater. I was eager to get underway. After all, I was a sailor and *Rowan* was a destroyer, and our place was at sea.

USS Rowan Underway. Pre-World War II. Note the portholes, large numerals and crow's nest.

Underway

27 December. 0700. "Go to your stations, all special sea and anchor detail."

I climbed the ladder to the fo'c's'le to join my unit. Waters led us to our station where we would handle mooring lines, dragging in the six-inch thick manila hawsers securing *Rowan* to her nest. We hadn't been drilled on this maneuver, and my first experience would be the real thing. We lined up along the hawsers and waited for the order to "haul in." Our job was to grab the line and drag it aft as far as we could, break off, run back to the head of the line, grab the hawser again and repeat the process until all of the line was aboard.

All around me, sailors quickly and competently carried out their assigned tasks. Next to me, the telephone talker, rigged with headset over his ears and sound-powered telephone mouthpiece hanging around his neck, informed the bridge, "Anchor detail, manned and ready." I couldn't hear the other stations, but I knew they were reporting in.

"Midship, manned and ready."

"Stern, manned and ready."

When Captain Harrison received all reports, he ordered a test of the whistle and siren.

Rowan's piercing siren split the air with a WHRRP, WHRRP, WHRRP, followed by a single deep blast of the whistle. VRROOOMMM!

"Single up," our talker said, relaying Harrison's order. When the line was in, he reported, "Fo'c's'le line singled."

"Take in the spring lines," the captain ordered, watching our actions from over the wing of the bridge. "Take in the stern line." *Rowan* started to drift away from her nest mate. "Take in all lines. Five degrees right rudder. All astern one-third." Amid swirls of water, *Rowan* slowly pulled clear of the buoy.

The union jack at the bow and the ensign at the stern were lowered and simultaneously, the underway ensign was two-blocked to the gaff up the main mast as the last line was cast off. The call sign signal flags, identifying us as DD 405, were hoisted and we were away.

Our lines secured and properly faked down, I took the opportunity to see what was going on. *Rowan* moved at headway speed, her screws throbbing beneath us. This was different from the sounds I had grown accustomed to. This was like a heartbeat.

"All stop. Right full rudder. All ahead one-third."

Rowan came about and sedately made her way toward the narrow harbor entrance. She headed out to open sea, following in a line with the other ships of our squadron; the flagship *Anderson*, then *Stack* and *Wilson*. Once clear of the harbor, she picked up speed, raising and lowering her bow in a graceful rhythm. As she rose to the top of a swell, she would lean slightly to port. Then the crest of the wave would swing her gently to starboard, lowering her bow to greet the next swell. She knifed her way through walls of blue sea, churning them into foaming white water. The wind quickened and the underway colors snapped smartly red, white and blue against the gray San Diego dawn.

I had little time to spare because I had to get to my first underway watch as lookout. In those days *Rowan* had no radar, and my station was up in the crow's nest. This was a circular metal box five feet high and three feet in diameter located about fifty feet up on the main mast. A destroyer rolls a lot and at that height, those rolls are highly exaggerated. Climbing up the mast to get to the crow's nest was the most fearsome part of the watch. It was like hanging on the outside of a moving roller coaster.

I climbed into the crow's nest and relieved the watch, a sailor named Britt Crowe. He was shook up. It turned out that he was in trouble with the OOD because of his name.

"I was just reporting the way I'm supposed to," he told me. "I said, 'Crow's nest, Crowe speaking.' Now I have to go below and prove that my name really is Crowe."

Someone had recently passed a ringing telephone and answered it "Charlie's Bar and Grill." It was a joke the officers didn't find the least bit amusing. The culprit hadn't been caught and no doubt Crowe was presently the prime suspect.

Crowe gave me the identification, location, speed and course of all the ships on the horizon. As soon as he finished, I said, "I relieve you." He wasted no time in scooting back down the mast to go clear his name.

Careful to do everything according to the book, I donned the telephone headset, draped the strap of the huge twenty-power binoculars over my neck and began scanning the horizon, one section at a time. Suddenly, I saw something that made my heart jump. It was big, off the port bow about five miles from our location. I focused the lenses but could not identify what I saw. If we continued on our present course, we would pass very near the object. My pulse pounded as I called, "Bridge, crow's nest."

An answering voice came back immediately, "Bridge, Smith speaking."

"Unidentified object, five degrees off the port bow," I reported. "Distance five miles." I kept the glasses focused on the mysterious object, at a loss for what it could be. It didn't look like a ship or a sub, but what was it?

After a few minutes, a call came back, "Crow's nest, Bridge."

"Crow's nest, Seeley speaking," I responded correctly.

"We see the object. It's a whale."

"Crow's nest, aye." I cringed a little as I thought what the log entry would look like. "Crow's nest sights enemy whale." Even though I felt foolish reporting a fish, I comforted myself that the reason I couldn't make the identification was that whales aren't generally seen in Illinois. I laughed as I held the glasses to my eyes again to study the first whale I had ever seen. I couldn't imagine that any living creature could be so big.

Although my first day at sea was not very exciting, it was what I had waited for all my life. While some of my shipmates were suffering from seasickness, I felt fine. I enjoyed the pitch and roll of the ship. In less than a day, I had my sea legs. There's nothing to this, I thought.

New Year's Day

The galley put out a big spread including ham, black-eyed peas and corn bread. I ate my fill but shortly after supper, the sea began to kick up. The constant rolling was annoying at first, then nauseating. In no time, I was as pale as an early-morning mist. The fish ate well that night as I leaned over the rail and deposited that fine meal into the sea. I sat down on the deck, wishing that the ship would hold still, when one of the old-timers came by and noticed my condition.

"Hey, sailor," he said with a lop-sided grin, "you feel okay?"

Too embarrassed to admit how rotten I felt, I sat up straight and said, "I'm fine. Just enjoying the night air."

"Right," he said. "If I were you," he advised, "I'd get up ahead of the stack. The smell back here makes me feel seasick when it's choppy like this."

Í nodded to him, praying he would go away and leave me to die in peace. But I had had enough of being sick. By force of will, I pulled myself together. Just for good measure, I headed forward, clear of the smoke. Soon, I started to feel better. The experience taught me that I could function even when I felt nauseated, an invaluable lesson for the days to come. I would get seasick many times, but never again bad enough to throw up. It was a performance I was happy never to repeat.

The sea remained rough and with frequent speed and course changes ordered by the captain as *Rowan* maneuvered in training drills, life in the galley was nearly impossible. Had I known what I was getting myself into when I decided to strike for cook, I might have had second thoughts. Being in port lulled me into a false sense of security. While underway, the work in the galley could be just plain frustrating. Even in calm seas, you couldn't count on anything staying where you put it. The captain never consulted with us before he ordered a ninety-degree turn or a sudden increase in speed. All we could do was stay alert and never let go of anything that couldn't stand to be dropped.

As I lurched around the galley, I noticed that Hatchell managed just fine. He moved naturally with the rhythm of the ship, grabbing hold of the overhead beams or cables whenever the pitch of the deck exceeded his ability to stabilize himself. The first few times I tried to imitate his moves I wound up awkwardly clutching the nearest stationery object. The big cook laughed and said, "You're going to have to develop faster reflexes if you want to save your skin." More seriously, he added, "Remember, Seeley, in the Navy, you always have one hand for the job and one hand for yourself."

That was not always possible and a short time later, Hatchell himself proved the results could be serious. He was beating some eggs, one hand wrapped around the mixing bowl, the other holding the whisk when the ship suddenly went into a deep roll. Instead of immediately dropping the beater, Hatchell waited a split second too long before grabbing for the overhead beam. His grasp fell short and his feet went out from under him. As the ship's roll deepened, he slid under one of the steam kettles, hitting the drain spigot as he passed by. This opened the valve, allowing the scalding water in the kettle to pour over him. The ship was practically on its side in the roll and the force of gravity pinned him in place. Hatchell screamed in pain.

There was nothing I could do. I watched horrified, unable to move for if I had let go I would have been thrown on top of him making a bad situation worse. I waited for an eternity until the ship began to right itself. Then I ran to shut off the flow of water.

D.K. Waxler, the boatswain's mate of the watch who was stationed just outside the galley door, heard Hatchell's scream and rushed in as soon as he could. He got to Hatchell about the same time I did and together, we helped the injured cook down to sick bay. Hatchell was pretty badly scalded but in a few days, he recovered enough to return to duty. While he was out, his workload fell to the other cooks and strikers, but we willingly took up the slack. Each of us knew that what had happened to him could as easily have happened to any of us. When Hatchell came back to duty, he was sporting a bandage and a renewed dedication to one-handed cooking. It was a lesson I never forgot.

A few days later, we were preparing to put out the supper meal while the ship was on maneuvers. In my hand was a towel, a small cotton terry cloth that was an all-purpose necessity used to wipe up a spill, handle a hot plate or dry your hands. Some cooks would tuck it into their waistband but I found it a lot more convenient to flip it over my shoulder. As I wiped my hands on the towel while checking on the coffee brewing in the steam kettle, the ship suddenly went into a deep roll to port. Having learned from Hatchell's experience, I flipped the towel over my shoulder and grabbed for the overhead beam in one motion. At least, I thought I had flipped the towel over my shoulder. When the ship was back on an even keel, I looked for it but couldn't find it anywhere. Supper was about to be served and I had no time to waste searching for it. I grabbed a replacement and went about my work.

After supper, the final job of clean up was to swab the deck. In order to conserve water, we used leftover coffee for the final rinse. Coffee, in those days, was around nineteen cents a pound but water, made by the ship's condensers and always in short supply, was considered far more valuable. Aboard ship, nothing goes to waste and at the end of the day, the undrinkable dregs of the coffee were used for clean up instead of clear water. We conserved water and got the deck squeaky clean and shiny.

I emptied the thick sediment from the urn onto the deck and on the bottom of the kettle, there was my lost towel. As I was about to close the galley door for the evening, Waxler called out to me, "Good coffee tonight, Seeley." As far as I can remember, that was the first and only time anyone ever complimented me on my coffee. It was also the only time I lost my towel in a steam kettle. I laughed to myself as I wondered if I would earn more words of

John Johnides

praise by using a dirty towel in the coffee all the time.

For all our frustrations in the galley, they were nothing compared to what a seaman from Ohio had to endure. John Johnides, who had been assigned as mess cook, had the job of carrying the food in tureens from the galley down one deck to the mess hall. There was always fresh air blowing through the portholes in the galley, but the mess hall relied on forced air for ventilation. Once you dropped down the ladder, the air closed in around you like a blanket. The smells could be overwhelming.

Johnides, who was prone to seasickness, would come to the galley, pick up the food, carry it down to the mess hall and throw up as soon as he got to the bottom of the ladder. He would clean up the mess and return for more food. That continued for several days. The medical department did not accept seasickness as a reason to be excused from duty. To his credit, Johnides never asked for relief. He kept performing his job as best he could. Finally, the men to whom he was trying to bring the food, despairing of ever getting a full meal on time, requested he be reassigned. He was.

10 January 1941

After a stop at Mare Island, near San Francisco, we headed down the coast to San Pedro, California. Everyone who rated it expected to get liberty as soon as we were moored but we got the word that it would be delayed. The scuttlebutt was that a new piece of equipment was going to be installed.

I generally put little stock in rumor. To get the straight dope, I struck up a conversation with Chief Boatswain's Mate Youtsey. He had five hash marks on his sleeve, meaning he had been in the Navy at least as long as I had been alive. His face was hard, which made him seem unapproachable. While he never talked about himself, when it came to ship's business, he was always willing to answer questions for the men. He told me it was degaussing gear, and explained that it was equipment that demagnetized the hull to repel submerged mines. It would be vital to our survival if war came.

The next day at 0800, most of *Rowan's* one-hundred-seventy crewmembers filed off onto the dock. As we stood at ease, a long line of dungaree blue, awaiting instructions, I noticed a piece of cable, about two hundred feet long and six inches in diameter, laying near the closest building. Before I had a chance to wonder whether this was the degaussing gear, we were ordered to move into position beside it. Another order was given and, as a unit, we hoisted it up onto our shoulders and carried it aboard.

Shifty Lanoue, one of the smallest guys on the ship, wound up behind Bill Ward, one of the tallest. I wouldn't have been surprised if the cable never even touched Lanoue's shoulder but to hear Shifty tell it, he bore the entire weight of it all by himself. I'd have argued that with him, however. For as sore as my back, neck and shoulders were for days afterward, I believe that honor fell to me!

I rated liberty but Bob had duty and couldn't come along. I went with Doyle Kelley, one of the new mess cooks. A recent graduate of the Naval Training Center in Newport, Rhode Island, Kelley had reported aboard the *Rowan* at the Mare Island Naval Shipyard. Redheaded and a face full of freckles, he had a ready smile and quick wit. I liked him immediately. I hadn't ever talked to him before but we had an enjoyable liberty together.

As often happened when we were on liberty, we met up with other *Rowan* men, including Goon Alderman, Steve Kess, and Ernie Karbowski. With no agenda in mind, other than to have a good time, we followed anyone with an idea of where to go. Bob Hill was from California and he told us about a place in Long Beach where we could hear a good big band play. It didn't look like much on the outside but inside, the music was all he said it would be.

When we got back to the ship before midnight, I went looking for my brother to tell him of my great evening, but he had already turned in and wasn't interested in conversation.

"Tell me about it in the morning," he grumbled, pulling the pillow over his head.

"Okay," I said, "but you don't know what you're missing! The story might not be as good tomorrow morning."

"I'll take my chances." He rolled over and did not stir again.

Having no one else to shoot the breeze with, I swung my hammock and turned in.

Goon Alderman
Ernie Karbowski
and Steve Kess

Hawaii

Monday, 13 January. 0345. Still feeling pretty good from liberty Saturday night, I rolled out of the sack and headed forward to the galley to report for duty. As always, a number of the men were gathered outside the galley drinking coffee and swapping yarns.

Waxler was one of them. A veteran of the Asiatic fleet, he was as colorful an individual as I had ever met. He had a story for every occasion and his tattooed body suggested to me that his stories were at least partly based on fact. Tattoos covered almost every part of his body. He had a spider web tattoo on his stomach, which had been done when he was young and slim. Now, nearing forty, he had put on weight in the midsection. The spider web had stretched with his stomach, making a gigantic pattern. He had hula girls tattooed on the calf of each leg, placed so that he could make them wiggle when he walked. It was always good for a laugh when he showed anyone how he could make them dance.

Even with his potbelly, he cut a dashing figure when he went on liberty sporting a tailor-made uniform that he got when he was in China. His bell bottom trousers had an exaggerated flair and the inside flap of his trousers and the cuffs of his jumper were embroidered with golden dragons. He wore his white hat crushed down with the outside rim forming jaunty ears on either side.

Almost any morning, Waxler could be found standing in the galley passageway sipping hot coffee and telling tall tales. His stories, rich and explicit, reminded me of the exotic South Sea Island tales I used to read. Waxler loved to tell stories and I loved to listen. As soon as the coffee was brewed in the morning, I'd grab a steaming mug, doctor it up with cream and sugar, and join him and the group for my morning ration of sea salt.

This morning, Waxler had some scuttlebutt. With mug in hand, he leaned against the door of the galley passageway and waited for all of us to give him our undivided attention. "You'll like this, Seeley." He took a sip to build the suspense, "Word is, we're going to be gone for a long time."

"Where are we heading?" I prompted enjoying Waxler's game.

He shrugged and said, "Maybe Panama, or Hawaii."

I thought he might be teasing me because I had said often how much I wanted to go to Hawaii. I didn't want to get my hopes up because it was just scuttlebutt. It could be weeks before we would find out for sure.

15 January 1941

Rowan, *Wilson*, *Anderson* and *Stack* left San Pedro and formed up with two carriers, *Enterprise* and *Yorktown*, and another destroyer squadron, heading southwest. Every day, we'd maneuver, change directions and take part in target drills, but our course remained southwesterly. After a few days, all bets were that our destination was none other than Hawaii.

20 January

We were not far from the islands and excitement left me tossing and turning all night. Waking from a dream in which hula girls were chasing me, I rolled out of the sack and hurried topside to see if I could see the island. The first hint of the Hawaiian dawn was painting the eastern sky with tinges of pink and silver. The spectacular sunrise splashed the drab gray ships of our destroyer squadron with rainbow colors as they formed up single file preparing to enter port. But the ships of our division did not capture my attention. My eyes were riveted to the wind-swept face of Oahu.

Hawaii! This was the land I had been reading about, dreaming of for years. Until now, it had existed only in my imagination. Now for the first time, I could see it with my own eyes. It was more beautiful than I ever believed. I drank in the beauty of that dawn like a man dying of thirst drinks of cool, sweet water. Although I would return to Hawaii many times over the next twenty-six years, never again would I experience feelings to rival the exhilaration of that first contact.

As we made our approach, Diamond Head loomed large off the starboard bow. Choppy seas had the ship rolling gently, not more than ten to fifteen degrees. Snappy winds gusting through the shrouds made the rigging flap and the signal flags stand out straight and stiff against the breeze. I had to hang onto my white hat to keep it from blowing overboard. I could hardly pull myself away to go to my duty station.

I was eager to get off the ship as soon as we tied up at Pearl, but that would have to wait. We were ordered to begin taking on fuel and provisions. Finally, liberty parties began at 1300, when the last of the supplies was neatly stowed. Bob was among the first to go but I had duty. I felt a slight twinge of jealousy as I watched him cross the gangway, but my chance would come the next day. I just had to wait a little longer.

With nothing better to do, I sat down on an ammunition box topside near the galley to write a letter home to the folks. A sweet fragrance wafted out across the water and I inhaled its aroma deeply. I wanted to tell them all about my first impressions of the island. The feelings I had wouldn't translate well onto paper. All I could tell them was, "I could write a book!" I didn't know how long it would take to realize that ambition. As soon as I gave the letter to the mail orderly, Frankie Rung, I went to my locker and pulled out my liberty uniform to be sure it was ready to go.

21 January

Two tugs came alongside and towed *Rowan* away from the pier. Then under our own power, we moved to the other side of Ford Island where we were moored to a buoy.

Since *Rowan* was the last ship of our squadron to arrive, we got the outboard position, farthest from the buoy in the nest of four destroyers. Whether you were inboard, outboard or in the middle of these destroyer nests, there were inconveniences to deal with. Outboard, whaleboats picked up and deposited passengers at your gangway twenty-four hours a day. In the middle, your ship served as a passageway for the crews from the other ships. Inboard, you had to march across several ships before you could go anywhere. No matter where you were, you could expect a steady stream of foot traffic crossing the gangways that connected one ship to the other. But our position in the nest didn't matter to me, as long as we were in Hawaii.

1300. My liberty began. I finished cleaning up in the galley and raced to change into my whites. Bob was already waiting for me on the gangway. Along with fifteen or twenty others from the *Rowan*, we boarded the liberty boat for a long, choppy ride to the submarine base, where we had taken on provisions the day before. When the whaleboat docked, we swarmed to the front door of the seaman's club. That was the terminal for the open-sided jitney cabs that would take us into downtown Honolulu.

Roy Danielsen
in Hawaii

52

The cabs were always full but if you missed one, another would be along in a few minutes. Bob knew exactly where we had to go and we were first in line to catch the next jitney that came by. We chose a couple of seats on the shady side of the cab and as we rode, I took in the sights. Honolulu was a small port city where everything seemed to run at slow speed. I loved its quiet, lazy charm but something was missing. There were palm trees but I saw no Hawaiian guitars being strummed softly under their branches. There were young ladies but no hula girls.

All day long, we walked around town, stopping once in a while to buy a soda or some trinket. One shop caught our attention because of the crowd of servicemen out front. Upon closer inspection, we saw it was a barbershop and all the barbers were fantastically female. Tempting as it was to have a beautiful young woman run her fingers through your hair, neither of us felt it was worth $5.00, when we could get a haircut aboard the *Rowan* for fifty cents! We bought some postcards for the folks at home. I found one with a sailor chasing a hula girl with a lawn mower. I hoped Mom would like it.

By 1800, we had seen everything we were interested in. The sun was setting and shops were closing. The only remaining forms of entertainment were drinking and carousing. Neither of us was so inclined and we had had enough walking. With the souvenirs we had purchased, we headed to the YMCA to board the jitney back to the ship, tired and a little let down. Hawaii was beautiful but it wasn't the paradise I had dreamed of.

As we rode along, a familiar odor assailed my senses. It reminded me of the perfumed breezes that had excited me when we first pulled into Pearl Harbor, only this odor was so strong, it was obnoxious. I leaned over to the jitney driver and asked, "Say, do you know what that smell is?"

"Yeah, bruddah," he said in a heavy Hawaiian accent. "Tha's from the pineapple factory up ahead." He nodded in the direction of the docks. "Tha's where they can it."

I sat back in my seat. It was yet another blow to my fantasy. There had been no perfumed breezes, only a pineapple factory. There were no lilting Hawaiian guitars and the only hula girl I saw was on a postcard! I was beginning to think some things are better enjoyed in your dreams.

Even though our sections rated liberty, neither Bob nor I went ashore again. We had lost interest. I doubted if there really were hula girls dancing under swaying palms. The truth was, I had just about drained all my recreational funds. By staying aboard, I knew I would not be tempted to spend money I didn't have.

Bob and I spent the evenings together, talking about our visit to Hawaii and about our illusions and disillusions. I turned in early on those evenings. If the real thing didn't measure up, I could still dream.

As I dreamed, I was unaware that this was the calm before the gathering storm.

Grumman Down

Like most Americans before the war began, I had only passing interest in the events taking place in the world. The Nazis in Germany and the Imperial Japanese fleet were too far away to be of much importance to me. As long as the United States was not involved, neither was I. But all of that was about to change.

The Nazis were swiftly moving ahead with their plans of conquest, disrupting sea lanes as they forced the nations of Europe to accept their domination. Countries fell one by one and after the fall of France, Britain stood virtually alone in opposition. To bring that proud nation to its knees, the Germans threw wave after wave of aerial attacks at the British Isles. After almost two years of pounding, the stalwarts were beginning to falter. Their fleet was devastated, their planes held together by chewing gum and bailing wire and their armies badly bloodied. The only thing that kept Great Britain from falling was the indomitable spirit of her people.

Prime Minister Winston Churchill knew his country could not stand alone much longer, and he appealed to Britain's former colony for aid. By the middle of January 1941, secret top level meetings were held in Washington, D.C., to discuss plans for collaboration between the British and American military forces.

In the months to come, those meetings would quietly move us to the brink of war. The drama unfolding in Europe would soon involve my country - and me - half a world away.

Aboard the *Rowan*, the indication of things to come arrived when we received word that there would be an inspection by Rear Admiral Husband E. Kimmel, then Commandant of the Naval District. We were unaware that his visit was part of an overall assessment of fleet readiness. For us, it was just another of the unexplained surprises the Navy presented from time to time. We didn't ask questions. We just got ready.

25 January 1941

Saturday. An admiral's inspection was a big deal and we spent three full days preparing for it. We scrubbed and painted, working right up till the last minute. At 0900, all hands shifted out of dungarees and into whites. An hour later, the crew was at quarters standing at parade rest when the admiral's barge came along the starboard side of the ship. Everyone was called to attention and those on the starboard side gave a smart hand salute to the approaching craft. In a gleam of white and brass, the admiral and his entourage came aboard. The boatswain's pipes shrilled as they passed through a welcoming committee of sideboys, an honor guard of sailors.

The ceremony surrounding the inspection was all I saw of the admiral's visit. My division stood at ease on deck until we were again called to attention for the departure of the dignitaries. Apparently there were no problems, for liberty was granted as soon as the admiral left the ship. Bob had duty and I wasn't interested in going ashore, so I spent the day writing letters and sitting on deck catching some sunshine. The peacefulness of the day gave no hint of things to come.

27 January

Monday. The entire fleet stood out to sea for a training exercise. There were the carriers *Enterprise* and *Yorktown*, battleships *Arizona*, *New York*, *Pennsylvania* and *Nevada*, cruisers

Philadelphia and *Wichita*, and two squadrons of destroyers, eight in all. From horizon to horizon stretched the ships of our invincible armada. This Navy was even grander than I had ever imagined.

The next morning, independent of the carriers and battleships, our destroyer squadron was ordered to commence target practice, firing our main batteries. Unlike the target practice on maneuvers with the Illinois National Guard last summer, the Navy gave us live ammunition to work with, and it packed a deafening wallop!

All seamen second class had to qualify at every position before they could advance in rate, and so I became familiar with the operation of *Rowan*'s main battery, four five-inch, thirty-eight caliber guns. These were dual-purpose, semi-automatic, rapid-fire weapons effective for anti-aircraft barrages, salvos at surface targets and shore bombardments. State of the art for their time, they had high-speed drives for training and elevation, a hydraulic rammer for loading, and both local handwheel control and remote director control. The guns could propel a fifty-four pound projectile as far as 18,000 yards, with a maximum aerial range of over six miles.

The average gun crew could get off a shot every four seconds and the best crews could cut that to less than three. Given the complexity of the gun, which required the combined skills of nearly every man aboard to score a direct hit, that was quite a feat. From helm to engine room, fire control director to magazine, everyone had to execute his job with something nearing perfection. After all, not only was the target moving, but also the ship from which the gun was fired.

The process of firing the gun began with retrieving the ammunition from storage in the magazine, a cramped room in the lowest level of the ship, which was lined on all sides by racks of shells and powder cans. To enter the magazine, a sailor had to slip through a hatch in the deck above, climb down the ladder and then dog down, or secure, the hatch behind him. When he received word through the sound powered headphones, he'd load a shell and powder can, smokeless for daytime use or flashless for night, onto a conveyor, which hoisted the munitions up to the upper handling room. There, two sailors pulled the shells and cans off the conveyor and passed them up to the gun mount above.

The swivel mount gun had an eleven-man crew. They were the pointer, trainer, fuse setter, sight setter and sight checker, shell handler, powder can handler, spade man, hot shell man, gunner's mate, and gun captain. As a team, they readied the gun and after the shell was fired and the breach opened to expel the spent powder can, the crew started all over, ready for the next round.

28 January

Tuesday. 0800. All gun crews were at battle stations. I took my position in the #2 upper handling room and awaited orders to commence firing. Our station reported our condition, "Number two upper handling room, manned and ready."

Off in the distance, I heard the sound of an approaching aircraft. I peeked out the scuttle, a small opening in the upper handling room hatch, and saw a single-engine biplane towing a target sleeve. Fire control lined up the shot and passed the coordinates to the gun crew chief. Above me, the gun mount trained around into position while the pointer brought the gun barrel to the proper elevation. The fuse setter set the fuse for detonation at the proper distance from the ship. The shell handler placed the shell in the breach, the powder can handler loaded the powder, and the projectile man rammed the load home. We were set.

"Commence firing," came the command. With that, we opened up. The first sharp report erupted from our guns but the shot came closer to the plane than it did to the target. We reloaded as quickly as we could and let loose another barrage. A miss. Reload. Fire. A miss. Reload. Fire. A little closer. For more than an hour, we blazed away at the target. Our marksmanship probably did little for that pilot's nerves. After a short period of rest and evaluation, we started again. For hours, we fired salvo after salvo, sharpening our skills. At the same time, we were learning to work together as a team, as if our lives depended on our abilities and each other.

The training exercise was moderately successful, but not good enough to earn *Rowan* an "E" for efficiency. That would have meant an extra five dollars a month for each member of the gun crew. Maybe next year. I wonder if we would have tried harder had we known that before the qualification period came around again, our guns would be firing at an enemy who would be firing back at us.

At week's end, we switched from guns to torpedoes. The "fish," as they were called, were twenty-one inches in diameter, weighed about 2,200 pounds, carried a payload of 500 pounds of TNT and cost the American tax-payer $10,000 each. Those early torpedoes had a lot of accuracy problems, but we gave the citizens their money's worth. I am pleased to report that on the training maneuver, we made a direct hit. That hit, to the best of my knowledge, was the only one made in *Rowan's* brief history.

President Roosevelt said publicly that he was trying to keep the United States out of the war but as early as February, 1941, the men of our crew were starting to believe that the shooting was about to begin. The incident of the *Panay*, an American ship sunk by the Japanese in the China Sea several years earlier, had bruised our national pride. As our crew practiced, we could hardly wait for the day to come when we could put a few five-inch shells or, even better, a torpedo or two, into a Jap ship. We were cocky, certain that the United States Navy would whip the Japanese Navy in just a few days.

1 February

I was on watch in the galley when I heard two blasts from a pocket whistle, the signal indicating attention to port. I glanced out the porthole to see a Japanese merchantman a hundred feet off our beam. According to naval tradition and courtesy, we rendered passing honors, dipping our flag in a salute to the Japanese ship. At the same time I could hear gun mounts swinging into position as our crews seized the opportunity to practice training our guns and torpedo tubes. We weren't at war, but it was a shaky peace.

3 February

Monday. After a weekend in port, we were out to sea again. This time, our destroyer squadron was screening the carrier *Yorktown*, forming a field of protection around her. *Rowan* was astern in the screen. Watch Condition III was set, where only one of three sections was on watch at any given time, and only certain stations were manned for training purposes. We had four hours on military watch, eight hours off.

I left the galley right after breakfast to take up my position as lookout on the port wing of the bridge. The man on watch told me our position and explained my duty during this exercise. When *Yorktown* launched or landed planes, I was to identify the aircraft. I would report the activity to Mr. Wyatt, the officer of the deck, so he would know how many planes were in the air. When the sailor finished filling me in, I said to him, "I relieve you," to complete the change of watch.

Lt. John Wyatt

Keeping an eye on those planes wasn't easy because sometimes they were hidden from my sight by the mass of the carrier. I was nervous, as I was any time I had to be on the bridge, but the nerves helped me concentrate. With the powerful field glasses raised to my eyes, I scanned the sky for approaching aircraft.

I spotted a Grumman F-1 biplane making an approach, and focused on him so I could report as soon as he touched down on *Yorktown*'s runway. As I watched, I realized something was wrong. Instead of making a smooth approach, the plane began to sputter. It fell short of the carrier and crashed into the sea. "Grumman F-1 biplane," I shouted to the OOD, "it's ditched, sir. It's in the water!" My hands shook as I tried to focus the binoculars on the plane.

Mr. Wyatt, a soft-spoken, gentlemanly officer from North Carolina, looked in the direction of the downed plane for half a second, assessing the situation. He quickly called to the helm, "Left standard rudder. Increase speed to twenty-five knots." He told the telephone talker who was trailing behind him, "Notify the boatswain's mate-of-the-watch away the rescue party." He came up behind me and asked, "Any sign of the pilot?"

"No, sir," I said, not taking my eyes off the plane. I drew strength from Mr. Wyatt's calm. *Rowan* vibrated with the increasing speed. I kept my glasses trained on the biplane. It was slipping slowly away. We'd never get to it in time. When we were still several hundred yards away, it vanished under the sea. We were close enough now. I lowered the glasses but kept watching the point where the plane disappeared so that I could aid in the rescue effort. I was sure that at any moment, I would see the pilot pop to the surface. "Come on," I urged him mentally. "Come on, get out of there." But there was no sign of life. A minute passed. Then two. Suddenly, I knew the pilot wasn't getting out. A coldness set in around my heart as I realized I had just witnessed his death.

I was relieved by the next watch. I gave my report but instead of going to the mess hall for chow, I stayed on deck watching, hoping. Although we searched for several hours, no trace of either the plane or the pilot was found. I went to my bunk at dusk and tried to rest before I went back on duty at 2000. Fighting back tears, I lay on my back, thinking about what I had seen. In the short span of time that I had the F-1 in my glasses, I had made a connection with that pilot. I never knew his name, never saw his face, but I felt as if I had lost a close friend. I wondered at how quickly and easily life can be snuffed out. What if I had not been watching? No one would have known how he died - not the way I knew. Was he frightened? Did he suffer long? Would his family hurt as badly as I was hurting?

If this was a preview of war, I did not like it.

Witnessing the pilot's death had affected me deeply, yet it could not prepare me for the future. I still didn't connect our preparations for war with the killing of men. For me, this practice was like the games we used to play as children, when boys would man make-believe machine gun and others would charge into them to be slain in their tracks. It was more fun to be the one killed because dying required more acting. Besides, you could "die" once and get up and go through it all over again. It was, after all, just a game.

Although our weapons were as real as the possibility of death, for me and many of my shipmates, doing battle meant excitement and adventure. We never associated it with mangled bodies or grief-stricken relatives. If anyone was going to get killed, it was the enemy. Death had little meaning to me - until today. I had my first bitter taste of death. Before another year passed, all of us aboard the *Rowan* would understand the reality of war with vivid clarity, and none of us would ever be the same.

Aunt Violet's Ring

April 1941. Upon our return to California from maneuvers in Hawaii, *Rowan* was scheduled for two weeks of yard availability to install new equipment and update certain systems.

This provided Bob and me with just the opportunity we had been waiting for. Since we would not be needed for regular ship's business during that time, we submitted our requests for a two-week leave. Both of us were cooks, and going together was a long shot. To our surprise, our requests were granted. Bob and I couldn't wait to see the folks again. All we had to do was figure out how to pay for the trip.

We were very frugal with our money, but we still didn't have enough to pay for two round trip train fares. We had one chance-Aunt Violet's ring. When we wired Mom telling her of our situation, she immediately took Aunt Violet's ring into town, got a loan against it, and wired us the fare.

The ring was the family heirloom and treasure. Since the beginning of the Depression, there were many times that we ran out of money before we ran out of month. That ring came to our rescue providing the cash we needed just in the nick of time.

Aunt Violet, Violet Beatrice Seeley, was my father's younger sister. A registered nurse, she loved her profession and served her

Violet Seeley

community in that capacity for twelve years. She worked at Springfield Hospital and later, St. John's Hospital in Springfield, Illinois, but she was never too busy or too far away to take care of her family when the need arose. Her nursing skills probably saved my life.

One early spring day when I was very small, my mother found me playing outside our house in the snowy slush. I was wet and chilled to the bone. I fell ill and within a short time, developed pneumonia. In those days, that was considered a death sentence. When Violet heard I was sick, she took a leave of absence from the hospital and came immediately to take care of me. Through the worst it, she stayed by my side night and day. She was a loving, caring, humorous person and I realize now that I loved her very much.

When Aunt Violet was about forty, she became engaged to a man named Troy. He gave her a diamond ring when he asked for her hand. They never married, however, because she developed cancer. Despite extensive surgery, on Tuesday, August 7, 1928, just five days before my tenth birthday, Aunt Violet died. I felt her loss deeply. She bequeathed her ring to my mother and I believe her spirit lived on with us through that simple piece of jewelry.

The ring itself was nothing special, just a plain white gold setting and a small diamond. Its monetary value was not great but it was priceless to the family. In time of need, Mom would take it into town and pawn it to cover an emergency loan. It was in and out of hock more times than I can say but it never stayed in long. Just as soon as Mom had the money, she would repay the debt and bring it home. With the arrival of our telegram, Aunt Violet's legacy once again made the trip into town. This time, it would provide transportation money for us to come home.

It was the middle of April when we got back to Macomb. The temperature was quite cool, especially since we had gotten used to the warmth of California and Hawaii. Nevertheless, the early spring of central Illinois was a welcomed sight to both of us.

The first thing Bob and I did was to spend some time with Dad. Everett Seeley wasn't doing well and I'm not certain he even recognized us. His stroke left him a total invalid, incapable of anything beyond the most rudimentary communication. It was hard for me to see him like that. When we were growing up, Dad seemed to possess boundless strength. He was a builder, skilled at all the trades - masonry, carpentry, concrete work, anything to do with building a house.

When times were good, he had several full-time employees and a large inventory of construction tools. We always had a late model car or truck. But after the 1929 crash, things started getting hard and Dad had trouble finding work. By 1930, the situation was desperate. Accepting welfare was terribly difficult for proud people like Mom and Dad. To keep us housed and fed, Dad took what assets he could gather and bought a farm. It seemed like the perfect solution - we would be okay as long as we could grow our own food.

Dad and my mother were enthusiastic about the move. They described the farm as a "one hundred acre paradise" just twelve miles outside Macomb. The five of us city-raised children didn't share their enthusiasm. To me, farming was just plain work! Work started too early in the morning and ended too late in the evening, and nothing was easy. But Dad had no choice. He had to provide for his family so every day, he was out trying to scratch a living from the unyielding earth behind a team of two draft horses and a

Seeley Family -- Lewis (standing, left); Back row, left to right: Mary (Mom), Everett (Dad), Maurice; Front: Myron, Freda, Bob, Mildred, Anne (Maurice's wife)

hand plow. While he tended the livestock, we boys would look for every opportunity to slip out to the creek for a swim. Seeing him now, I was not very proud of that part of my life.

Our time at home passed quickly. The last evening we were home the whole family came over, Myron, Freda and the baby, and Maurice and his wife, Anne. Mom made her famous biscuits and gravy, and Bob and I talked about our great adventures. We had everyone's rapt attention and we tried to tell Waxler's best sea stories, cleaned up, of course. Every time I'd get to the punch line of a joke or a story, I'd forget how to say it, or leave out an important tidbit of information. It didn't matter. We laughed at everything whether it was funny or not.

In quieter moments, we talked some about the world situation, the prospects of war, and what it all might mean to family and friends. There was an undercurrent in our talk that we had never felt before. It was like an awareness of a great, dark, unknown future and we all carried our private, inexpressible fears. But we didn't dwell on these thoughts because our hearts were too full of the love we had for each other. Our laughter was a cloak to shield us from an inevitable tomorrow that we were yet unprepared to face.

After dinner, we moved to the living room and gathered around the Gulbranson, a fine old player piano. It was one of the few survivors of the time before the Depression that Mom clung to. Myron and I pulled out guitars and we sang some of our favorite songs.

For fun, Tip, Bob and I went down to the square to watch the people go by, just as we had during the Depression when we didn't have a nickel in our pockets. Friends and neighbors were happy to see us and made a big fuss over us, all decked out in our uniforms. Then we joined Myron at the dance hall where he was playing guitar with the Harold Benson orchestra. He had taken my place when I joined the Navy, and I enjoyed listening to him play. Mildred, never one to shy away from the spotlight, needed little encouragement from us to get up and sing a song with the orchestra. She was very good and she loved to perform.

We were all together as we had always been, but it was like a visit into the past, a last look at a page before it is turned forever. It was a rare and precious moment but like a morning mist, it would soon be gone. We were changing, going our own ways. Our paths would never again be along the same course. None of us could have guessed then that it was the last time all of us would be together.

Bob and I had mixed feelings about leaving. Our visit was warm and satisfying but our lives were at sea. The house on Carroll Street was where Mom and Dad lived. For Bob and me, the USS *Rowan* (DD 405) was now the address we called home.

Good Clean Fun

May 1941. When we returned to the ship, *Rowan* was in the yard at Mare Island to be stripped of all non-essential personal gear. Even the captain's private sailboat had to go in the "strip ship" process, to make room for increasing the ship's complement from one hundred seventy men to a wartime crew which would eventually reach two hundred seventy. One especially appreciated upgrade was the installation of extra bunks, which meant Bob and I no longer had to sleep on hammocks in the mess hall.

Experienced crewmen were being reassigned, replaced by a larger group of recent boot graduates. It became difficult to get to know all the new men. But two I did manage to get acquainted with were Bob Abbott and Bob Icenogle.

Lankford and Abbott

By the end of May, we were out to sea again. Although we didn't know it then, we would never return to a California port. After a few days heading in the general direction of Hawaii, we met up with the cruiser *Philadelphia* and turned southeast on our way to the Panama Canal. From then on, we would be operating in the Atlantic.

With every passing day, the mercury climbed, humidity rose and sea becalmed. The only thing that saved us from the suffocating conditions was our steady speed of twelve knots. Forced air blowers barely made the crew quarters habitable. If you had the bottom bunk, which got the best circulation from the blowers, you could stay cool enough to sleep. Otherwise, all you could do was lay there in a listless, sweaty stupor.

The days turned into a week at sea. Then two. Aside from daily drills and crew exercises, there wasn't much to ward off monotony. We entertained ourselves by watching passing porpoises and tortoises, and writing letters home. After sundown, they'd show a movie back on the fantail. Trouble was, even when we swapped movies with the other ships in the squadron, the selection of films was limited. Two of those unforgettable titles were *Boom Town* and *Flying Down To Rio*. They became a running joke. When anyone asked what the movie was for that night, the answer was always *Boom Town* and *Flying Down to Rio*.

31 May

We were off Panama. We'd soon be in the Atlantic where our ship movements would come under the scrutiny of the Germans. The United States had not declared war against the Third Reich, but the Germans treated us as an enemy. They did not trust us. The feeling was mutual. To make the spies' job of reporting ship movements to Hitler a little harder, we were ordered to paint out the numerals on our bow and lash a hammock across our name on the stern before went through the canal.

Our first stop in the Atlantic was Guantanamo Bay, Cuba, where we stopped for refueling. Then we headed north to Philadelphia, and entered the naval yards for more repair and upgrade work.

Decker and I were working together in the galley when I mentioned to him that I had to go ashore to draw small stores, like aprons and towels, etc. Because of an earlier incident, he was about half way through a sixty-day restriction. He jumped at the chance to go with me. Going ashore to get replacement uniforms was permitted and he was eager for any excuse to get off the ship.

1300. Decker and I handed our passes to the man on duty at the gangway and headed ashore. When we got to the small stores building near the docks, we discovered it wasn't open. We should have gone back to the ship right away but Decker was not in any hurry to return. "Aw, come on," he cajoled. "What will it hurt if we just stop at the Base Exchange beer hall for a couple of cold ones?" We had plenty of time on our hands and since we weren't going to leave the base, I thought, "What's the harm?"

One beer led to another, and another, and another, until we were both feeling okay. The more we drank the more our sense of right and wrong blurred. Decker was just starting to get back in the good graces of Captain Harrison. Stopping for the beers was pushing his luck. But after a while, it didn't seem to matter to him. If it didn't matter to him, why should it matter to me?

I'm not certain how or when we arrived at the decision to go into town to continue drinking but next thing I knew, we were making plans. The first step was to go back to the ship and change into whites. Then there was the matter of a liberty card. Getting one was no problem for me; I rated it. For Decker, it was a different story. I didn't think he'd manage but when we got to the gangway, he produced a liberty card. I didn't ask any questions. I just took it for granted that he knew what he was doing. He was a petty officer third class. I was just a seaman second.

We found a friendly tavern in downtown Philadelphia where the radio was tuned to the Louis-Conn boxing bout. The two of us listened to the fight and downed a few more beers with the other patrons of the bar. Decker was having a good time and when the fight ended about 2330, he didn't want to leave. But liberty was up at midnight and I knew we had to move.

After a bit of a struggle, I got him out into the street where I was able to hail a cab. As soon as he saw the taxi pull up, he started telling me he wasn't going back to the ship, he was going back in for a few more beers. With a flare of anger, I grabbed him by the arm and shoved him toward the open cab door. In his intoxicated condition, he failed to duck and his left cheek slammed smartly into the roof of the cab. At that, he changed, like Jeckyl and Hyde.

As the cab pulled away from the curb, Decker began mouthing obscenities at me, arguing that we should return to the tavern to continue our good time. Then he went too far; he called me a son-of-a-bitch. That did it. I hauled back and clobbered him with a sharp left to his already injured face.

The taxi driver stopped the cab immediately. He whirled around and looked at us with a face as hard as granite. "Knock it off, you two," he said. "Any more fighting and you'll find yourself walking back to your ship. Got it?"

I got it. I guess Decker did too, because he was sullen and subdued the rest of the trip. It really hadn't been much of a fight - just the one clout, but Decker's mouth was bloody from his collision with the roof of the cab, and he was as mad as a wet hornet. We got back to the ship at five minutes after midnight - late, but not late enough to go on report.

Somewhat unsteadily, Decker made his way back to the crew quarters. Knowing his state of mind, I had my doubts that he was going to turn in and peacefully go to sleep. I decided to let him cool down before I hit the sack, myself. I sat topside on one of the torpedo tubes, where I could shoot the breeze with the petty officer of the watch and keep an eye on the ladder coming up from the crews quarters.

My intuition had been right. In a short time, I spotted Decker coming back up on deck, looking for me. As he weaved his way up the ladder, I saw a flash of light glinting off the blade of a knife, which he had tried to conceal down the back of his jumper. When he was close enough to me, I wrapped a restraining arm around him and slipped the knife from his jumper. The petty officer of the watch called Mr. Hirschhorn, the OOD, who quickly and accurately assessed the situation. He ordered Decker handcuffed to his bunk for the rest of the night. After that, I was able to turn in, secure that I would not wake up dead the next morning.

Decker was in trouble again. I felt sorry for him. When he was sober, he was a good sailor but he and alcohol didn't mix. I'm sure he felt I was in part responsible for his latest mess, but to his credit, he never let his feelings carry over to his job. Drinking was drinking. Work was work. In all of this, I learned a valuable lesson: Some of my shipmates were better drinking buddies than others. I never went ashore with him again.

3 August

0450. Naval Ship Yard, Norfolk, Virginia. We had arrived yesterday and had taken on supplies and more personnel. In other words, it was business as usual. In the pre-dawn hours, I was putting the coffee into the kettle to start it brewing for breakfast when a sleepy-eyed, blond-haired sailor came into the galley and leaned against the door.

As he fought back a jaw-cracking yawn, he offered a muffled, "Mo'nin'."

I looked up at him and answered in kind, "Morning." As I replaced the cover on the kettle, I asked him, "What brings you here so early? Breakfast isn't until 0630."

Ernie Harvey

"Well, in a way, that's why I'm here," he offered in a slow, concise Southern drawl. "I'm having just a little trouble getting my heart started this morning and I was hoping you might have a cup of java to help me out."

I shook my head. "It'll be at least ten minutes. I just put the coffee on to brew. If you don't mind last night's coffee, I have some in a pitcher." I pointed to a stainless steel pot sitting on the counter to my left. "It's cold and strong - for emergency use only."

"I'll take it," the sailor replied firmly.

As I poured him a cup, I asked him, "You new aboard?"

"Yep. Came aboard yesterday. Three of us were supposed to be on the *Bernadou*, but she took off without us. We've got temporary duty here until she comes back for us." He took a sip of the coffee and made a face. "Wow! You weren't kidding about it being strong. Do you have anything I can use to disguise this? Like a sweet roll, or something I can dunk?"

I laughed at his request. "I don't give anyone but the captain such special treatment, but you're in luck. I just happen to have a few leftover cinnamon rolls in the issue room. They're a little stale, but you can have one."

"I'm beginning to wonder about your talent for understatement, but I don't mind if I do." When I returned and handed the pastry to him, he said, "Much obliged." Before he took a bite, he held the roll up and said, "Now, you see? My daddy was right. He told me that the first person to make friends with on a ship is the cook. That way, you'll never go hungry." He dunked an end of the roll into his coffee and took a big bite. "This is just fine, thank you...uh...I don't think I caught your name."

"Seeley," I said. "Lew Seeley. And yours?"

"Ernie Harvey." He held the sweet roll in his teeth and reached forward over his mug to shake hands with me. Past the pastry, he managed to say, "I'm from Georgia."

"Illinois," I replied.

"Well, sir, you're a real gentleman, for a Yankee."

"I don't think anyone's ever called me a Yankee before," I said with a laugh. "Sorry you won't be aboard for long. I've never had a Southerner for a friend before."

It was his turn to laugh. "Well," he said as he finished the roll, "we have a little time to get acquainted." He licked the last crumbs off his fingers and said, "I'm your mess cook."

I started chuckling. Harvey was a real character and in the space of a few minutes, I already considered him a friend. "Maybe your ship won't come back for you," I said. "But meanwhile, we have a meal to put out. How are you at peeling potatoes?"

"I'm a whole lot better at eating 'em, but I'll do my best."

A few days later, the three sailors, including Harvey were returned to the receiving station to wait for their ship, but as it turned out, the *Bernadou* didn't come back for them. Captain

Harrison, who needed a few extra men, learned that they were still unassigned and requested they be posted to *Rowan*. They were.

I was happy to learn Harvey had been reassigned but he never came back to the galley to mess cook. In fact, he spent very little time on the deck force because of another piece of advice his father, a merchant marine, had given him: Strike for a rate where you can see what's going on, he was told. To Harvey, that meant the bridge. Following his father's advice was the beginning of a mutually beneficial friendship. He was always welcome in the galley for a cup of coffee and whatever leftovers I could scrounge, and he always provided me with the latest and most reliable scuttlebutt.

24 June

Puerto Rico. After we returned to port from target practice and gunnery drills, the Captain urged us to form softball teams and go ashore for some R & R (Rest and Recreation). Bob was the first to volunteer. He pitched and I, being one of the few left-handers, played right field.

It was a hot day and the beer which had been provided for us, flowed freely. Quite a few of the men had more than enough. As the game was winding down, for reasons known only to them, a minor scuffle broke out between Decker and another of our crew, Louis Vogel. They were separated but the hostility simmered until they got back aboard. Then, down in the mess hall, a full-blown fight erupted between them. Vogel had Decker down and was pounding him up one side and down the other. After a full day in the sun and too much beer, neither of them had enough energy to do much damage, but what they lacked in power, they made up for with enthusiasm.

The spectators - that is, the entire crew - who had assembled to watch the melee, were both vocal and divided in their support. Some were for Vogel, some for Decker. This time, no one attempted to put a stop to the scrap. Everyone was having too much fun until a simple shoving match among the crowd escalated into fisticuffs. Pretty soon, it was a free-for-all as the spectators became combatants. The action spilled out of the confines of the mess hall.

They fought from the fo'c's'le to the fantail, chiefs, petty officers, and seamen. It seemed that everyone was fighting - except me. Although I have always enjoyed watching a good fight, I had enough of pugilism back in the CCC's when I had been the sparring partner of Bill Thompson, a little guy with a long reach who kept my mouth bloodied every time we strapped on the gloves. From my secure vantage point in the galley, I had a ringside seat to one of the best fights I have ever seen.

After a while, everyone seemed to run out of gas and the fight finally fizzled out without any outside intervention. There were plenty of bruised faces the next morning but no one bore any grudges. It was just a good clean brawl that drained off pent-up emotions.

We never had a repeat of that kind of action because, as it turned out, we didn't have time or energy to get into trouble once we got back to Philadelphia. The Navy claimed all we had. Contrary to what I had hoped for when I began striking for cook, working toward a rate did not exempt me from work on the deck force. From the moment we hit port, I spent more time with a paintbrush in my hand than I did with an apron around my middle.

This time, the paint we were using was not the familiar navy gray. It was black. The new color changed *Rowan*'s appearance completely - which was the whole idea. Everyone knew German submarines, called U-boats, were operating off the East Coast, and painting the ship was a ploy to confuse the enemy about our actual numbers.

Sporting our new paint job, we went out to sea for a few days on maneuvers with the carrier *Wasp*, the cruiser *Tuscaloosa*, and other ships of our destroyer squadron. When we got back, we received orders to repaint the ship in camouflage colors, with big spots of gray, slate blue, and black arranged in random shapes. Again, we let the Germans have a look.

Mid-July

Back in Philadelphia, we received orders to repaint *Rowan* a third time. This time we were to remove paint from all surfaces, down to bare metal. Day and night, you could hear chipping hammers. This was tedious work that made wire-brushing and red-leading seem easy by comparison. To make matters worse, with the non-stop racket, no one got any sleep. And there would be no liberty until we finished.

A few of us decided to take out our frustrations when we got to the director trunk, a circular tower that ran from the fire control director up topside, through the captain's cabin just off the bridge, and down into the galley. We wanted to be sure the captain knew we were busy. If it bothered him, well, that would be a bonus. The captain took our petty protest with good grace. I'm sure he didn't enjoy the experience any more than we did. His silence on the matter showed his compassion for our lot.

Rowan got a spray-painted coat of fire resistant primer. Then the job was finished off, stem to stern, from keel to the top of the mast, inside and out, with a coat of fire-resistant navy gray paint. Nothing was left uncovered. From then on we no longer had to polish brass. The word was simply, "If it moves, salute it. If it doesn't, paint it."

This was yet another sign of our inexorable move toward war. Even though December 7, 1941, came as a complete surprise to most Americans, we knew from mid-summer on that the fighting was about to begin.

Initiation

July 1941. When President Roosevelt declared a three hundred-mile United States territorial water limit, the ships of the U. S. Navy were for all intents and purposes, at war. Under the banner of "neutrality patrol," fully six months before the Japanese bombed Pearl Harbor, we began escorting convoys transporting British troops from U.S. ports in cooperation with Allied Forces.

The duty of the destroyer was to run interference for the slow-moving, unarmed cargo ships. This firepower helped to discourage the well-armed, silent and illusive German U-boats, or submarines. Although America was still considered a neutral country, that stance was hardly more than a thin veneer that was being stretched to the limit. Our orders were not go looking for trouble, but we would not shrink from it, either.

10 November

Rowan, as part of DESRON 8 (Destroyer Squadron 8), was assigned to escort a convoy from New York to somewhere near the equator, where a British convoy was to relieve us and continue to Capetown, South Africa. Scuttlebutt had it that we might be back in time for Christmas, which was fine by me.

Before we left New York we took on more food than I had ever seen in my life, enough to last for three months. Space was at a premium and we had to get pretty inventive about places to store the food. Potatoes got tucked behind a gun mount and eggs wound up ahead of the stack. As we were struggling to stow everything, Bob cheerfully observed, "That means we eat, anyway. What more could a man ask for?"

Our schedule in the galley was tighter now than it had been. There were more mouths to feed, and Hatchell's hitch was up and he left the ship in New York. We were sorry to see him go. He had been a good teacher and a hard worker. To make matters worse, the cook who came aboard when Hatchell left was not much help. We had no sooner gotten underway than he became ill and spent the first part of the cruise in the sick bay. That meant extra duty for all of us.

14 November

0530. I didn't have watch until 0800 and I was enjoying a peaceful sleep. The men on the midnight to 0400 watch had turned in a short time before and had about half an hour to grab some shut-eye before dawn general quarters at 0600. All was quiet.

Suddenly, a violent bump and roll of the ship jolted everyone awake. I was almost thrown from my bunk. Groggy and confused, for a moment I thought we had been hit by a heavy sea swell. At that instant, the ship's siren began to scream out the collision alarm. I hit the deck running, stopping only long enough to ram my feet into my shoes. Hastily, I grabbed my life belt and merged into the flow of men heading topside. In the commotion, I heard someone hollering for us to abandon ship, although no one heeded that order.

When I got to my collision station, I looked to port and saw *Mayrant* backing away. Ernie later told me that *Mayrant* had crossed ahead of us a little too closely and we rammed her. *Rowan*'s bow was crumpled but aside from some considerable damage to a davit and whaleboat, *Mayrant* came away with only a few dents. But the damage to our reputation as a well-oiled fighting machine was more extensive. The confusion that followed the collision signal was a clear indication that we needed more drill. Had this been an actual emergency, we would have been in trouble. For a while, everyone had a story to tell about where he was and what he was doing when the event happened, which made for some lively conversations between drills.

The day after the collision, *Rowan* left the convoy and headed into Puerto Rico to have a steel patch welded to our bow. We were there through the weekend, which meant liberty for those who rated it. Some liberty. They told us to keep our mouths shut because our mission was secret, stay away from the locals, who could be hostile to strangers, and keep out of the water because of sharks. We may as well have stayed aboard.

That advice didn't discourage Decker. Just as soon as liberty parties started going ashore, he was off the ship and into town. I had duty but Ernie didn't. He was about to get his first introduction to Cicero Decker.

The bar they went to was a real waterfront dive. The smoky, dimly lit saloon was filled with seedy looking characters hunched over drinks at a long bamboo bar, or at round, tightly packed tables. Next to each table, waiters would place a twelve inch, round three-legged table for the patron's order, usually a self-serve fifth of rum and a couple of bottles of cola.

Ernie found a seat in a corner and ordered a rum and cola. He had just settled back to watch other people watching him, when he noticed a sailor entering the bar. He leaned a little to his left to see if he could identify the sailor. Sure enough, it was Decker.

Like John Wayne in a Western movie, Decker swung open the saloon doors, and stopped to look around. He spotted two local men standing side by side at the bar. Instead of picking a less crowded spot farther down, he went right up and elbowed his way between them. The two locals took exception to his action. In

81

response, Cicero pulled out the knife he liked to carry in the laces back of his bell-bottoms, and flung it boldly onto the bar. The tip stuck into the wood and the shaft shuddered menacingly. The two men took a hostile stance, daring him to fight. Even before downing his first drink, Decker was all too happy to oblige them.

The atmosphere of the bar became charged with electricity. Chairs scraped back as locals came to the aid of one of their own and sailors headed over to lend a hand to a man in uniform. Women screamed. Voices rose in pitch. With the first blow only seconds away, the bar owner ran out into the street to call the Shore Patrol. Then the fists began to fly. With the free-for-all in full swing, three SP sailors and a lieutenant burst through the door. Whistles blew, adding to the pandemonium. More women screamed and bodies pressed for the door.

Harvey, who didn't court trouble, decided to slip out the back. Someone made a grab for him. To avoid getting sucked into the melee, he dove under a nearby table and inched toward the exit. He looked back to size up the situation and saw the SPs trying to subdue Decker, who had a small table in one hand.

Bury, Bxybe, Hagen and friend

Decker broke free of the restraint and using the table like a baseball bat, brought the weapon around in an attempt to clobber one of the fellows he had been fighting. The SP standing in front of him ducked just in time to dodge the blow but the lieutenant, who was behind the SP, didn't see the projectile coming. He took the full force of it right across the jaw and teeth flew like dice at a crap game. The stool kept flying and wound up crashing through the mirror behind the bar. Whiskey bottles broke, glass flew everywhere and all hell broke loose.

Decker was really in trouble now and apparently, he knew it. With the attention of the SPs momentarily focused on the injured officer, Decker headed for the hills with the SPs in hot pursuit. Our shipmate wasn't seen again until early the next morning, just as we were singling lines, preparing to cast off. Ernie was up on the bridge when, from off in the distance, he caught the wail of approaching sirens. He looked over the wing of the bridge and watched as two SP motorcycles squealed to a stop in front of the

pier. In the sidecar of the first motorcycle was a shackled Cicero Decker, muddied, bloodied and subdued. He looked as if he had spent the night in a swamp, which, it turned out, he had.

The SP officer, a different lieutenant from the one last night, stood on the pier and shouted out to the *Rowan*. "What do you want us to do with him?"

Captain Harrison leaned over the wing of the bridge to assess the situation. *Rowan*'s gangway had already been pulled up in preparation for getting underway. The captain was well acquainted with Decker. He shook his head and said, "If he can jump this far,

William Mihans,
Shore Patrol

83

he can go with us. Otherwise, throw him in the brig until we come back."

Decker was no fool. He knew he stood a lot better chances with the captain than he did with the local constabulary. As soon as they unlocked the manacles, he backed up a few steps and made a running leap, landing with a thud on the quarterdeck. I believe he spent the rest of the cruise doing extra duty. He was busted to seaman first - again. After that, he requested a transfer back to the deck force. It was granted.

With *Rowan's* nose job completed, we had to catch up to the convoy. Doing twenty-five knots all the way, we headed down to Trinidad where the rest of the ships were taking on fuel. The following morning, the convoy turned southeast, bound for the equator. We would soon be crossing the line and that meant fun for the shellbacks who had made the crossing before, and trouble for us pollywogs, who hadn't.

By navy tradition dating back to the days of the old sailing vessels, every pollywog had to go through a rite of initiation, which included fair amounts of hazing and shagging.

For almost a week, the shellbacks gathered in impromptu meetings, discussing what they would do to us, and concocting their evil plans. They had us save all the garbage from the galley, including coffee grounds, eggshells, leftover food servings, potato peelings and grease. To get the right consistency, liberal amounts of cooking fat and fuel oil were added and the mixture left in barrels on the fantail near the depth charge racks so it could properly age in the heat of the South Atlantic sun. It was so foul, I wouldn't have touched it voluntarily even if I had been wearing gloves. Whatever they had in mind, I was sure I wasn't going to like it.

20 November

1200. Notices appeared on the bulletin boards around the ship. One, for example, read:

"Davey Jones"

POLLYWOGS TAKE NOTICE
UNIFORMS FOR LOOKOUTS

WATCH CAPS WORN OVER EARS,
JERSEY, PEA-COAT,
REGULATION GLOVES, SHORT
SKIVVIES AND BLACK SHOES
WITHOUT SOCKS OR LACES.

LOOKOUTS WILL PROVIDE
THEMSELVES WITH "FOGHORNS"
AND BINOCULARS.

ALL LOOKOUTS WILL MUSTER ON
FANTAIL AT 1255 FOR
INSPECTION.

ALL LOOKOUTS WILL MARCH TO
THEIR STATIONS SINGING
"ASLEEP IN THE DEEP."
BY DAVEY JONES' LEFT-HAND MAN
ASSISTANT GESTAPO CHIEF

Shellbacks could assign pollywogs any task they chose, and could force us to stand trial for the slightest perceived infraction. More notices appeared.

TO ALL SLIMY POLLYWOGS--TAKE NOTICE
ALL POLLYWOGS SENTENCED TO "STOCKS" AND "BARREL"
WILL BE ENTERED IN A BATHING BEAUTY CONTEST.
ALL CONTESTANTS WILL GIVE EXHIBITIONS OF DIVING,
FANCY SWIMMING, AND POSING. THE WINNER WILL BE
DECIDED ON FORM OF FIGURE, DIVING FORM, AND SWIMMING
GRACE.

```
                    ATTIRE:
      LONG HANDLED SKIVVIES AS BATHING TRUNKS.
   NECKERCHIEF TIED AROUND HEAD AS BATHING CAP.
   SHEETING OR RAG TO COVER "BUST" OR "TITS", AS THE
   CASE MAY BE. NAME OF HOMETOWN, PRECEDED BY THE
   WORD "MISS" MUST BE PROMINENTLY DISPLAYED ON
   PERSON. THE CONTEST WILL OPEN WITH A SOLO, SUNG
   BY (GEORGIA) GRAY, SINGING "BEBO" IN E-MINOR,
   FOLLOWED BY A GRAND CHORUS BY ALL CONTESTANTS
   IMITATING THE "MISSES" THEY ARE.
                             THE SEA PUPPY
```

22 November

Saturday. All pollywogs were ordered to have nothing for breakfast but bread and water. I, being a wise guy and a cook, went to the galley and prepared bacon and eggs for myself. I thought I had pulled a fast one and felt rather smug about it. I had overlooked the fact that Brown, the cook on duty, was a shellback.

1300. King Neptune and his court came aboard. Captain Harrison met him at the bow and turned the ship over to him. Neptune, Chief Boatswain's Mate Youtsey, was dressed in a long robe fashioned from a sheet. On his head was wig made from the string end of a swab, topped by a crown, and in his left hand, he carried a trident, which one of the shipfitters had made. He glowered at us pollywogs.

After the welcoming ceremonies, Neptune took over the ship, according to custom. He ordered all pollywogs to assemble on the fantail where they would be initiated into the Royal Order of Shellbacks. There was only one way to survive the initiation - you had to go along with it. If you struggled or failed to see the fun in it, it would have been a nightmare. I decided to cooperate.

All pollywogs, except for those on duty, had to strip nude and go through a slop chute, a long piece of canvas which was sewn together to form a tunnel just big enough for a person to crawl through. It was filled with the slimy, moldy grease-garbage combination we had been saving for the past week. One end was held open with a wire arrangement but the rest of the chute lay flat on the deck, ensuring that all who entered it got thoroughly coated by the ooze. We had to use our heads to push up the collapsed canvas. The smell was bad enough but the shellbacks added to our tribulations. Armed with homemade canvas shillelaghs, they took whacks at the passing pollywogs.

Once clear of the slop chute, we had to run about twenty feet through a double line of shillelagh-armed shellbacks, each trying get in his whacks. Then, we had to stand before the Royal Baby, a part played by Electrician's Mate Second Christiensen, a cherubic looking fellow clothed in a diaper with some chocolate dribbled down his leg. He wore a baby bonnet and sat on his chair sucking a lollipop. We had to kiss his knee before being passed on to the Royal Judge.

As each pollywog came before the judge, the magistrate would ask if any shellback had charges to bring against the initiate. Complaints could be anything. Men were accused of such crimes as breathing, or being ugly. If anyone had a complaint, the pollywog was sentenced immediately - and you could count on being sentenced, no matter what.

When my turn came, Brown, the cook who had observed my bacon and egg breakfast, was only too happy to stand up and accuse me. There was no defense. I was immediately sentenced to another trip through the slop chute.

Next came the Royal Doctor, who examined me with an electric probe, which produced an uncomfortable shock when he passed it across my stomach. When I opened my mouth in response to the discomfort, he pushed a walnut-sized quinine pellet into my mouth. For good measure, he followed that up with a squirt of quinine water. He ordered me to swallow it but its size made that impossible. I had to let the bitter thing sit in my mouth as it slowly dissolved.

The Royal Barber gave me a haircut, which was only a snip with scissors, finished off with a big dollop of heavy grease to my head. With a solid push to the chest, he shoved me backward into the tank of seawater where several shellbacks were dunking pollywogs. Every time the initiates came up for air, the shellbacks would ask them, "Are you a shellback or a pollywog?" Before they could answer, they were dunked again. I formulated my plan of action just as my head was being shoved under water for the first time. As soon as I was dunked, I spat out the quinine pill and when they let me up for air and started yelling, "I'm a shellback, I'm a shellback!" With that, my initiation was complete.

Although I'd never want to do it again, I knew no one was trying to hurt me and it was, after all, a way to break up the monotony of a long cruise. And I wasn't alone in this playful misery. In addition to all the sailors who were initiated, five pollywog officers, including one commander, had to take their medicine right along with us. Rumor had it that one of the officers, a passenger aboard *Rowan*, had gone to the captain in protest, saying that the initiation was beneath the dignity of an officer. Harrison told him bluntly that he'd take what was coming to him and like it.

Only a few men escaped. Bob was one of them. He had duty in the gun and before he could go through the initiation, a sub was sounded and everything was called to a halt. The vintage slop went over the side and all hands went to general quarters. That garbage was one offering I don't think even the sharks would have eaten. We lost the contact but we didn't go back to the initiations. Although we were not at war, we were in unfriendly waters and that reminder took a lot of the fun out of the game.

The build-up to the initiations had provided us with some diversion from a long, monotonous trip. Now that it was over, there was a letdown. Every day, we watched for the British escort so that, as soon as we turned the convoy over to them, we could head for home. That was supposed to take place somewhere around the equator but we were now well south of that point and there was no sign of them. Lookouts kept an uneasy eye on the horizon.

No official information was available but there was plenty of scuttlebutt. Maybe we were going to go all the way to Capetown. Maybe we were going to Australia. Maybe we would turn around tomorrow. With no reliable dope, each man believed the rumors that best suited him.

27 November

Thanksgiving Day. There would be a real spread with turkey and ham and all the traditional trimmings of candied sweet potatoes, mashed potatoes, fresh baked bread, dressing, peas, pumpkin and mincemeat pies. It was a lot of extra work for the galley crew and we had to report to duty at 0300 to start all the boiling, baking, frying and roasting. The baker made bread the night before and the aroma throughout the ship was heavenly.

This was the first time I had ever celebrated the November holiday in ninety-degree weather. It was also the first time I had spent it so far from home. It was a fine meal, but as I cleaned up the galley, I found myself thinking of Mom and Dad. After dinner, Bob headed for his bunk and got some much-needed rest. I went down to the mess and watched the movie with Ernie.

Each day found us farther south. Our hopes of being home for Christmas evaporated but no one said much about it. We were kept busy with dawn general quarters, drills and exercises. The torpedomen pulled out the torpedoes to overhaul them. Gunner's mates stripped, cleaned and oiled their guns. We held a field day in the galley to clean off built-up grease. All hands scrubbed, mended and repaired clothing. Some men were fortunate enough to sew on new rating badges. The daily routine went on.

As the cruise dragged into December, we got more indications that we were approaching all-out war. One was a notice that was posted for all hands to read. It offered a twenty-five dollar reward to the person who first sights and reports a sub. It was supposed to keep everyone on his toes, but Bob made a joke of it. "We get twenty-five dollars if we sight the sub first, and if we don't," he said, "our folks get six months' death benefit." It was almost as if he knew.

USS Rowan transferring cargo at sea.

Contact

2 December. Midnight Watch. *Rowan* had the point position of the convoy, stationed about ten miles ahead of the rest of the escort. I was the phone talker watch on the bridge. I felt uneasy because my responsibility was to pass the word between the OOD or the captain and the action stations throughout the ship. If I misunderstood an order or passed the wrong information, it could be disastrous. My job was an important link in the chain of command and the outcome of our action might depend upon my ability to perform efficiently. I did not feel very confident.

The weather was cloudy and a slight fog hung in the air. The sea was moderate, giving us a soft up and down motion and an occasional roll of about fifteen degrees. We had been receiving reports of German raiders operating nearby, disguised as innocent neutral vessels. These ships were heavily armed and had been known to approach a victim within range of their big guns without causing alarm. Then they would suddenly shift colors, striking the flag of a friendly or neutral country and raising a German flag to reveal their true identity. Within seconds, they would remove the covering from their guns and open fire with all the advantage of surprise. They had been very successful in sinking a number of cargo ships carrying supplies to the Allies. As escort vessels, we were alert to the possibility of encountering one of these German ships.

"Ship bearing ten degrees off the starboard bow," called the starboard lookout.

The OOD, Lt. John Wyatt, moved quickly to the starboard wing of the bridge and spotted the ship through his binoculars. I followed him closely, awaiting his orders. "Call the captain," he said quietly. I passed the word to a messenger. A moment later, Captain Harrison appeared on the bridge to take command. My responsibility now shifted to him.

After studying the vessel for a few moments, the captain, who was standing next to the signalman, said, "Challenge him." The starboard signal light blinked as the signalman sent out the challenge. No response.

"Try again." The challenge was repeated. Still no answer. He turned to Mr. Wyatt and said tersely, "Inform flag."

Mr. Wyatt went to the TBS (Talk-Between-Ships system), held down the open lever and said, "This is DD 405. We've sighted an unknown and we are investigating."

"Let's get a closer look," the captain said. "Standard turn. Ahead full." I was following him from one side of the bridge to the other with my phone wire trailing behind. His voice was soft and I was afraid I might not hear all he said. "Have control get on the target," Harrison ordered. I passed the word. Immediately, I could hear the motors grind as the director trained around.

"Target bearing 0010, range 3,800 yards," came a report from the fire control director. I repeated the information to the captain.

"Very well." His calm voice did little to soothe my anxiety. "Try another challenge." Our signal light blinked again. Still no response. The target vessel seemed lifeless. There were no lights or visible activity of any kind. "Train guns on him."

I repeated his order into the phone. Again, I could hear the grinding sound as #2 gun swung around to the bearing.

"Should I sound general quarters?" Mr. Wyatt asked.

"Not yet," replied the captain. "I want to get in a little closer. Flank speed." The ship vibrated as the screws started to turn faster.

"Target bearing dead ahead. Range 1,200 yards," came the report from control. I relayed the information and the captain acknowledged with a short nod. Our speed was twenty-two knots and increasing. The vessel was now visible without binoculars.

"Target dead ahead, range eight hundred yards," I reported.

"Very well." The suspect ship was moving in the opposite direction of the convoy and its course would take it between the troop ships and the escort. We were accelerating and closing rapidly. "Challenge again," the captain ordered. The signal light blinked out the message. No answer.

"Target dead ahead. Range one hundred yards," I said. It was a big ship. It could easily have been a raider. We were now almost upon him.

Rowan was moving at top speed - around thirty-five knots. No ship, not even a nimble destroyer, can stop short. I glanced nervously at the captain, thinking we had better slow down or we'll ram him.

"Illuminate," he ordered. I passed the word and instantly our searchlight came on. The powerful beam was focused on the target ship's bridge. We were close enough to have read the fine print on a legal contract. At the very last second, a feeble light blinked out the code that let us know she was a friendly ship. Harrison, satisfied with the response that almost came too late, said quietly, "Douse the light." I repeated the words into the telephone and the searchlight went out.

"All stop." The engine room telegraph to my left clanked as the lever was moved to the 'All Stop' position to relay the captain's orders to engineering. "All astern." Still making headway, we were much too close to the target ship for my liking. Its massive silhouette loomed before us. "All astern full." Reversing the engine seemed to have little effect on our forward progress. "Emergency astern." *Rowan* seemed to stand on her tail momentarily until the screws finally bit into the sea, swirling the water around the stern in giant whirlpools. We were almost touching the merchant ship with our bow. I didn't breathe again until we began to back away.

Captain Harrison called to the OOD, "Inform flag, friendly ship. We are returning to station." My heart was beating like mad. I fully believe he would have rammed that ship if he had not received an answer to his challenge. As it was, he could not have waited much longer to give the order for us to stop.

We finally had a comfortable distance between the ship and ourselves. About the time my breathing was back to normal, the port lookout reported, "Captain, a cruiser is crossing our stern."

Calmly, Harrison ordered, "All stop." *Rowan*'s screws stopped turning. "All ahead one-third. Left standard rudder." We eased away from certain collision with the cruiser. With the ship at last out of danger, the captain turned to the officer of the deck and said, "You have the deck, Mr. Wyatt. Get us back to station. I'm going below."

8 December 1941

Monday. We got word that the Japanese had bombed Pearl Harbor. We had heard that the battleship *New Mexico* had been sunk. This really shook up one of the guys whose brother was on that ship, but the *New Mexico* had left Hawaii a few days earlier. Another rumor was that the *West Virginia* that had been destroyed. Neither source was correct. It was the *Arizona* that had gone down with over 2,000 men aboard.

Perhaps it was the lack of information that caused us to accept the news so calmly. Perhaps it was because we had been unofficially in a state of war for almost six months. Although the declaration of war that followed the attack gave us something to talk about, little was made of the day. We went about our work, business as usual.

The next day, however, a notice appeared in the plan of the day for all hands to read, a notice that gave me a cold chill.

> *The attention of all hands is called to the fact that in the past few weeks of cruising, we have more or less avoided trouble with prospective enemy ships. However, the situation has changed since the formal declaration of war and we are now looking for trouble instead of running away from it.*

War

9 December. Bob and I marked our first anniversary aboard the *Rowan*. Two other events of note took place that day: the United States declared war on Japan - and would declare war on Germany two days later, and *Rowan* arrived at Capetown, South Africa. The only one of those three events we took much note of was our arrival. We celebrated by refilling our depleted storerooms and fuel tanks as soon as we tied up.

14 December

Underway again, escorting American troop transports around the tip of Africa. Scuttlebutt was that we were going all the way around the world to Australia and then back to Hawaii. Like most scuttlebutt, it had no basis in fact.

At 1400 the following day, we met up with a single British cruiser. A short while later, *Rowan* and the other ships of our squadron got a message releasing us from convoy duty, thanking us for our fine work, and wishing us a pleasant voyage. We returned to Capetown and stayed there overnight.

Only the captain seemed to know where we were heading next, although scuttlebutt persisted that we would sail around the world. A year earlier, it might have sounded glamorous to me but considering how dull four weeks at sea had been, I wondered what another three months would have been like on top of the one month we had just finished. That was one test we didn't have to face, for we were heading home.

Bob and I received word that we had made Ship's Cook Second Class. We had firmly established ourselves in the galley as good workers who were willing to work hard for advancement.

20 December

The chief commissary steward had been a baker before he made chief but after his advancement, he needed to find someone he could train to take over the job. Bob, always eager to acquire new skills, grabbed the chance.

Bob's first run of bread came out around 2345, just when the mid-watch was taking over the duty. The galley blowers exhausted just below the bridge and the smell of freshly baked bread was irresistible. Almost everyone coming off watch was hungry. Even if they weren't, the aroma was enough to spark their appetite. A few couldn't resist stopping by to try to talk Bob out of a sample.

B.H. Desch

Bob was a friendly kind of guy and the fact that he was the keeper of the bread only added to his popularity. But bread was a vital component of the ship's daily rations. If the weather turned rough or if we had to spend long hours at general quarters, the ninety loaves were hardly enough to make the sandwiches we needed to keep the crew going. In spite of the pitiful requests from starving friends, like Desch, Paez and Laakman, Bob kept a tight rein on the supplies.

It wasn't easy, as there were some that wouldn't kowtow to anyone for a crust of bread. These rugged individualists would try to slip in when Bob wasn't looking and snitch a loaf. Others were more open about it, like some of the officers, who were the hardest panhandlers to discourage. Once in a while, one of them would come down and make a "friendly" request for a sample, a request a ship's cook found hard to refuse.

25 December

Near the Equator. We would not be home for Christmas this year. Instead, we celebrated both the crossing of the equator and Christmas with a "happy hour" on the fantail. It was the most unusual Christmas I had ever experienced. At 1600, it was one hundred eight degrees in the shade. Undaunted by the heat, we made the most of our Christmas so far from home.

Goldman, an electrician, had a guitar. I borrowed one from one of the other guys. Ferguson played lead and I played rhythm while everyone sang Christmas songs. I had never heard Bing Crosby sing "White Christmas" at that time, but I was dreaming of one anyway. In spite of homesickness, we had a good time. A few of the officers put on a Jack Benny-type program to entertain the troops. It wasn't professional quality but it was the only entertainment we had, and we enjoyed it.

As we proceeded north, there was an occasional sonar contact of what we believed was a submarine. We never dropped any depth charges because we either lost contact before we could take action, or it turned out to be a false alarm. We investigated another unidentified merchant ship, without the excitement of the last one, and found it to be a Cuban ship heading to Capetown from New York.

There were plenty of alerts but no action. Bob groused about this situation, complaining that "our Navy was built for beauty only. As far as I'm concerned," he stated flatly, "we're safe as bugs in a rug." Others felt the same way. After all our practice, we were getting anxious to pit our skills against the Germans.

It never occurred to us that we could also be the target.

Death Comes Aboard

1 January 1942. All correspondence now would be censored before being mailed. We could not write home to tell about our trip to South Africa or the exciting things that had happened. Bob's diary, which he had been carefully maintaining for months, was now illegal and could not be sent home by mail. Fortunately, he was able to smuggle it home in his luggage when he went home on leave.

4 January

The Virginia coastline appeared on the western horizon, a gray shadow against the brightening sky. Shortly after we arrived, a boat pulled up alongside and delivered several large bags of mail. At mail call, I had a stack waiting for me. Among the letters was a notice from my local draft board telling me to report for registration, as I was classified as 1-A. I had some small satisfaction in replying that they were too late. The Navy already had me booked for the next five years.

We returned to a different United States from the one that we had left just two months earlier. It was now wartime and signs of war were everywhere. The yards were crowded with new ships under construction, both merchant and man-of-war. Young men were joining the service, eager to "do their part." Everything was moving a little faster and sacrifice became a way of life. If anyone complained about shortages, he would be told, "There's a war on, you know."

There was an unfamiliar feeling in the air, like a motor running a little too fast. It felt as if all the old familiar underpinnings of the pre-war world had been knocked away. Although disorienting, it was exciting. It was a time when I felt more alive than I ever had felt before. If the war was the reason that we felt this sense of purpose, then so be it. We could take whatever came our way. The world had changed and so had we. Although we had not yet faced the test of fire, that time would not be long in coming. We would soon find out what this war really meant in human terms.

14 January

Underway again. Our first assignment was target practice. The last time we had taken part in these accuracy drills, we had been in Hawaii where the sea was calm, the weather warm and the skies clear. Here in the wintertime Atlantic, it was a different story. The sea started out choppy and as the day wore on, got progressively worse. We still didn't rate an 'E', but our aim had improved over the year before.

As soon as we secured from the drill, I headed into the galley to start preparing dinner. This was one of those days when a cook really earns his keep. We were rolling around so much that it was hard to keep from spilling food. The deck became slippery and staying on your feet was a job. Our top priority was getting the next meal out which, because of the weather, would be Spam sandwiches. With less than two hours before chow down, we had to work fast. We never could have made it if we hadn't had an informal agreement among all the cooks that in circumstances like these, both watches would come in and lend a hand. In the tight confines of the pitching, rolling galley, all of us worked together to turn out a mound of sandwiches and plenty of hot coffee.

15 January

1118. *Rowan* and *Mayrant* received word that the British tanker *Coimbra* had been torpedoed and sunk about sixty miles south of Block Island, in Long Island Sound. We were ordered to proceed and search for survivors. Weather conditions were not favorable for spotting survivors either in the water or in a small lifeboat. Even *Mayrant* would frequently disappear from sight, swallowed up by ocean swells.

After an hour and a half of searching in the vicinity of the coordinates we received, the lookout on the port wing of the bridge spotted the bow of the tanker sticking straight up into the air, its stern apparently resting on the bottom thirty fathoms below. The merchantman, which had been carrying lube oil from New York to Halifax, was abandoned. Any survivors had to be close by. *Rowan* and *Mayrant* each lowered two whaleboats and formed a scouting line, each boat staying within visual range of the other. They headed downwind, 110 degrees true.

Bud Desch, in the rescue party, faced a fierce twenty-knot wind that whipped his exposed skin raw. The air temperature was twenty-five degrees; the water was around forty-six. Swells twenty to thirty feet high. He and the other rescuers were cold even before they shoved off. The survivors, if there were any, had been out there nearly thirteen hours. They would be unimaginably cold. One thing was certain; if they were still alive, they were running out of time. That thought helped the rescuers forget their own discomfort and press their search even harder.

The searchers had been out for half an hour when one of the men of the *Mayrant*, his voice nearly swallowed up by the wind and waves, shouted to the *Rowan* crew that he had spotted something near their location. One of *Rowan*'s rescue teams investigated, only to find an empty raft.

Meanwhile, Desch's whaleboat crew came upon a lifeboat with the name *Coimbra* stenciled on the side. As they neared the craft, Desch could see that it was half-filled with frigid, oily water. Bud reached out and pulled the other boat close. As he did, he looked down in the bottom and there, huddled together against the bitter cold, he saw two men, sitting upright against the gunnels. A third was lying on his side. The survivors, W.L. Pinder, First Mate, and E. Randall, Chief Radio Officer, were white with cold, suffering from extreme exposure. There were three other men slumped over in a heap, face down in the water, obviously already dead. With half frozen fingers, Desch secured a line to the lifeboat. The coxswain then turned back toward the *Rowan* and opened the throttle full.

Back aboard the ship, Harvey waited on deck to help bring the survivors aboard. He stood at the ready when the lifeboat bumped to a halt against *Rowan*'s port side. As he waited for the boat to be secured, he looked down at the survivors. At that moment, Chief Randall feebly looked up in Harvey's direction and their eyes met. On the Chief's face was an expression of gratitude and peaceful resignation. He tried to smile but could not. When rescuers tossed him a line, he was unable even to raise his hand to grab it. It was all he could do to hang on to life for a few more minutes. Rescuers jumped into the boat and tied a rope around the Chief to haul him up.

Harvey would never forget that haunting look of one who is seeing Death. It shook him to the core. That night, he would cry himself to sleep with the Chief's peaceful gaze burned deeply into his memory.

At the same time the first survivors were being brought aboard, *Mayrant*'s whaleboat found another *Coimbra* raft with five men, M. Burns, Seaman; P. Roberts, Fireman; H. Pease, Seaman; Jr. Cover, Second Cook; and D. Ralph, Able Seaman, all clinging to life. They were nearly frozen

Willis Doyle Kelley

to the bone. Seaman Burns looked more dead than alive. The men needed immediate medical attention and so were towed to the closest ship, the *Rowan*.

Doyle Kelley, in the damage control party, was standing by to help bring the men aboard. When the boat was secured alongside, Kelley reached over the lifeline to help haul up Burns, the most critical. Kelley realized right away that the man had stopped breathing, and took charge. Getting a better grip on the man, he said to Tex Taylor, "You grab his legs. Let's get him out of the weather." They took him into the shower room, which was closest warm place with enough room to lay the man down.

I followed them, a mug of hot coffee in one hand and a woolen blanket in the other, ready to offer them to the survivor. I realized at once that the man was in no condition to accept them.

Kelley gently laid him on the shower room floor, rolled him onto his stomach and began artificial respiration. He pushed down on the middle of his back, then pulled up on his arms. Down on the back, up on the arms. Down on the back, up on the arms. Like some kind of tireless machine, he repeated the maneuver over and over again, trying to force life back into the dying man's body.

Chief Pharmacist's Mate Estabrook came in and checked Burns' pulse and respiration. There was none but Kelley would not stop. A few minutes later, Estabrook checked again. Nothing. "He's gone, Kelley," he said gently.

Kelley paid no attention. Again and again, he repeated the life-saving motion. Down on the back, up on the arms. Down on the back, up on the arms. Over and over. Five minutes. Ten minutes. He worked with unwavering focus to resuscitate the man. He gave it all he had. The sweat from his physical and emotional exertion beaded up on his forehead. Burns was dead and no amount of effort could bring him back. Still, Kelley would not stop. Finally, Estabrook stepped in and put his hand on Kelley's shoulder. "Let him go, son. He's gone."

Kelley sat back on his heels and wiped the sweat from his brow. He stared at Burn's body for a long moment, then hung his head. He watched without blinking while two men came in at Estabrook's direction, to take the body away. He slowly got to his feet and left the shower room. I had never seen anyone so devoted to saving the life of another. It was the first time I would witness the character of Willis Doyle Kelley but it would not be the last.

The next day, the bodies of all those who died were laid out on deck, bound in canvas and weighted. Under the monochromatic sky and slate-colored, windswept sea, a brief service was held and the bodies were committed to the deep. This was the first such burial most of us had ever experienced. It was also the first time death had come aboard the *Rowan* and in that instant, the war became starkly real. For an hour afterward, everyone went about his business and quietly reflected upon his own mortality. While all of us took the death of the frozen sailors to heart, I think Kelley took it the hardest.

10 February

Three weeks after the *Coimbra* incident, *Rowan* was moored next to *Rhind* in the warm, peaceful waters of Bermuda. By late the next afternoon, we were underway again in the company of USS *Rhind*, and two British cans, H.M.S. *Duchess* and H.M.S. *Kent*. We had hardly cleared the breakwater when general quarters was sounded and gunnery drills commenced.

Two hours after leaving port, a blinding rainstorm came up quickly and intensely, visually cutting us off from the other ships of our squadron. The downpour got heavier by the minute and the sea began to swell. Every lookout strained his eyes trying to locate the ships. *Rowan* turned around to search for them but in the failing light of evening, it was unlikely that we would find them before the next sun. Throughout the night lookouts continued the vigil, uneasy in the storm, aware that U-boats could be out there patrolling, waiting to pounce on a lone shiplike the *Rowan*.

The morning dawned as foul as the night before. Still, there was no sign of the squadron. Anxious eyes scanned the horizon. Sonarmen listened for telltale pings indicating an enemy presence. Finally, after nearly twelve hours, off the starboard beam, the lookout spotted the silhouette of *Rhind*. *Kent* and *Duchess* were close by. *Rowan* returned to her place alongside the others and turning north, headed to New York without further incident.

15 February

By the time the squadron tied up in Brooklyn, everyone was ready for liberty. Bob, Bud Desch, D.K. Duckworth and I boarded the subway at Sands Street and rode uptown to Times Square. We wanted to visit the city's most famous skyscraper. Hailing a taxi, we told the driver to take us to the top of the Empire State Building. He said his taxi went only to the front door. We settled for that.

At sunset, we headed back to Times Square where it seemed there was a nightclub every few feet. Jack Dempsey's, The Latin Quarter, and The Brass Rail were a few of our favorite nightspots. The *Rowan* crew usually wound up at Jimmy Dyer's Sawdust Trail. It was a friendly bar where you could buy a beer and make it last all evening while you talked to your buddies about the ship and girls.

Then there was Chin Lee's Restaurant. On our next visit to port, something would happen there that would change my life.

Convoy

By late February, the U.S. Navy had two missions to accomplish in the Atlantic theater of war. The first was to keep open the transportation lanes by providing protection to convoys of merchantmen and troop transports to and from Europe and Africa. The second was to safeguard coastal shipping lanes off the Eastern Seaboard from Canada to South America, through the Caribbean and the Gulf of Mexico. Like all the destroyers and their crews in the Atlantic during this time, *Rowan* would play a key role in accomplishing those tasks.

19 February

Underway. Forward in the screen were *Trippe, Mayrant, Rowan* and *Rhind*. Astern were four other destroyers. We cleared Ambrose Channel in New York harbor and fanned out, each ship searching for submarine contacts. As soon as the coast was clear the capital ships - the battleship *New York*, and the light cruiser *Brooklyn* - and fifteen merchantmen and troop transports, left the protection of the harbor. The convoy formed into columns with the flagship *New York* near the center, leading one of the columns of merchant ships. The escorting destroyers formed a screen along the perimeter, in harm's way.

Our distance from the convoy was calculated to do two things: make it hard for a submarine to fire off a lucky shot outside our line of defense, and make it difficult for the enemy to penetrate our screen and pick off a merchantman from within the perimeter. If a U-boat were out there, it would have to get past a picket line before it could get to the convoy.

We began a zigzag course, challenging our amateur navigators to guess where we were going. Everything was secret but shortly after leaving port, we got our first clue about our destination. All weather deck watches were issued cold weather clothing, including a heavy, lined and hooded jumpsuit made of a canvas-like waterproof material. The last two items were the most telling - heavy gloves and a mask that covered the whole face, leaving only slits for eyes and mouth. We were heading back into the icy reaches of the North Atlantic. I would come to appreciate that winter gear although it would still prove painfully inadequate to the demands of the journey.

Within six hours of leaving port, we had it all - snow, sleet, freezing rain, strong winds and low temperatures. The exceptionally heavy swells made forty-degree rolls commonplace. And then it got worse. The following morning, frozen ocean spray covered all weather decks and riggings in ice. No one was allowed topside. In an emergency, you could try the newly installed catwalk, but before you could use it, you had to break enough ice off the lifelines to give you something to hold onto. It was better than nothing, but not by much.

The weather was only one of our problems. Another was traveling in convoy. Our speed was determined by the fastest speed of the slowest transport which most cases, was eight knots. Just to slow things down, we never traveled in a straight line. The theory was that frequent course and speed changes confused the enemy and a "fish" fired off when we were changing course would miss. Of course, there were those who said that as many ships were lost through an unfortunate zag as were saved by a fortuitous zig.

Traveling in this manner was tedious and highly inefficient, and the merchant captains were not convinced of the merits of zigzagging. Antagonistic about taking orders from naval officers, especially ones who were telling them to do something they thought was just plain ridiculous, they argued that they could do a better job of getting their cargo through if they struck out on their own. Under the best of conditions with good weather and willing crews, getting twenty to thirty ships to turn to a new course simultaneously was difficult. Trying it in the tempestuous North Atlantic with uncooperative captains was nearly impossible. The Germans, however, supplied us unexpected help in persuading the recalcitrant merchantmen. When the wolfpack submarine forces began picking off stragglers, the tough-minded captains had a sudden change of heart.

21 February

Rowan arrived in Halifax, Nova Scotia, pausing briefly while the crew steamed and chipped off the build-up of ice. After refueling, we got underway again in heavy snow and calm sea.

The numbing cold made standing watch almost unbearable. The air temperature was near zero, the water temperature just above freezing. It was so cold, in fact, we were told that in case of a man-overboard, no attempt would be made at rescue. The victim would freeze to death before help could get to him.

Convoys were stalked by submerged submarines. To keep us informed as to the location of the underwater threat, two *Rowan* radiomen were on duty in the radio shack at all times when we were at sea to receive messages from NSS, the Navy Shore Radio Station. This Washington, D.C.-based round-the-clock transmitter sent continual encoded reports on sub locations. The radio crew passed them on to the duty officer who decoded them and informed the captain of their content. We knew the wolfpacks were out there, but the trick was to find them before they found us.

Sounding them was difficult, complicated by rudimentary sonar equipment, inexperienced sonarmen and the convoy itself. The noise of some thirty ships effectively camouflaged any echo a sub might send back. Whenever a suspicious sound was detected, we went to general quarters and fired off a few depth charges, or ashcans, as we called them. If we were to err, it had to be on the side of caution. To do otherwise could have been fatal. We had to stay vigilant at all times.

23 February

A submarine was sounded. As usual, the "Y" guns were fired and a few ashcans dropped. But this time, the port "Y" gun was loaded improperly and instead of flinging cans out a hundred or so yards from the ship when the gun was fired, the charges rolled out onto the deck with a dull whump. Depth charges are relatively harmless until activated by the hydrostatic pressure for which they have been set.

Harmless though the charges may have been, they still had to be removed from the deck. With the sea running high and heavy, that wasn't easy. The strongest men, Doyle Kelley and Tex Taylor were assigned the task of rolling the hundred pound charges off the deck. Even 6'3" Bill Ward was recruited out of the after Radio Shack to lend a hand. It took all their combined strength to roll the charges over the side.

24 February

Another sub was sounded. More depth charges were fired off but the weather was so rough that even if we had killed a submarine, we would never have known it. I heard rumor that we had hit something but Harvey told me he was pretty sure the only thing we contacted was a school of enemy fish.

A month later, we were back in New York. Some of the crew left for new assignments. Jack H. Harrison, an enlisted man, had an opportunity to go to aviator training, and he jumped at the chance.

27 March

We would be in Brooklyn for fourteen days for yard availability. Early afternoon on a rainy, windy day, we proceeded up the East River past Hell Gate Bridge to the Brooklyn Navy Yard. By Friday, everyone who was eligible for an extended liberty was making plans for seventy-two hours away from the ship. Steve Kess was heading up to Connecticut to visit his family. Bud Desch invited Bob to go with him down to Columbia, Pennsylvania, to spend some time at his family's home.

Ernie and I couldn't get away on leave because of duty. Our liberty would start at 1600 and we could stay out all night as long as we reported each morning at 0800. The two of us were among the first to get across the gangway. We were looking forward to a typical New York liberty, which included a good time around Times Square.

After visiting a number of nightspots, we wound up back at Chin Lee's restaurant, one of our favorite haunts. There we met two young women, Cecile Coburn and Anne Quinn. After dancing and late-night bowling, Ernie asked for, and received Anne's telephone number.

Over the next two weeks, he went out to the Bronx to see Anne two or three times, although I never went with him. With Bob on leave, I had double duty in the galley, and getting away wasn't easy. When Bob came back, I went on leave down to Pennsylvania where my mother was a guest at the Desch home. When I returned, Ernie had a lot to tell me about Anne's family, and especially her beautiful sister, Helen. I was interested.

5 April 1942

Easter Sunday. Harvey had an invitation to go out to the Bronx for Easter Sunday dinner at Anne Quinn's house and asked if I wanted him to arrange for me to go with him. The offer was tempting but I had duty. I would have to wait until the next time we were in New York to visit the Quinn's.

Maybe I'll call her on our next liberty in town, I told him. Ernie advised me not to wait too long. Fortunately for me, I heeded his advice.

San Jacinto Rescue

11 April. 1600. At sea. I was in the galley when I became aware that the ship had slowed down. Glancing out the porthole, I could see the battleship, *South Dakota*, in the distance steaming toward us in all her majesty. She took her place in the middle of the screen and by the time she was comfortably tucked in, the convoy was back up to cruising speed, heading south. Scuttlebutt had it that we were to escort her through the Panama Canal and on to Australia. All I could think of was the song that went, "I joined the Navy to see the world. And what did I see? I saw the sea."

The biggest problem with long cruises was monotony. After you had laundered and repaired everything in your sea bag, you could go to the ship's "library," a six by six navy gray bookcase located on the port side of the mess hall, and try to find something you hadn't read before. During the day, you could lie out in the sun and work on a tan and in the evening, see a movie. You could try to catch up on some sleep or, when all else failed, talk with a buddy about your last liberty. That was Bob's favorite pastime. He could often be found in the laundry room next to the galley, with Rudy Paez, Freddie Laakman or, most often now, Bud Desch. Bob had met Bud's sister, Dorothy, on his visit to Pennsylvania and he was completely taken with her.

I liked to hang around with Harvey and talk about almost anything. He was a keen observer and as a storyteller, he had no equal because he always tried to get his facts correct before opening his mouth. He rarely dealt in rumor and since his duty station was on the bridge, I went to him if I wanted to get the straight dope. During this long cruise, he mentioned Anne Quinn's sister from time to time. He was piquing my interest.

Music was a great way to pass the time. Bob and I liked to stand out by the break of the fo'c's'le outside the galley and sing popular songs. Sentimental ones were the best. With Bob singing the lead and me on harmony, we'd do a great rendition of "Wishing." I don't know how good we were but we enjoyed it.

Others preferred to listen to prerecorded music. The radiomen were in charge of the phonograph, and they were the ones who selected the music that could be heard all over up topside. The selection of music was limited and some songs got played a lot. *Princess Pupuli*, by the Andrew Sisters, became a favorite of the radio shack crew. It was played about every other song, probably because of its somewhat suggestive content. According to the lyrics, the princess in question had lots of a favorite tropical fruit, which she generously gave away. The end of the song suggested that now she was selling her wares.

After a while, the constant repetition started to irritate Mr. Walters, the executive officer. He sent word to the radio shack that they were not to play that record so often. That only seemed to make the song more appealing. But an order was an order. Instead of playing the record every other time, they started playing it only every third or fourth time. That didn't cut any ice with Mr. Walters. He sent word that the song not be played, period. The radio crew waited about six songs before slipping it back onto the turntable. That was the last straw for Mr. Walters' patience. He marched furiously into the radio shack, grabbed the record, broke it in two and flung it over the side. And that was the end of that.

18 April

We reached the Canal Zone and remained there approximately four hours, just long enough to throw a coat of paint on the fo'c's'le deck and take on fuel. Then we started homeward. Our division, DESDIV 16, joined Task Group 38.5 to escort the SS *Aquitania*, a large passenger liner, to New York. We took off at twenty-two knots. At this speed, we'd be in New York in a few days. That would more than make up for our lack of liberty in Panama.

22 April

0700. A distress signal was picked up by convoy radiomen from a passenger/cargo ship, the SS *San Jacinto*. The word was that the ship had been torpedoed and its passengers included women and children. At 0730, the flagship USS *Brooklyn* ordered *Rowan* to detach from the convoy and proceed to latitude 32.10 N, longitude 70.45 W to search for and pick up survivors.

These were dangerous waters, patrolled by German U-boats traveling in wolfpacks of two or more submarines. Wolfpacks had been responsible for sinking some fifty-six ships in the first three months of 1942. Their favorite targets were tankers and cargo ships that they sank almost at will. Survivors, if any, were often strafed.

In April, however, wolfpack warfare entered a new phase. The German High Command instructed U-boat captains to surface and, courteously and apologetically, to inform the passengers and crew of the target vessel that they were about to be sunk. Victims were given ample time to radio their exact location before abandoning ship. This was no humanitarian gesture. The U-boats would torpedo the hapless vessel and then lay in wait for rescuers, like the *Rowan*. With luck, they could pick off two or more ships just by being patient.

Captain Harrison did not know the German plan, although he may have had his suspicions, but it would not have made any difference. Our orders were to pick up survivors regardless of the risk. Increasing speed to twenty-eight knots, *Rowan* turned northeast. Alone against the threat of a submerged wolfpack, our speed would offer some protection. Underwater, a U-boat can travel only at a speed of about ten knots. Still, we would have to remain alert. For more than five hours we proceeded, scanning for U-boats and for *San Jacinto's* survivors.

1240. Off the port wing, Signalman John Jilcott spotted signal flares. "Very stars about six miles off the port beam," he reported. *Rowan* changed direction to run down the flares while cautiously making a sweep of the area, checking for submarines before approaching the survivors. Sonar contact was negative but the probability was very high that the attacking subs were still in the vicinity.

1253. Lookouts spotted six lifeboats from the *San Jacinto*, with a total of more than one hundred survivors aboard. The boats were all bunched together like sheep huddled against a predator's attack. When we were still three thousand yards away, Captain Harrison ordered, "Slow to five knots. Away the rescue party."

On his command, the davit winches whined as the whaleboats located amidship, port and starboard, were lowered to the bulwarks. The whaleboats were snubbed tightly against the side of the ship while the rescue parties, including the engineer, coxswain, bowhook, signalman, pharmacist's mate and gunner's mate, boarded. They had orders to keep the survivors together and render first aid where needed. The engineers cranked over the motors and in less than a minute, the boats were lowered into the water.

Rowan slowly circled the survivors as the rescue party was being lowered. As soon as the whaleboats were afloat, the davits, first aft, then forward, were released. It was extremely dangerous to stay in one place any longer than absolutely necessary, so as soon as the rescue parties were away, the captain ordered ahead one-half to conduct a further sonar and visual sweep of the area. When the first circle was completed, the rescue teams would tow the lifeboats full of survivors back to the ship.

Rowan's whaleboats approached the survivors and by coincidence, the *San Jacinto* captain was in the first boat they reached. The agitated skipper reported that the German sub that had sunk them had surfaced shortly before we arrived. They were setting a trap for would-be rescuers, using the survivors as bait. The U-boat captain, he said, had asked for their cargo manifest, tonnage, and passenger information. The German captain was polite but left no doubt that the cooperation of the *San Jacinto* crew was mandatory.

Signalman Koch, in one of the rescue boats, turned toward *Rowan* and relayed the message back to the ship. Harvey, on *Rowan*'s starboard wing, had Koch's whaleboat under observation. Through his high-powered binoculars, he carefully read the semaphored message, acknowledged it and passed the word to the captain.

On previous orders from the captain, we were already underway, proceeding to conduct a sonar search of the vicinity. The transceiver located on the after portion of the bridge, sent out a constant ping every five seconds. No return echo. If and when a signal were picked up, the sonar operator would quickly determine range and bearing and immediately inform the captain. So far, nothing was in range - but the subs, at least two of them, were out there. The captain ordered a wider sweep of the area on our way back around to the survivors.

Our circuit complete, Harrison ordered a wary approach. Bob "Shorty" Icenogle, at the helm, pulled us up alongside the lifeboats as the captain ordered all stop. This was extremely risky. We had to get those people aboard as fast as possible. A rope net was rigged over the side and all hands on deck reached down to render assistance, sometimes bodily pulling the survivors aboard. It wasn't easy, especially with so many children.

Heglin and Hunter

Among the women, several were pregnant. We kept urging them to "Hurry, hurry!" With everyone moving as fast as they could, we had retrieved three boatloads of survivors, probably seventy-five or eighty in all, in just over five minutes. We had to get underway. Being at a full stop was like sending the Germans an engraved invitation. If they knew exactly where we were, they could even now be lining up their shot.

Suddenly, Harvey noticed "Muscles" Heglin, the forward lookout nicknamed for his scrawny physique, pointing out ahead of us and jumping up and down. He was so agitated he couldn't speak. He just kept stammering and pointing forward. Harvey looked in the direction the lookout was indicating and saw the unmistakable wake of a "fish" heading our way. "Torpedo!" he shouted to alert the bridge. "Fifteen degrees off the starboard bow!"

"Hard right rudder," Captain Harrison barked. "Full astern starboard screw. Full ahead port screw." The quick evasive maneuver pivoted the ship and put the torpedo harmlessly off to port. Icenogle had to carefully maneuver the helm to steer around the lifeboats that were now clustered ahead of us.

Ted Smith

Back on the fantail, Radiomen Ted Smith and Bill Ward had been standing by, watching the rescue proceedings. Almost simultaneously, both men sighted two separate torpedo wakes, one about twenty yards astern, the other crossing our bow about fifty yards ahead. "Torpedoes!" they both called to the bridge, reporting the position of their approach.

"Contact bearing 275 degrees true, 60 degrees relative. Range 1800 yards," sonar reported. That was too close for comfort, as a torpedo could be fired with reasonable accuracy at a distance of 2000 yards.

"Hard right rudder," Harrison ordered. "All ahead flank speed." The captain turned *Rowan* around and straight into the attacker. Range was decreasing. 1400 yards. 1200 yards. 1000 yards and closing. Seconds later, another torpedo broached the surface, veering dangerously close to our bow. Abbott, the gunner on the 20-mm gun, opened fire on the torpedo with no effect.

1317. Harrison was unruffled by the near miss. He turned to Torpedoman Jack Goodpaster and said, "Set depth charge attack for shallow barrage."

"Aye, aye, sir." Goodpaster passed the word to let loose a barrage of three six-hundred-pounders from the fantail racks and six three-hundred-pounders from the "Y" guns. Behind us, the sea erupted in

Jack Goodpaster

geysers of saltwater spray as the explosive charges blew up only twenty feet below the surface. Although there was no indication that anything was hit, that bombing probably shook the U-boats up enough to get them to back off. Harrison wasn't satisfied with that. He told the helm to circle in to maintain contact with the enemy vessels.

Bud Desch, the coxswain of one of the boats, had been shepherding a group of survivors toward the *Rowan* when he looked up and saw her rev up and take off without so much as a "see you later." His mouth dropped open as he watched her disappear over the horizon. Moments later, he heard an explosion and saw spouts of water rising in the air. For tense moments he waited, not knowing what had happened, wondering who had just gotten the worst end of the encounter. Fear gripped him that *Rowan* had been sunk.

Aboard the *Rowan*, sonar reported, "Target bearing 0000 true, range 800 yards."

In response, Harrison told Goodpaster, "Give 'em another hit."

"Aye, aye, sir." When sonar reported that we were directly over the target, seven more one hundred fifty-pound cans were flung out from the "Y" guns.

Moments later, another contact was made. "Bearing 0040, range 1000 yards."

"Torpedo broaching two points off the starboard bow," called the forward lookout.

"Right full rudder," the captain commanded. A second torpedo broached about 200 yards off the bow, bearing 0020.

"Torpedo astern fifty yards!" the after lookout called.

Harrison ordered another depth charge attack, dropping a pattern of six ashcans astern from the rack on the fantail. Detonation was set for fifty feet. Moments later, a U-boat broached the surface, pushed up by the concussion of depth charges exploding directly under it. Its conning tower and deck appeared above the water for a few seconds, then sank from sight.

"Oil bubble dead astern," the after lookout reported.

Harrison leaned out over the starboard wing, looking aft. When he spotted the oil bubbling to the surface, he nodded, satisfied that we had made a kill. Just for good measure, he ordered a barrage of another five depth charges. No more contacts were made. With the wolfpack either destroyed or in retreat, he ordered *Rowan* about to pick up the remaining survivors and the two whaleboat crews.

1454. All during the attack, the survivors, who were still out in the lifeboats, could only see the sprays of water and hear the explosions. They sat terrified, silently watching the horizon and praying. Finally, they saw a ship approaching but it was too far away to be identified. The whaleboat crews told the survivors that if it were a German ship coming back to strafe them, they should all dive into the water. That would be their only protection. Statue-like and dead quiet, they watched and waited.

The ship was closing. Suddenly, Desch called out, "It's her! It's the *Rowan*!" Everyone started cheering and clapping and hugging each other. When *Rowan* pulled up alongside, survivors and whaleboat crews bounded aboard in record time.

1518. As soon as the last one was out of the water and the whaleboats were hooked up to the davits, Harrison, who had been watching from the starboard wing of the bridge, ordered, "All ahead full. Take her up to thirty knots." Turning west, we headed for Norfolk, Virginia.

The galley crew had to turn to and get some chow out for the *San Jacinto* survivors. They had been in the water for more than eight hours and were hungry and thirsty. We broke out cold cuts and put out some sandwiches and made up a fresh pot of hot coffee, enough to serve double our regular ship's compliment. It was chaos. There were people all over the place. Most of the passengers were Puerto Rican and spoke no English. None of *Rowan's* crew spoke Spanish, so it was like the Tower of Babel on deck. I was happy to retreat to the relative calm of the galley.

Estabrook had the busiest day of his career patching cuts and bruises and passing out seasickness medicine. As if he didn't have his hands full enough, one of the pregnant women, who was very large with child, went into labor. You could hear her periodic cries as her baby tried to see its first light of day while at sea. Estabrook, with no background in obstetrics, was a nervous wreck. Sprains and cuts were his specialty - not babies. Once everyone quieted down, the woman's labor pains subsided as the baby held off its debut until after we arrived stateside.

1835. We came upon a lifeboat from the freighter SS *Steelmaker* with six crewmen aboard. They were clad only in their underwear. When we picked them up, they told the same story as the *San Jacinto* survivors. Some of them had been sleeping when two subs had surfaced and ordered them to heave to. They had only minutes to abandon ship before they were torpedoed. The men were tired, hungry and grateful to be rescued.

Bringing them aboard took less than twenty minutes and we were off again at thirty knots. Survivors were bunked down, women and children in the chief's and officer's quarters and the men in the crew's quarters. It was an uncomfortable night for everyone but at our present speed, if all went according to plan, we would be in port by morning.

But everything did not go according to plan. Jack Burgess, *Rowan's* oil king, had the responsibility of keeping the oil in the ship's port and starboard fuel tanks balanced so that we stayed on an even keel. He kept a close eye on levels and on his check shortly after picking up the survivors of the *Steelmaker*, he noticed that we were dangerously low on fuel. He reported the information to Lt. McDowell, the chief engineering officer, who in turn reported it to the captain.

"At this speed, Captain," said Lt. McDowell, "we'll be out of fuel a half hour before we reach port."

Harrison wasn't pleased but he compromised. "Back her down to twenty-eight knots. Will that do?" he asked.

The engineering officer shrugged. "It'll be close."

The haste was not without reason. Bill Ward was receiving reports that nine enemy subs had been spotted in our area. Fortunately, we made the rest of the run without further incident.

Scuttlebutt had it that there was a German among the *San Jacinto's* multi-national crew. Someone said that before they were approached by the sub, he had been seen flashing a light out to sea. It was believed that he was signaling the enemy. Others claimed he acted suspiciously when they were abandoning ship, although no one made any specific charges. Whether it was true or just wartime hysteria, I do not know. Nevertheless, when *Rowan* got into Norfolk, the suspect was turned over to the FBI for questioning.

It was a tremendous relief to unload our passengers. *Rowan* was not designed with civilian passenger comfort in mind, and having so many people aboard had been inconvenient, at best. In spite of that, we were proud to have brought so many back to safety with our own skin still intact.

Our brush with death had been a little closer than any of us may have realized. We had nearly met the Grim Reaper on 22 April. The old boy had sat out there on the high seas, swinging his scythe, gleefully laughing and watching as the German subs unloaded more than half a dozen torpedoes in our direction. But his victory cheers would have to wait for another time, thanks to the skills and ingenuity of our captain and well-trained crew. On this particular adventure, the Angel of Death had been repulsed. Score one for our side. So go the fortunes of war.

With the passengers unloaded and our fuel tanks once again reading full, we proceeded north to New York where we would rejoin our division. Bob was planning another trip to Columbia, Pennsylvania with Bud Desch, and I was planning to go with Harvey out to the Bronx to meet Anne Quinn's sister.

Helen

Sunday, 26 April. Harvey was all set to go at noon but I would not finish my watch until 1300. Just as soon as I could remove my apron and shift into blues, we took off, heading for the Bronx.

The subway trains did not run as often as they did during the week, so it took us nearly two hours to get from the ship to the Quinn's house. It was raining on and off, but despite the prospects of a long, soggy trip, Harvey and I were eager to go ashore. The opportunity to visit a friend, especially an attractive female friend, made the trip worth the effort.

It was about a mile walk from the ship up Sands Street to the BMT subway. At the station, we caught the train to 42nd Street. When we got off the train, we climbed the long flight of steps to street level and headed straight for one of the many telephone booths that lined the walls. Harvey dropped a nickel into the slot and dialed the Quinn's phone number.

"Hello, Anne?" he began when the line was picked up.

"No, this is Helen." I could hear the reply as I leaned close to the receiver. "Anne isn't here right now. Who is this?" she asked.

"Ernie Harvey."

Helen J. Quinn

"Oh, hello, Ernie. When did you get in?" Her voice sounded pleasant.

"Late last night," he said. "I was hoping to come out to see Anne. Will she be home?"

"She's working until 8:00 this evening, but you can come out, if you like."

"Well, uh, I have someone with me. A buddy of mine from the ship."

"Oh, you mean the cook?"

"He's the one." Ernie gave me with a thumb's up as he said, "You heard about him?"

"I did. Why don't you bring him with you. I'd like to meet him," Helen said. Then she arranged with Harvey to pick us up at West Farms Road.

Harvey finished the conversation with, "Just look for two good-looking sailors wearing blues. We'll see you soon."

The trip took us about an hour longer than we had anticipated. By the time we arrived, Helen and her younger sister Bernadette, were waiting for us with the family's 1939 Dodge. Harvey had met Helen only once before but with his eye for detail, he had no problem picking her out of the crowd. With a wave, he called to her.

Apparently, she had already decided we were the ones she was looking for. A smile lit her face as she waved us over to the car.

Love at first sight is a cliché but in my case, it was true. From the moment I first laid eyes on Helen Quinn, I knew she was for me. She had shoulder-length brown hair and dark brown eyes that sparkled when she smiled. Her grace and charm knocked me off my feet. I wanted nothing more than to get to know her better. I had only one major obstacle to overcome - I had to meet with her mother's approval.

Delia Quinn was a large Irish woman with a thick brogue and a sharp eye. She had a way of quickly sizing up a person to see if he or she was the kind that she wanted calling on her children. With five daughters and two adopted nieces in her charge, she got plenty of practice. She was a strong-willed woman, a real survivor. She had come to America in 1910 with only one suitcase, "and that wasn't full," she would say. In just over thirty years, she and her husband, James Jerome Quinn, also an Irish immigrant, had raised a family of seven girls and two boys. Though times had been hard during the Depression, they had become successful, though perhaps not in the monetary sense. Their wealth was in the family, itself. They were all healthy, employed, and living in a warm, comfortable, happy home.

Kathleen, James, (seated), Helen, Joe
Bernadette (seated), Elizabeth and Anne

Shortly after we arrived at the house at 1615 Hone Avenue, we all went into the living room to get acquainted. Mrs. Quinn sat on a straight-back chair, arms folded across her chest, feet firmly planted on the floor. Her gray hair was rolled in a tight bun at the back of her head. "Well, now, tell me about yourself," she began. She seemed friendly but there was purpose behind her questions. Ernie glanced at me out of the corner of his eye. Apparently, he had gotten the third degree the first time he had come for a visit, though he had forgotten to mention it to me.

Mrs. Quinn asked me about my rate, my family, and my hopes for the future. She must have been satisfied with my answers because at eight p.m., she announced that tea was ready. As everyone made a move for the dining room, she said to Harvey and me, "I hope you boys like Irish soda bread."

I had no idea what it was but if it meant spending more time with this family, I would love it. I didn't know then that this invitation was her way of telling Helen, "He's okay." If Mrs. Quinn hadn't approved, there would have been no invitation to tea. Instead, she would have sternly told Helen, "Remember, you have to go to work tomorrow." At that, Helen would have said good night and that would have been the end of it. Happily, we were invited to tea.

Later, all us young people returned to the living room. There was a piano in the corner and I asked who played.

"No one," Helen replied. "We inherited it. When we moved into the house, the piano was here. The former tenants said they were sending someone for it...in a few days...but that was several years ago. It's a good conversation piece and it's not really in the way."

"Do you mind if I play?" I asked. I wasn't prepared for the enthusiastic reception I got from everyone. So I sat down and started with *Twelfth Street Rag* and *Happy Days Are Here Again*. I hadn't practiced since before I joined the Navy and I was pretty rusty. As an excuse, I pointed to my right hand and said, "I sliced my thumb when Bob and I had a chicken cutting contest a few days ago. It's still sore."

Helen came over and sat beside me. "You poor thing," she said, and took my hand. That was it for the piano and me. I spent the rest of the evening sitting close to her and holding her hand.

Helen's older brother Joe, asked us if sailors liked to shoot dice. Ernie and I admitted that some sailors were known to shoot craps. Helen said, "Why don't you show us how to play. I have some dice upstairs." She jumped up and went to get the ivory cubes.

When she came back, I showed everyone how to play but Joe said, "This is no fun. If we're going to shoot dice, we have to play for something of value."

It was Helen's turn to roll. "What will we play for?" she asked.

Joe could see the sparks between Helen and me. He said, "Why don't you play for Lew?"

"Fine!" With a gleam in her eye, Helen rolled the dice. "Seven!" she shouted triumphantly. "Hey, I won you!"

I smiled happily and said, "You ain't kidding!" My words were hardly audible but I wanted to shout them out loud.

It was nearly 2200 and Ernie and I had to get back to the ship by 0100. Helen offered to drive us to the train station. It was late and there are no trolleys running at this hour.

"No," Joe said. "The car's low on gas. With rationing, we can't get any more until Tuesday. I don't want you running out and getting stranded somewhere. I'll drive them back." I have always suspected that he volunteered to drive because he decided Helen needed a chaperone.

"We'll both go!" Helen said firmly. "You drive," she told Joe, handing him the key. Ernie and Anne got into the back seat and Joe, Helen and I rode up front. Since Helen didn't have to drive, her hand was free so I could hold it a little while longer.

At the station, Helen and Anne walked Ernie and me to the stairs leading to the elevated platform. Helen said she didn't want us to accidentally get on the wrong train. Any excuse to be with her a little longer was fine with me. I just wanted to get my arms around her. When we were saying good bye, she reached up and gave me a quick hug and I knew then and there that I would see her again. "Is it okay if I write to you?" I asked.

"Oh, yes. Please do!" From the pocket of her coat, she produced a piece of paper with her name, address and phone number on it. She must have jotted it down before we left the house. I was beginning to think she liked me, too. "Next time you're in town," she said, "call and come out, okay?"

"You bet I will!" I replied. The train was coming, so I took the initiative this time and gave her a friendly kiss. It felt so good! But it was not nearly enough.

"Come on, Seeley," Harvey said. "We've got to get aboard."

Helen stood at the foot of the steps until we disappeared inside the train. As the doors closed behind me, I looked back to see if I could catch another glimpse of her. She stood there, waving until our train rounded a corner and she disappeared from my sight.

When we sat down, Harvey poked me in the ribs and said, "Didn't I tell you?"

I just grinned.

On that rainy Sunday in April 1942, I fell in love for the first time and I knew that from then on, my life would never be the same.

PQ-17

21 June - the longest day of the year. The mild and clear weather felt like an early spring day back home. Bob and I decided to stay up to see if the sun really didn't set. Just after midnight, the large orange orb dipped slowly to the horizon. Then, before it disappeared totally from view, it once again began rising higher in the sky. I wished for a camera to share the moment with our family at home. How do you describe something so breathtaking? In this case, a picture would have been worth a thousand words.

About this time, scuttlebutt began circulating that we would be out to sea for at least another four months, probably escorting a convoy to Russia. My heart sank. All I could do was hope the rumor mongers were wrong. A year ago, I might have been excited about the adventure, but now all I wanted was to get back to New York. If we were gone that long, Helen might forget about me. I didn't want that to happen. I ignored the scuttlebutt and instead, sat down to write another letter to her.

30 June

We put into Seydisfjordur, Iceland, a small harbor town with only a few scattered houses here and there. As we entered the harbor, the thing that struck me most was the unspoiled landscape of majestic beauty. In stark contrast to the towering cliffs of blinding white ice walls was the cobalt blue water. The low-hanging sun cast long and unrelenting shadows across the land. To my eye, the surreal vista seemed like a scene from a Jules Verne novel.

Captivated, I stood by the break in the deck, soaking in the splendor and thinking about the other beauty in my life - Helen. For those few moments, the war seemed far away, almost like a bad dream. But it was closer than any of us knew. And it was about to become a nightmare from which we could not soon awaken.

1 July

Rowan received orders to put to sea with a cruiser/destroyer force to escort the convoy designated PQ-17. This convoy of twenty-two American merchantmen, eleven merchant ships of other countries, three rescue ships, and a fleet oiler was routed around the western and northern coasts of Iceland. Bound for the war effort in Russia, the freighters carried millions of dollars of urgently needed supplies.

From the British Royal Navy, the escort consisted of the cruisers H.M.S *London* and H.M.S. *Norfolk*, six destroyers - *Keppel*, *Offa*, *Ledbury*, *Wilton*, *Fury* and *Leamington*, two flack ships, two submarines and eleven smaller craft. From the American forces came the cruisers *Wichita* and *Tuscaloosa*, and two destroyers, *Wainwright* and *Rowan*. The Allied Covering Force responsible for keeping an eye on the German heavy units reportedly berthed in Alten Fjord, Norway, consisted of a British battleship, an American battleship, a British aircraft carrier, three British cruisers, a squadron of British DD's and corvettes, and the American destroyers *Mayrant* and *Rhind*.

PQ-17's planned route was along the northern coast of Iceland, north-by-northeast past Jan Mayen Island, north between Spitzbergen and Bear Island, then east and southeast through the Barents Sea, past the Kola Peninsula and into the entrance of the White Sea. Our destination was Archangel, Russia. This was dangerous territory, within easy reach of German land-based forces. It would take everything we had to get our charges through safely.

The German Admiralty was well informed of the composition and movement of PQ-17 and as determined as we were to reach Russia, they were equally determined that we would not. They planned a combined air-surface-underwater operation to annihilate this sea train. To this operation, which the Germans labeled "Knight's Gambit", were assigned the battleships *Tirpitz, Scheer, Hipper*, the pocket battleship *Prince Eugen* and seven destroyers. German dive-bombers and a wolfpack of as many as six U-boats waited along the coast of Norway for their opportunity to strike.

Rowan had hardly taken up her position in the screening force when lookouts sighted an enemy plane in the distance. Every now and then, one of the cruisers fired off a round or two to let the pilot know he had been spotted. The plane stayed just out of range but never out of sight. Its job was to keep the German High Command informed of the convoy's every move and there was nothing we could do about it. We had other, more immediate problems on our hands, courtesy of Mother Nature. At times we passed dangerously close to heavy ice floes, and a thick blanket of fog fell like a curtain across the Strait of Denmark, obscuring from sight the ships in our charge.

Late afternoon. One of our merchantmen ran aground. A short time later, another collided with an iceberg and was so damaged that it was ordered to break off from the convoy and return to port. Suddenly, the captivating beauty I had enjoyed only a few days before took on a much more menacing aspect. It didn't take long for us to realize that this convoy was likely to be the most perilous we had ever been a part of. Word was that we would be engaging the enemy this week, a chilling thought in these frigid Arctic waters. We didn't have long to wait.

2 July

0700. *Rowan* was sent to refuel from the fleet oiler, the British tanker *Aldersdale*, which was within the body of the convoy. On the way, we passed through a fog bank as thick as pea soup. When we broke out of it, lookouts immediately sighted three or four Heinkel torpedo bombers circling the merchant ships, preparing to launch an attack.

General quarters was sounded and as I raced to my battle station, I saw one of the bombers making a low pass across our bow. Before we emerged from the fog bank, he had been maneuvering to attack from the port bow of the convoy. Our sudden appearance must have shaken up the attackers. They hadn't planned on any targets that could return fire. With a destroyer on station, it would not be the turkey shoot they had hoped for.

Captain Harrison's orders came across my headset. "Bring us broadside of the target." As *Rowan* swung into position, our guns came around and locked onto the closest Heinkel off the port side at a range of 8,000 yards. "Commence firing with the main battery."

The crew inside the #2 upper handling room quickly passed charges and projectiles, and the gun crew above unleashed the salvo. The report from the port lookout came back, "Target is breaking off the attack."

"Very well," the captain said coolly. "Let's see if we can drown his buddy."

Our guns trained around as we tracked the second plane. "Target at 7,000 yards."

"Fire." With all four of our guns blazing away at him, the second pilot quickly abandoned the fight. He joined the first plane in a hasty retreat.

Fire control, meanwhile, was sighting in on the third Heinkel. The forward lookout called in, "Target crossing our bow to starboard. Range 5,000 yards." Lt. Brown in fire control brought our guns to bear. "Fire," the captain ordered.

All four guns hurled salvo after salvo at the incoming fighter, but this one didn't back off. For about twenty seconds he kept coming, ignoring the flak bursting under him. Lt. Brown ordered

a few adjustments to the targeting and the next shell exploded right under the Heinkel, setting it ablaze. With black smoke trailing out behind, the torpedo plane glided down into the drink.

One of the other Heinkels that had broken off the attack returned, coming in low, following his buddy down. Although flak was bursting all around him, he managed to avoid being hit. In an amazing feat of skill and courage in battle, the pilot landed his plane on the water right next to the downed craft, some 10,000 yards from our location. The disabled Heinkel was sinking and its crew abandoned ship. They scrambled aboard the rescuing plane like cowboys swinging into the saddle in a Western movie. They weren't even fully aboard when the second pilot throttled up and, though his plane was greatly overloaded, powered his way out of the water and back into the air.

I could feel the ship vibrate as Captain Harrison ordered flank speed to chase down the plane. *Rowan* was out of range but at this speed, we would be on them within minutes. Our gun crew loaded another round and prepared to fire as soon as the order was given.

Over the telephone headset, I heard Jilcott on the wing of the bridge shout, "Torpedo! Off the port bow!" One of the Heinkels had taken deadly aim at us and if we didn't move fast, we would be a chalk mark on the side of a Nazi plane.

Almost immediately, the ship heeled over as the captain ordered evasive maneuvers and we were forced to break off pursuit of the rescue plane. We could only watch as it passed by a British destroyer, which peppered the air with flak. The Brits did not score a hit. Had the Heinkel pilots not been the enemy, we might have cheered them for their bravery and skill. But as it was, we knew that the escape of the Heinkel was bad news. It meant that two German crews had survived to fight another day

Shortly, we received a message from the British destroyer H.M.S. *Keppel* saying, "*One bird in water. Do you claim?*"

Captain Harrison's reply was understated. "*Fired on plane which flew away streaming smoke.*"

When I turned in that night, my whole body ached from the tensions of the day. I was afraid I wouldn't be able to sleep but thankfully, as soon as my head hit the pillow, I was out like a light. I would need all the rest I could get because the Germans were determined to stop the convoy at all costs and they had the firepower to back their intentions. The crew of the *Rowan* would have to be sharp to face what the enemy would throw at us next.

4 July

The ship plodded along at a sedate eight knots and there was scarcely any chop to the sea. I glanced out the porthole. It was pea soup, just as it had been the day before. I said a silent thank you to God because until that cover burned off, the Germans planes would be grounded. I hoped it would stay that way, to give us a respite while we celebrated our country's birthday.

The brief Arctic night ended at around 0200, and from the brightness of the sky even at that hour, I was sure the cover wouldn't last. It didn't. As the ships of the convoy emerged from a heavy mist, enemy planes were waiting for us. At 0300, German Heinkels and Junkers swooped down out of the sky and sighted in on the SS *Christopher Newport*. They dropped their lethal payloads and sank the unarmed freighter. It was just the first of the day.

The torpedo planes came in, wave after wave. Allied Forces got three of them but by late afternoon, the Heinkels had hit the SS *William Hooper* and the Russian tanker *Azerbaodjan*. Miraculously, the Russian damage control team kept her afloat. Our flagship, USS *Wainwright* took a pounding, though thanks to her skipper's quick reflexes, she escaped with only minor damage and no loss of life. So far, PQ-17 was holding its own.

1400. I was relieved from my general quarters station to begin the evening meal. A short time later, when I was about to put a pan of ham into the oven for the Fourth of July dinner, I felt a change in the sound of the screws. Curious, I glanced out the starboard porthole to look at the other ships of the convoy as I had done many times before. This time when I looked, I was surprised to find that the ships of the convoy were not where they had been. I crossed over to the other side of the galley and looked out the portside. I couldn't believe it! The entire escort force was making a one hundred-eighty degree turn and was heading back toward England.

At my earliest opportunity, I tracked down Ernie to find out what was going on. He told me that the convoy had received orders to scatter. The message from the British Admiralty stated simply,

> *Cruiser Force withdraw to westward at high speed owing to threat from surface ships. Convoy is to disperse and proceed to Russian ports. Convoy is to scatter.*

The British Admiralty, fearing the superior strength of the Germans and the potential loss of such a large and irreplaceable escort force in what could prove to be a turning point in the war, sent word for us to quit the convoy. It seemed we had reached a critical point in our journey just south of Spitzbergen. Archangel was still a long way away but here, German forces were the strongest. Our screening force was pulled back to support a second cruiser division in anticipation of engaging the German heavy units, which were rumored to have left their base at Alten Fjord, Norway. The merchant ships would have to disperse and make their way to Russia any way they could. As they proceeded, Russian ships and aircraft would give them what protection they could which, at the moment, was precious little.

We received a signal from the Admiral commanding Cruiser Squadron One to all ships and company. It read:

"I know you will all be feeling as distressed as we are to leave that fine collection of ships to find their own way to harbor. The enemy, under cover of his shore-based aircraft, has succeeded in concentrating a vastly superior force in this area. We were therefore, ordered to withdraw. We are all sorry that the great work of the close escort (the destroyers) could not be completed. I am sure we shall all have a chance of settling this score with them soon."

The message was supposed to reassure us, but it didn't. We still believed we could lick any enemy in the world and so it was hard for us to understand why we were running from a fight, leaving those defenseless ships, thirty-three in all, to fend for themselves. We wished only the best for the merchantmen on their perilous journey, though we knew their chances were poor to nil.

For as bad as we thought it would be for those men, we would learn some time later that the toll was far worse than any of us could have imagined. One by one, the ships of the convoy were picked off by U-boats, bombers and torpedo planes. The *Washington, Carlton*, two British freighters, the Dutch freighter *Paulus Potter,* SS *Olopana, Fairfield City, Daniel Morgan, Samuel Chase,* SS *Hoosier*, and the SS *El Capitan* were lost. Also sunk were *Alcoa Ranger, Honomu, John Witherspoon, Pan American, Pan-Kraft,* and *Peter Kerr.* British merchantmen *Earlston, Empire Byron, Bolton Castle,* and the *Hartlebury* went down. Finally, the Russian rescue ship *Zaafaran,* damaged in intense bombing, had to be scuttled by her crew.

In all, twenty-two ships and crew went to the bottom. Only eleven battle-scarred freighters survived to limp into Murmansk on 25 July. History showed that the expected battle for which we had been pulled away from escort duty, never developed because the German battlewagons never left port. But PQ-17 was devastated.

Nursing bitter feelings over having left so many of our countrymen and allies to die in the cold waters of the Barents Sea, we returned to Hvalfjordur, Iceland. We did not comprehend the British decision to retreat. Perhaps our inability to understand was because we had only been in this war less than a year. The British had been fighting for three. They knew that the loss of even a few capital ships would have been an enormous blow to the defense of their island nation.

In retrospect, it is clear that if the PQ-17 escort had continued, there would certainly have been many casualties and many U.S. fighting ships would have gone down along with the merchantmen. The Germans, parked only twenty or thirty miles away from our shipping lanes, could have attacked us with impunity. The British decision was the only reasonable one they could have made, for in trying to protect PQ-17, we would have been engaged in a fight we could not have won.

It was hard for us to disguise the feeling we had that the British had betrayed the convoy of merchant ships. We couldn't wait to leave them and the ugly memory of PQ-17 behind.

14 July

It was a relief for us when *Rowan* was released from duty with the British Home Fleet. In the company of the battleship *Washington* and the destroyers *Wainwright, Mayrant* and *Rhind*, we headed home, arriving in New York on 21 July.

I couldn't wait to see Helen. Seeing her again might help erase some of the horror and the hollow emptiness I felt.

At that point in the war, the future looked grim. We could see that our objective of keeping the shipping lanes open would be won only at high cost in dollars and lives. The Germans were asserting themselves with surprising strength and we had no assurance that we could whip them.

As the stark realities of war touched us more closely than ever, our proud bravado of only a year earlier evaporated. Through the fire of battle and the pain and suffering we felt about that terrible loss of life, a loss we believed we might have prevented, we of the *Rowan* were galvanized into a seasoned fighting force. Never again would we underestimate our enemy. We swore never again would we abandon a friend. We were more resolute than ever to win this war at any cost.

We did not know just how high that cost would be.

Friendly Fire

12 August. Underway with *Livermore, Intrepid* and *Kearny,* heading toward Newport, Rhode Island. It was a big day for Bob, Britt Crowe, John Goldman, Carter and me. We were all celebrating birthdays. Bob and I baked a white sheet cake and decorated it with a half dozen candles, and the five of us birthday boys sang "Happy Birthday" to each other. It was an especially big celebration for Bob. He was now twenty-one, old enough to vote.

When we got into Newport the next day, I went ashore with Crowe and Goldman, intending to celebrate our birthdays with a couple of drinks - but I turned into a party pooper. I hadn't regained my taste for drinking after an incident that had happened the month before when I was on a three-day leave. On a crowded train from Boston to New York, the only standing room I could find was in the club car. After the four hour trip, I had had too much to drink and to put it mildly, was just a little inebriated by the time I got to the Quinn's house. Although none of the family realized my condition, the incident embarrassed me so much that I decided to lay off alcohol.

I was back aboard the ship by 2000, grabbed a pen and paper and as the last glow of day faded from the sky, sat down on the locker outside the galley to write to Helen. I wanted to get a letter in the mail to her before we shoved off again the next morning.

16 August

0400. *Livermore, Kearny, Intrepid, South Dakota* and *Rowan* weighed anchor, set a course of 180 degrees south at a speed of 22 knots. Our amateur navigators guessed that we were bound once again for Panama. They were right. The weather was clear and bright and the sea calm. If it hadn't been for the Germans out there, the trip would have been downright pleasant.

We were jolted back to the reality of war when, early the morning of 19 August, lookouts sighted a lifeboat with what appeared to be a number of survivors aboard. *Rowan* was ordered to investigate. As we approached, it was discovered that the "survivors" were actually sea gulls sitting quietly on the gunwales of the otherwise empty boat.

20 August

Colon, Canal Zone. Liberty was granted until 2200. I was still off booze and determined to avoid temptation. Harvey, who was never much of a drinker anyway, came along with me for a stroll into town. The steamy, tropical port city was not much to look at and if you weren't interested in drink, or...other things...there wasn't much to do. The only reason Harvey and I were in town at all was to escape the close, stifling confines of the ship.

Around 1800, we met a couple of our shipmates, Prettyman and Carter, near the nightclub district. They were heading over to catch one of the floorshows and invited us to join them. With nothing better to do, Harvey and I figured we might as well. The club was what you would expect in a port town like Colon - hot, dark, smoky, and noisy. The four of us found a table on the edge of the stage and within minutes, a couple of pretty Panamanian "B" girls came over to us and asked if we'd like to buy them a drink. We agreed and pulled up chairs for them.

A waitress came by to take their drink orders. In heavily accented English, the first dark-eyed beauty asked for an Especial. The other wanted a Blue Moon. Although we didn't know it, both beverages were non-alcoholic and the only difference was the price. The Blue Moon cost twenty-five cents more.

The floorshow featured some rather scantily clad women performing an energetic dance. One of the dancers came close to us and whipped Prettyman's hat off the table. She hugged it to herself and began to rub it seductively across her body and down between her legs. Prettyman's eyes bugged halfway out of his head. He went to grab his hat, but the dancer was too quick for him. The *Rowan* man figured out the game right away. The next time the girl shimmied close, he didn't grab for the hat but for the area of her body across which she was rubbing it. He missed the hat but scored a direct hit on the body, and the girl dropped the hat. We laughed so hard tears were streaming down our eyes. Prettyman picked up his hat to an enthusiastic round of applause. He took a deep bow, then sat down with a permanent grin on his face.

23 August

0530. Helen's birthday. I was in the galley thinking about her as I honed my knives before starting breakfast, when Waxler came in for his morning cup of coffee. As usual, he had a story to share. He leaned against the bulkhead in the galley passageway, mug in one hand and one hairy arm crossed over his bulging belly. "I got a good one for you, Seeley," he began. "Did ya hear the one about the ninety-day wonder?"

I looked up at him and shook my head no. I knew how he felt about the green college boys who were sent to Officer Candidate School and graduated ninety days later with their commissions. Like the doctor who became my drinking buddy on the train from Boston to New York, in that scant three months' time, these civilians were supposed to come out with the leadership and seamanship skills that men like Waxler spent years developing. I figured any story he had to tell concerning ninety-day wonders had to be a good one.

"There was this whaleboat coxswain came alongside a cruiser requesting orders from the officer of the deck. Turns out this OOD is a ninety-day wonder, fresh out of OCS. The OOD shouts down to the coxswain, "'Take your boat forward and tie it to the yardarm.'"

I chuckled at the improper use of terms. The yardarm is a crossbeam located close to a hundred feet up on the main mast. What the OOD should have said was to take the boat forward and tie it to the boat boom.

Waxler continued, "Well, this coxswain starts circling the ship at full speed. Round and round he goes, faster and faster all the time. After several passes, the OOD calls him alongside and asks him what the heck he's doing. The coxswain said, "I'm just trying to get up enough speed to fly up there, sir."

I laughed at the joke, but I didn't share Waxler's disdain of the ninety-day wonders. Although many sailors, especially the old salts, had a few good laughs at the expense of those instant officers, in reality many of them turned into fine leaders. They learned through experience gained at a time when there was little room for error. If they were lucky, they lived to talk about their mistakes. But the learning process could be dangerous. That was never as clear as it was the night we met patrol craft PC 491.

It was just after sunset and normal cruise conditions were in effect. The hour around dusk was the most vulnerable time for ships in this area. U-boats would track ships silently until nightfall, then under cover of darkness, surface, fire torpedoes and slip away unseen. The 2000 to 2400 watch came on duty. The new watch included Harvey, signalman of the watch; Goodpaster, torpedoman; and Lt. Glenn, officer of the deck. The watch going off duty filled them in concerning any conditions or information they would need to know. All was quiet and there was little to report.

2045. Radar picked up a contact and general quarters was sounded. Within seconds, Captain Harrison was on the bridge to take over the con. "Unidentified craft six thousand yards dead ahead. Speed six knots," Glenn told the captain

"U-boat?" Harrison asked.

"Unknown, sir. I don't think they know we're here," Glenn replied.

Harrison frowned. "That doesn't sound very German," he mused. "Bring us broadside to the target," he ordered the helm. Then turning to Harvey and said, "Challenge him."

"Aye, aye, sir," Harvey replied and began blinking out the challenge in standard Morse code. He waited, scanning the surface for some sign of reply. Nothing. "No answer, sir," he said to the captain, who was standing right behind him.

"Try again," Harrison grumbled. "Try without the suppresser. Maybe he doesn't see us."

With a well-practiced hand, Harvey flipped the lever transmitting the challenge. The shutter clacking open and shut was the only sound to be heard as all hands on the bridge focused on the horizon, trying to catch a glimpse of a response.

Long seconds passed. Nothing.

"Still no answer, sir."

"Stand by to open fire." Harrison stared off the starboard wing of the bridge, muttering, "Something's wrong here. I can feel it." Ordinarily, a competent and seasoned captain like Harrison might have opened fire by now but the captain hesitated.

Reports from throughout the ship were coming into the bridge. *Rowan* was trimmed for action. Guns were loaded and targeted in. At a simple command from the captain, *Rowan* was prepared to unleash a deadly barrage from her five-inch guns and within seconds, the unidentified threat on the horizon might vanish forever beneath the waves. The bridge telephone talker, trailing behind the captain as he paced, stood ready to give the command to fire as soon as he was ordered to do so. But the captain hesitated.

Harrison glanced at the talker and in response to the ready reports, he said softly, "Stand by." Then he nodded to Harvey. "Try another challenge."

"Aye, sir," Harvey replied. He turned and repeated the message, slowly and carefully.

Harrison spoke quietly to Lt. Glenn. "This just doesn't seem like a German vessel. The only enemy in this area would have to be a submarine, yet this is a surface vessel and shows no sign of submerging."

Lt. Glenn, who was looking out toward the target, interrupted his superior. "Excuse me, sir!" He pointed to the horizon and said, "I see flashes ahead. I think they're firing on us!"

Harrison turned to follow Glenn's direction. "Dammit!" he responded almost under his breath. "Stand by to open fire," he barked.

As a reflex action, everyone else on the bridge crouched as low as possible waiting for the projectile to reach them. Everyone, that is, except Goodpaster, who had nowhere to crouch. He could only paste himself flat against the bulkhead and hope for the best.

Forward lookouts reported that the anticipated projectiles had missed by more than a hundred yards. When the word reached Harrison, the captain banged his fist on the chart table. "Now I'm sure they're not German. The Krauts are better shots." He turned to Lt. Glenn and said, "I think it's one of our own yokels out there without enough sense to respond to our challenge." He jerked his thumb in the direction of the Talk Between Ships system and said, "Try him on the TBS. Maybe that'll rouse him."

Lt. Glenn went to the TBS, pushed down the talk lever and called out *Rowan's* recognition signal. "This is the USS *Rowan*, DD 405. Cease fire! Cease fire!" His voice was calm but firm, leaving no room for misunderstanding.

Just then, another shell exploded from the guns of the darkened target. Everyone on the bridge of the *Rowan* ducked again as this shell landed within fifty feet of the bow. "I say again," Glenn called over the TBS. "CEASE FIRE. This is the USS *Rowan*, DD 405. CEASE FIRE!!!" Glenn paused a few seconds to wait for a reply, keeping a watchful eye for indications of another salvo.

Finally, a shaky voice came back over the squawk box. "Uh, this is PC 491. Sorry. We didn't recognize you."

Captain Harrison shot Glenn a weary glance and said, "Secure from general quarters. And have that idiot report to me immediately." Shaking his head in disgust, he settled back in his chair, drumming his fingers on the arm rests.

A few minutes later, a whaleboat grated alongside *Rowan* and a sheepish-faced lieutenant (jg) clambered up the sea ladder. Lt. Glenn was there to meet him and without a word, escorted the young officer to the bridge where Captain Harrison sat, grimly awaiting his arrival.

When the PC boat captain arrived, he saluted Captain Harrison, a gesture that the senior officer acknowledged with a wave of his hand. For an uncomfortable moment, Harrison said nothing. Then quietly, in an almost fatherly voice, he began, "How long have you been in the Navy, son?"

The young lieutenant (jg) cleared his throat and said, "About eighteen months, sir. I've been in the Navy about eighteen months, including OCS."

Goodpaster rolled his eyes toward heaven.

"And how long have you been in command of that PC out there?" Harrison asked turning to stare in the direction of the PC's dark silhouette.

"Six months, sir."

The captain shook his head imperceptibly. Without moving his gaze, he asked, "Do you anticipate a long life?"

"Yes, sir!" the young officer answered firmly.

Harrison slowly turned to face the young man again. "Do you have any idea how close you came to ending that life tonight? Can you estimate how many of your crew might have been killed if I had been as trigger-happy as you? I had a full broadside trained on you that would have blown you out of the water," he said with a sudden motion of his left hand, as if he were swatting a fly. The movement made the young man wince. When the hand came back to rest, the captain said, "Only a hunch kept me from firing, an action that we both would have regretted...had you survived."

The lieutenant swallowed uneasily. "I'm sorry, sir, but I thought you were a submarine...."

Harrison leaned forward suddenly, cutting off further response. "What bureaucratic snafu gave you a command?" Harrison growled. "Are you trying to tell me that you are so stupid," his anger was mounting, "that you can't recognize a destroyer silhouette from a submarine?"

"I was...it was...I mean...I was as sure as I cou..."

"Shut up, you son-of-a-bitch," Harrison roared, losing what little control he had maintained to that point. Rising out of his chair, he said, "If you're that dumb, you shouldn't be in command of a ship! I intend to prefer charges against you as soon as possible." He stood up and said more calmly, "How in the hell the Navy ever put anyone as incompetent as you out here is something I'll never understand."

Rowan's skipper clasped his hands behind his back and said, "Your first shots missed us by over a hundred yards. The second came much closer, but if we had actually been an enemy, you would never have gotten past the first shot. That is not good gunnery. You are directed to report to your commanding officer tomorrow morning and request target practice. See if you can't come a little closer next time. One day, it may actually be an enemy you encounter."

He took a step closer to the young officer and glared coldly at him. "You are also directed to administer additional training to your signalmen and bridge lookouts. They ignored the attempts we made to contact you by light before you so rashly commenced firing on us." Raising his voice half a notch, he added, "Is that clear, mister?"

"Y-yes, sir," the cowed lieutenant quavered.

Harrison turned away. "You are dismissed. Return to your ship."

The lieutenant (jg) saluted and left as quickly as he could. His ego was bruised, but at least his skin was still intact.

With the PC captain gone, Harrison shook his head again, looking drained and worn. He glanced in Lt. Glenn's direction. Returning command to the junior officer, he said simply, "I'm going below."

Captain Harrison was one of a kind. He expected a lot from us, and pushed and prodded until he got it. But he also showed us a great deal of consideration. Firm when he had to be, he was always fair in his dealings with enlisted men. His officers knew they were trusted and that trust inspired confidence. Many of the crew had been with him since he put *Rowan* into commission in 1939. We had been through good times and bad. With him at the helm, we knew we could do just about anything.

Therefore, it was with mixed feelings that we received word that he had been promoted to full commander. His promotion was well deserved but it meant he would be transferred. Captain Harrison's leaving was hard for all of us. We took up a collection among the crew and bought him a cap with "scrambled eggs" on it, the Navy slang for a captain's cap insignia. We wished him hail and farewell and hoped for the best with our new captain.

Operation Torch

10 October. Casco Bay, Maine. The new skipper took command. Annapolis graduate Lt. Comdr. Robert S. Ford, arrived and in a brief ceremony on deck, we saluted him to welcome him aboard.

Dark-haired and blue-eyed, Captain Ford wasn't a very tall man but he carried himself rigidly erect, giving him an air of unapproachability. Although he had previously served aboard the destroyer *Eberle* as executive officer, *Rowan* would be his first command. Within the next twenty-four hours, he would discover that *Rowan* wasn't the *Eberle*, and we would find that Ford wasn't Harrison.

For us, the changeover to the new captain was trying, at best. Ford was much less forgiving than Harrison. For example, in the interest of our physical and mental well being after the combat duty we had been through, Harrison had allowed some latitude in certain details of maintenance. The ship was always neat and well cared for, but looked like what it was - a man-o-war. This situation did not meet with Ford's approval and with an almost religious fervor, he set about bringing *Rowan* up to his standard of perfection. This did not endear him to the crew.

The new captain ruled with an iron fist, insisting on strict adherence to the book of Navy rules and regulations. He stated categorically that he was appalled by the condition of the ship. Under his command, he would tolerate nothing out of line. He was unconcerned that we had been through severe conditions. A poorly maintained ship was a liability. Everything was to be put in tiptop condition, immediately.

Robert S. Ford, when he retired as Rear Admiral

We had thought our training excessive under Harrison but it did not compare with how we were drilled and practiced after the change of command. Even before he had unpacked his gear, he started drilling us. We had gunnery drills, general quarters drills, emergency drills, collision drills, fire drills, drill drills. Then there was clean up, scrubbing, painting, sweeping, swabbing, inspections almost daily. Maintenance parts had to be inventoried and updated, a tedious, tiresome, dirty job that everyone hated. It was enough to get on anyone's nerves.

To make matters worse, once underway, Ford seldom left the bridge and by this action, expressed little confidence in his officers. He drove his executive officer mercilessly to get the ship cleaned up. Day and night, he watched the crew like a hawk, always jumping on the slightest infraction. Even the laid-back Georgia boy, Harvey, was about at wits end. As far as the crew was concerned, no one could replace Harrison. Although none of us considered Ford heaven-sent, he was in command and it was our duty to conform to his methods.

Ford seemed unaffected by our dislike for his style of management. He was not there to win a popularity contest. He was there to help win a war. No one but he knew that concern for the crew's well being was his chief motivation. He alone knew how frightened he was that a lack of preparation or readiness might cost him the lives of his men. And only he had any inkling of what lay ahead. History was about to toss him, untested, into one of the most trying crucibles of the war. Within one month of assuming command, he would be taking us into the teeth of what would be, up to that time, the biggest naval war operation ever staged in the history of the world.

13 October

Between late September and mid-October, I went to see Helen every time we were near New York. When we put into Boston for yard availability, I took the first train I could down to New York. I was more convinced than ever that she was the woman for me.

While in New York, I asked her to come to Boston for a few days while the ship was in the yard. It was easier for her to get off work and if she came to the ship, we could spend more time together. With her mother's okay, she agreed and we made plans. I had to get back to the ship but before I left, I told Helen I would call her from Boston the next day as soon as I had a place for her to stay. Then I'd give her specific instructions as to where and when we would meet.

The train from New York to Boston left at 1800, and I was very reluctant to go. The only thing that made my leaving any easier was knowing that I would see her again soon. All the way back, I kept thinking of how wonderful it was going to be when she came up. I could hardly wait. I got back to the ship just before liberty expired at 0100. Exhausted, I tumbled into the sack and fell fast asleep. Little did I know the surprise the Navy would spring on me the very next morning.

19 October

Monday. The boatswain's whistle shrilled out the message, "Go to your stations all the special sea and anchor detail."

We were getting underway! I was near panic. Helen was expecting me to phone her about coming up but there was no way I could get off the ship to call. Within the hour, we had weighed anchor and were clearing the breakwater, heading north. With a heavy heart, I watched the shoreline recede behind us. I only hoped Helen wouldn't think I had abandoned her. I prayed we would be in some port soon so that I could get to a telephone to call her and let her know what had happened. For all I knew, we might have been on the way to Timbuktu! There was nothing I could do but wait.

The following afternoon, we pulled into Casco Bay, Maine, and at 1600, liberty was granted. I was the first one across the gangway. I dove into the nearest vacant telephone booth to place my call to Helen. She was glad to hear from me, although she had been wondering what had happened. She showed me a part of her that I would grow to love and appreciate - her flexibility and understanding. I was determined never to take undue advantage of it.

With my mind finally at ease, I could notice my surroundings for the first time. Moored in the bay were a number of heavy fire-support warships. There were the battleships *Massachusetts, New York*, and *Texas*, five cruisers, including the *Augusta*, seven carriers, a dozen or more destroyers, mine vessels and auxiliaries. When I checked around for scuttlebutt to see what was going on, no one seemed to know. What ever was happening was heavily shrouded in secrecy.

24 October

The day dawned frosty and clear. I was just cleaning up after breakfast when I heard the special sea and anchor detail call echoing throughout the ship. Since the galley was my duty station, I went on about my business, the now-familiar sounds of the ship getting underway scarcely attracting my attention.

I did take the opportunity to grab a final view out the porthole. I could see the last of the autumn leaves cascading down from the trees clinging to the shoreline. The brilliant reds of the maples had faded, but the butterfly-yellow birch leaves still shimmered in the morning sun. I tucked away the memory of that morning just in case it would be a long time before I saw American soil again.

We got underway escorting the *Massachusetts*. The destroyers *Woolsey, Edison, Tillman*, and *Boyle* formed our squadron under the flag of Captain J.B. Heffernan. Two days later, we rendezvoused with ships that had left from Hampton Roads, Virginia.

28 October

The air group arrived. When all ships were present and accounted for, the captains of the fleet got together for a very high-level meeting. At that conference in the middle of the Atlantic, the scope of this ambitious, history-making operation, dubbed Operation Torch, was laid out for those who would execute its orders.

There were three main objectives: First, transport Major General George S. Patton's 37,000 men, along with their war machines, to French Morocco for beachhead landings along the Atlantic coast. Second, support Patton's efforts with a concurrent assault on Casablanca, a vital seaport that would be a staging area for a future drive to Tunis, Tunisia, and a second front in Oran, Algeria, in the Mediterranean. Third, establish a striking force that could assure Allied control of the Straits of Gibraltar. This all-important sea lane was the gateway to the Mediterranean, the link between Great Britain and the oil-rich lands of the Middle East, and the shortest route to the Indian Ocean and the Far East.

It was hoped that this massive Allied invasion at Rommel's back door would force Germany's Afrika Korps to pull back from the Suez Canal. This would set up a new front, relieving some pressure on Russia, and perhaps turn the tide of the war. After the powwow at sea was over, this massive armada that spread out over some one hundred fifty square miles of ocean, turned southeast at a speed of twenty-one knots.

The invasion was scheduled for 8 November, weather permitting. It must have been through divine intervention that the Germans never got wind of the more than one hundred warships amassing off the coast of North Africa. That gave the Allied forces the advantage of surprise, and we would need all the help we could get.

In the port of Casablanca, the Axis powers had a flotilla of their own. There was the Vichy light cruiser *Primauguet*, three flotilla leaders, six destroyers, twelve subs and a number of auxiliaries.

And then there was the unfinished battleship *Jean Bart*. Although she could not move from her berth, her awesome sixteen-inch guns were in perfect working order. In spite of her immobility, she was the single biggest threat to our forces.

6 November

Rowan, screening the cruiser *Augusta*, arrived off the coast of Morocco in the early afternoon. The ships were ordered to stay well out of sight from lookouts in Safi and Casablanca. The following day, we prepared for action. The weather was clear and we were ready. We waited. Our orders were that we would not fire a single shell until the Vichy first fired on us. No one knew what kind of resistance there would be. After all, the French were a proud people and their defeat and subsequent coerced cooperation with the Germans might make them unlikely to fight a pitched battle. The hope was they would put up only token resistance and then surrender. Wishful thinking.

8 November

H-Hour for the operation was set for 0400. Stealth was required because it was hoped that the port could be taken without the destruction of the vital marine facilities ashore. If the enemy got wind of the impending attack, they would destroy that cargo handling equipment, equipment needed to unload Patton's tanks, rather than let it fall into Allied hands.

Thirty minutes before H-Hour, two assault destroyers detached from the fleet. They were the World War I vintage four-stackers *Bernadou* (DD 153) and *Cole* (DD 155). Significantly altered so that they could not be recognized as American destroyers, they headed toward the breakwater outside Safi, about 125 miles down the coast from Casablanca. Their job was to capture the docks and pave the way for the troop landing craft trailing behind them. At 0410, they were challenged by shore lookouts. *Bernadou* signaled back an identifying code, which seemed to satisfy the Moroccan guard.

Rowan stood off the coast near Fedala, a small fishing village fifteen miles north of Casablanca and about 150 miles north of the action just getting underway near Safi. Along with us were cruisers *Augusta*, *Brooklyn*, and *Cleveland*, carriers, *Ranger* and *Suwannee*, and destroyers *Wilkes, Swanson, Ludlow, Murphy, Bristol, Woolsey, Edison, Tillman, Boyle, Ellyson, Forrest, Fitch, Hobson*, and *Corry*. In addition, there were fifteen transports and cargo vessels standing by, waiting for a path to be cleared for them to land some 20,000 Army troops and invasion equipment. All were waiting for word that *Cole* and *Bernadou* had successfully slipped through the lines.

Bernadou glided quietly into the channel at Safi. Her uneventful entry into the port was deceptive, the calm before the storm. Eighteen minutes after responding to the Moroccan challenge, she braced herself against the first salvo from the shore batteries and the game was on. "Play ball," the American destroyer called back to the fleet over the TBS. With that, the landing boats following the two destroyers opened up to full throttle. 0430, the first wave of assault troops hit the beach.

0604. As the sun was peeking over the eastern horizon, French shore batteries at Chergui and Fedala blazed to life. 0620. Up in Fedala, our Task Group got the word to "Play ball!" American troops came upon sailors from four French destroyers that had previously been sunk by Allied ships. These men formed a defensive line between the Americans and the shoreline. Even if there had been no other resistance, they would have single-handedly made life miserable for our troops. In addition, the French corvettes *La Gracieuse* and *Commandant de Large* were firing into U.S. troops from off shore.

The shore batteries were not *Rowan*'s problem, however. We had to deal with the French ships that were meeting us head on. Along with *Augusta* and destroyers *Edison, Boyle*, and *Tillman*, *Rowan* was dispatched to drive away the two corvettes. But that left the *Jean Bart* with her sixteen-inch guns and ten-mile firing range.

Bob Icenogle was in the chart room just below the bridge going over the maps of the area when he heard a strange noise that seemed to be getting closer. Curious about what it was, he opened the chart room door just in time to be hit in the face by a gusher of water. It was caused by one of *Jean Bart*'s shells that missed us by less than ten yards.

155

Harvey, up on the bridge, got the same dousing, but he was actually grateful for it. It covered evidence of what could have otherwise been embarrassing traces of wetness inspired by the sheer terror of watching the shell's approach through his binoculars. In the #2 upper handling room, I looked out the scuttle to find out what was making the approaching sound. I didn't get wet from the spray but the shock of coming that close to meeting my Maker broke me out in a cold sweat.

Clearly visible in the water beside us was the yellow dye marker trail, a gunnery targeting aid, from the *Jean Bart* shell. *Jean Bart* had missed us, but if we didn't get it in gear, we might not be so lucky the next time. Ford ordered hard to port, all ahead flank. Seconds later, another shell whizzed past us just behind the bridge. It was so close that Harvey later complained that the heat of it singed his eyelashes.

Rowan was too far offshore to return fire but *Massachusetts* was not. The big battlewagon opened up in our behalf and the two giants exchanged thunderous salvos.

11 November

Even with aircraft from the carrier *Ranger* joining in, *Jean Bart* was slow to surrender. She held out for three days until American assault troops stormed the gates of Casablanca. By that time, we had covered the landing of some 16,500 troops.

After the beachheads were secured, *Rowan* was ordered to screen the tanker *Chanango* down the coast to Casablanca. The French may have capitulated but the Germans were just getting warmed up. In two day's time, U-boats sank four U.S. transports off Fedala, and three other ships, including the destroyer *Hambleton*.

Rowan played a minor role in the invasion of North Africa. But a minor role in that operation was significant. After the emotional pounding we had taken from PQ-17, we all felt justifiably proud of what we had accomplished.

4 December

With Casablanca secured, *Rowan* received orders to head back to the states. Luck was with me. Our destination was New York. At my earliest opportunity, I called Helen and arranged to have dinner with her.

After dinner, she asked if I'd like to go to a new Humphry Bogart movie that she wanted to see. Naturally, I said yes. Movies were always a good excuse to hold hands. When we got to the theater, the marquee almost dropped me in my tracks. In bold black letters was the word CASABLANCA. I couldn't believe it! How in the world had Hollywood managed to get a movie out so soon about this top-secret mission? I couldn't wait to see it. Boy, was I disappointed. It had absolutely nothing to do with our recent operation. My enthusiasm for the film flagged instantly, but not my enthusiasm for Helen. Halfway through the picture, I leaned over to her and whispered, "Why don't we go find someplace where we can dance."

I caught the gleam in her eye as she nodded yes. Holding hands is nice. But the close contact of dance is far more enjoyable. Years later, Helen and I did see the entire showing of *Casablanca*, and we enjoyed it very much. That was after we were married and weren't as distracted by being close to each other.

31 December

As 1942 drew to a close, I danced to the music of Tommy Dorsey with my girl. The turmoil of war seemed so very far away. But its tragedy would soon touch me right there in New York.

Man Overboard

With the tempo of the war picking up, *Rowan* was at sea most of the time. The respites, when they came, lasted only long enough for major repair work or equipment upgrades to be completed. I was grateful that from late November 1942 through mid-January 1943, *Rowan* operated close to home. This gave me precious time to court Helen, time I put to good use. I knew the situation was too good to last.

19 January 1943

We were assigned to escort convoy GUS-3 from New York to Casablanca. Someone up there must have been looking down upon us favorably or maybe it was just Helen praying for me. Whatever the cause, the result was that, unlike our first visit to North Africa, this trip was without incident. Life at sea was beginning to lose some of its glamour. I wanted little more than to spend time with Helen.

7 February

Rowan dropped anchor in the river outside the Brooklyn Naval Yard and with the current running out to sea, the ship came around to face the flow. As a standard safety precaution, before entering the yard where workers would be using welding torches, all explosives had to be removed from the ship. A barge was due to come alongside to receive our munitions. Supper was hardly over when the word was passed for all hands to turn to and begin the unloading process. No liberty would be granted until the job was completed.

That was sufficient incentive for everyone to pitch in and get the ammunition topside and ready for transfer as quickly as possible. From the bowels of the ship, brass powder cans and service shells were passed hand to hand and neatly stacked up on the fo'c's'le and aft on the fantail near the handling rooms awaiting transfer. The work detail was a happy bunch. After all, we were within sight of the city and just as soon as the job was completed, we would be off the deck and onto the streets of New York. The misty night air was warm for mid-winter, around 40 degrees, warm enough to work comfortably with just a jacket and gloves.

As soon as the galley was cleaned up, Bob, who was on duty, shifted into dungarees and headed up on deck to lend a hand. He spotted me and came over. He looked puzzled for a moment and asked, "Something's different. What is it?"

I looked up in the direction he was facing. "Oh," I said, "it's the lifelines," referring to the safety lines that ran along the perimeter of the ship. "They're down." They had been dropped down from the stanchions so that the explosives could be off-loaded more easily. He nodded once, satisfied with my answer, and went back to stacking shells near the aft depth charge racks.

Word was passed to take a break. There was no more room on deck for ammo and the barge still had not arrived to pick up the load. There were no lights in the harbor because of blackout regulations, and I was amazed how dark it was this early in the evening. I mopped my brow with the back of my hand and leaned back against the depth charge rack. Bob, who was a little winded from slinging shells, joined me to tell me about a trip he was hoping to take down to the Desch's house.

As we relaxed, we noticed a group of the guys from the black gang horsing around with Bob Rettig. Now fireman first class, Rettig had a crazy laugh and a good sense of humor. The tall, slim sailor from Michigan was unusually ticklish and sometimes, all you had to do was point a finger at him and he would jump. The five or six guys from the black gang, including Rettig, were laughing and whooping it up.

After a few minutes of roughhousing, Rettig called for a time out to catch his breath. In a comical gesture, he crossed his legs and reached his hand back to lean against the lifeline. But the lifeline wasn't there. As if in slow motion, Rettig just kept going, falling downward into the water. I saw his face as he went overboard and there was a look of complete disbelief in his eyes. It was as if he couldn't understand why there was no support behind him. As soon as he hit the water, I heard him cry out in a shrill voice, "I can't swim!" He coughed once and shouted again, "I can't swim!"

Everyone became silent for a stunned heartbeat. Someone shouted, "Man overboard!" I stood up and started moving toward the stern. At the same moment, a blue blur flashed past me. It was Kelley, stripping off his jacket, shoes and hat as he went. By the time he reached the fantail, he was at a full run. In a graceful movement, he passed between the depth charge racks and made a headlong dive off the deck and into the icy water. I heard the splash but in the darkness of the mid-winter evening, I could not see him or Rettig.

Any sounds they might have made were blotted out when the ship's alarm blared out with a steady B-U-R-P, B-U-R-P. Rescue crews dashed to the boats and began to lower away. Up on the bridge, Harvey began flashing the light signal identifying DD 405 so that the whaleboat could find us in the darkness. The rest of the crew crowded around the fantail, hoping to be of assistance, hoping to spot the two men in the water, hoping to be able to help them aboard to safety.

Then, one of the electricians snapped on the high-powered searchlight on the after deck house and swung it around to light up the dark waters. The action could not have come at a worse time, as we learned later. Kelley had Rettig in sight and almost within reach. When the light came on, it caught him full in the eyes and temporarily blinded him. In the few seconds it took him to adjust to the brightness, he lost sight of the drowning man. He never saw Rettig again.

The current was running swiftly, carrying the two men ever farther from the ship. The boat crews were away now, but they couldn't see either man in the water. They proceeded at a painfully slow pace, trying to keep from accidentally passing the men in the darkness. Even the sound of the whaleboat's motor worked against them because it drowned out any cries for help.

Meanwhile, the ammunition barge arrived and all hands went back to work. I turned away, certain that Rettig would be rescued. Rettig had graduated boot camp with Bob and me, and the three of us had come aboard together. Losing him would be like losing a part of my own life. As that thought passed briefly through my mind, it left me with a hollow, cold feeling inside.

The rescue party was gone a long time, though because I was involved in the unloading detail, I could not judge how long. I recall hearing the whaleboat return. Work slowed down as everyone looked up to see if Rettig had been found. He hadn't. The man that was brought aboard wrapped in blankets was Kelley, blue-cold and very near death himself.

Only one man died that night. It might easily have been two. Kelley lived to tell us his story. By the time he lost sight of Rettig, he told us, he himself was a good distance from the ship and the current was carrying him farther away every second. He knew he would not have the strength to swim against the current. In the icy water, his arms and legs were like lead. All he could do was find some place to hang on and hope that rescue would come in time. That place turned out to be the anchor chain of a moored merchantman. The cold was rapidly sapping the life out of him. Five minutes longer and he might have joined Rettig in Davey Jones' locker. The rescue crew had to pry his nearly frozen fingers off the line to bring him aboard.

A month later, we got word that Rettig's body had been located, well down river of the incident. No memorial was held for him on the ship, though we all mourned his loss. It was a deeply personal tragedy to see a friend laughing one minute, and the next to see him swept away forever.

Heroes like Kelley don't come along every day. He was cited for bravery by Captain Ford.

He received the following award.

The Secretary of the Navy
Washington
The President of the United States takes pleasure in presenting the
NAVY AND MARINE CORPS MEDAL to
WILLIS DOYLE KELLEY
MACHINIST'S MATE FIRST CLASS
UNITED STATES NAVY
CITATION:

For heroic conduct while serving on board the USS *Rowan* in attempting to rescue a shipmate from drowning while his ship was proceeding to anchor off Tompkinville in New York Harbor, February 7, 1943. Upon hearing the cries for help from a man who had fallen overboard, KELLEY stripped off his winter clothing and dived over the side into the icy water. In spite of complete darkness and a strong ebb current, he exerted every effort to locate the man, gallantly remaining in the water until exhausted and numb from exposure and giving up the search only when he was physically unable to continue. His courageous initiative and disregard for his own safety in attempting to save another were in keeping with the highest traditions of the United States Naval Service.

For the President,
(s) James Forrestal
Secretary of the Navy

Rowan on the Rocks

Mid-February 1943. This was a time of great uncertainty and so each day was precious. We never knew where we would be going, or how long we would be staying, or if we would be coming back.

For my brother and me, times were even more uncertain because of our concern about Dad. His failing health often weighed heavily on our minds and every time we were in port, we'd place a long-distance call to Macomb to find out how he was doing. That concern offered us an ironic relief from the war. If we hadn't been so worried about him, we might have been more worried about ourselves.

I had more than Dad to occupy my thoughts and in that respect, I was more fortunate than my brother. Although Bob was also in love, his relationship was a stormy one. Mine was not. Helen was a great source of strength for me and I thanked God for her love. I couldn't believe that anyone as wonderful as she was could love me, but she did. And that made me the happiest man alive. While the world around me was full of chaos, in her I found peace. She made me feel rich beyond my means.

For nearly a month, the *Rowan* had been operating in and out of ports on the eastern seaboard. During that time, Helen and I got together often and began to talk seriously about the subject of marriage. The war had been a popular excuse for a lot of couples to get married on a whim. But Helen and I weren't interested in making a snap decision. We wanted to build a marriage that would stand the test of time.

5 March

I was excited and nervous about getting married but I didn't have a lot of time to think about it because *Rowan* received orders to join Task Force 33, under the command of our old skipper, Captain Beverly R. Harrison. We were pleased to learn that Harrison, who was aboard the USS *Champlin*, had received another promotion and was now a full four-striper (captain).

Our duty was to escort USG-6, a convoy of forty-five merchantmen, from New York to Casablanca. The escort was small: only six ships, including *Wainwright, Mayrant, Trippe, Hobby, Champlin* and *Rowan*. These were the only ships that could be spared for the job. Even though the tide of the war in the Atlantic was beginning to turn in our favor, U-boats were still a big problem. In five months, from November 1942 until March 1943, three hundred and thirty four ships had been lost, along with nearly 2,000,000 tons of cargo. This cruise would take us right through one of the most dangerous zones, an area near the Azores that had earned the nickname Torpedo Junction.

Rescuing survivors from the sea was of primary concern for all escort ships, and thanks to an innovation that Captain Ford instituted, *Rowan* was well equipped for the task. Neatly coiled in various locations on deck were some thirty lifelines and several cargo nets. Fitted with snap hooks and rings, these lines could be tossed into the water toward survivors while we were still underway. It was a definite improvement over our experience with the *San Jacinto* rescue. The new system would allow survivors to snap a loop around them so they could be hauled aboard with minimal effort on their part. This could prove particularly valuable if a survivor was either in bad shape or too exhausted to help himself. We expected trouble and it wasn't long in coming.

6 March

Although our first rescue was from an unexpected source of trouble, we were ready to handle it. A few days out from New York in the dead of night, a Norwegian motor ship blundered into the convoy, colliding with SS *Alcoa Guard*. Both vessels were severely damaged but due to faulty radio communications, their SOS was picked up by only one ship in the convoy. That ship, the SS *Richard A. Alvey*, dropped out of

Eileen & Bill Ward

formation to pick up survivors. The Norwegian ship went down, but *Alcoa Guard* stayed afloat and was ultimately towed to Bermuda.

Bill Ward was receiving regular radio messages about the location of U-boats. Word was, there were four submarines shadowing the convoy and six others moving up to intercept. This was a slow convoy with a top speed of around six knots, easy pickings for the enemy. With so few escort ships on station, the crews of the destroyers had to be alert. In spite of our best efforts, every evening at dusk our silent stalkers would surface and launch an attack. They would look for any ship that had dropped out of formation and target in on it. Their success rate was high.

13 March

Sunset. SS *Benjamin Harrison* was the first victim to fall to the wolfpack when she took a torpedo hit and was badly damaged. SS *William Johnson*, the closest merchantman, diverted to pick up survivors and *Rowan* was dispatched to assist. *Benjamin*

Harrison lay dead in the water, a listing, dark silhouette against the black night horizon. Now a threat to navigation, she couldn't stay there. She had to be scuttled.

When the last survivor was rescued, Captain Ford ordered torpedoes launched. The fish hit their target dead on but failed to detonate. An extremely unhappy Ford ordered the ship to be sunk by our five-inch guns. For a moment, the darkness lit up as the shells exploded into the merchantmen's hull near the waterline. A little while later, the burning wreckage slipped beneath the waves.

Evidence of the wolfpacks' handiwork was everywhere. The SS *Keystone* developed engine trouble and had to drop astern as repairs were carried out. For some unknown reason, *Keystone* didn't take the route designated for stragglers but her fate might have been no different if she had. No escort could be spared and the ever-watchful U-boats seized the opportunity. She was lost with all hands.

14 March

2340. *Rhind* picked up twenty-two survivors of a Norwegian cargo ship. They had been adrift since 6 March. A few nights later, the SS *Wyoming* took two torpedoes fired at the no-miss range of six hundred yards and went down in eight minutes.

17 March

The night began with deceptive calm. But as darkness closed in around the western sky, you could feel the tension building aboard the *Rowan*. We were expecting an attack, though we did not know from which direction it would come. Unseen by our lookouts, a U-boat surreptitiously surfaced and fired off four torpedoes at random into the convoy. Two of them passed harmlessly under a merchantman. The other two passed deep under the oiler USS *Chiwawa*, then sped on their way into the body of the convoy. Rising to the surface, one of them scored a hit on the SS *Molly Pitcher*. The merchantman was severely damaged, but she still had power and steerage.

Fearful that U-boats would come and finish her off, her crew abandoned ship over the protests of the escort captains, including

Captain Ford. There lay the merchant ship full of valuable cargo and lit up like a Christmas tree, a derelict with no one aboard. No amount of coercion could convince her crew to try to salvage the damaged vessel. *Molly Pitcher* had to be scuttled to clear navigation lanes and to keep her cargo from falling into enemy hands. That duty fell to Captain Harrison's ship, the USS *Champlin*. The fatal rounds were fired and *Molly Pitcher* joined *Benjamin Harrison* at the bottom of the Atlantic.

In heavy seas, *Rowan* screened as seventeen survivors of the *Molly Pitcher* were taken aboard the SS *William Johnson*. We circled around to search for any indication of U-boats in the area. While on a sweep later that evening, we came upon a lifeboat from the *William Johnson* with fourteen more survivors from the *Molly Pitcher*. The weather hindered the inexperienced *William Johnson* boat crew and they were unable to get back to their ship. We hastily picked them up and got underway again.

On this cruise, perhaps more than any other I can remember, nights were long and tiring. Sonar contacts were constant, general quarters frequent, and attacks commonplace. Despite the long hours and small size of our escort, we kept losses to a minimum. In the sixteen days it took us to make the transatlantic crossing, we lost only five merchantmen. Although we always tried for zero losses, for the six destroyers of Task Force 33 this was a job well done.

21 March

Casablanca. When we arrived, the waters outside the breakwater were churning with whitecaps and rolling ground swells. Inside the breakwater was somewhat better. At least there were no ground swells though the gusty winds forced tide waters into the harbor in a way that made it feel as if we were tied up off the coast.

Rowan was secured in the typical Mediterranean moor - bow facing out held in place by the anchors, stern secured to a breakwater constructed of stones, some of which weighed as much as two tons each. The gangway ran from the fantail to the breakwater, where a level walkway had been built to provide a smooth path for crews going into the city. After three weeks at sea, it wasn't surprising that crewmen of all the ships of the convoy turned their eyes shoreward. Once the escort got the forty remaining merchant ships of the convoy safely into the harbor, it was time for liberty.

Bob and I eagerly crossed the gangway in search of solid land and souvenirs. What we found was a little disappointing. Unlike Bogart's Casablanca that I had started to see at the movies with Helen a few months earlier, the real McCoy had little to offer tourists. The only thing we found that was of any interest to us was a few fresh fruit stands lining the crowded but clean city streets. Bob and I found a stone bench under a palm tree, placed the bag of oranges between us and like kids who had just raided a candy store, peeled a couple and bit into some of the sweetest fruit we had ever tasted.

As we munched on the juicy oranges, we were spotted by a few of our shipmates. They asked us where we had made our purchase. "Just down the street," we told them, not realizing the consequences of our openness. When we returned to the stand the next day to bring on stores for the ship, we found that the price had doubled. "Supply and demand," the vendor said with a shrug and a grin.

The sweet taste of the fruit faded when we learned that the locals used human feces to fertilize the trees. Aboard ship, we were ordered to drop the oranges into boiling water before serving them. Fortunately, the hot bath did not diminish their rich flavor. Bob and I suffered no ill effects from our feast. I don't think it would have bothered anyone to know the farming practices of the Moroccans. In this case, what we didn't know didn't hurt us.

23 March

1730. We were moored in the outer harbor at Jetty Delure with *Swanson* to starboard and *Edison* to port. The wind picked up to force five, between seventeen and twenty-one knots, and began pushing ground swells in through the breakwater. We were rolling around as if we were in a storm at sea. With the current ebbing, the securing lines began to slacken and the nest of destroyers drifted to port. A potentially dangerous situation was brewing. If a ship came in contact with the stone breakwater, it could sustain significant damage.

Rowan's engines were off line so that needed repairs could be carried out, but when a discretionary order was given by the harbor master to move from our mooring, immediate steps were taken to get the ship in a ready status. The situation was deteriorating. As *Edison* was preparing to get underway, her stern drifted too close to the breakwater and with a grinding crunch of stressed steel, made contact. Within minutes, the harbor pilot arrived and with a tugboat, assisted her clear.

Rowan and *Swanson* were still in danger. Ground swells rolled the two ships around, pushing them stern first toward the breakwater. In an attempt to ward off trouble, the order was given to heave in the starboard anchor line to compensate for the lower tide. But the anchor didn't hold. *Rowan* hit stern first, slightly damaging port depth charge racks. Fortunately, the charges had already been removed.

The weather showed no sign of letting up. With winds and sea still mounting, *Rowan* had to move to a safer location.

I had secured from the galley for the evening and gone out on deck to grab some fresh air and watch the rising storm. As I settled down on the ammunition box outside the galley, I noticed a couple of tugs arriving on the scene. The first one took up a position along *Rowan's* port side and began pushing her off the breakwater. The other took a line from *Swanson's* starboard side and pulled that ship clear.

1930. When *Rowan* was in a safer anchorage, the harbor pilot came aboard to readjust the mooring. Winds had calmed and everything seemed secure but just in case, engines were put on notice to get underway immediately for the remainder of the night. Before dawn, the wisdom of that precaution would be clear.

As I slept, the wind picked up again and *Rowan* began drifting astern toward the breakwater. On the bridge, efforts were started to stabilize our position by turning the port screw gently several times as preparations were made to slip the mooring. Moments later, I was jolted awake by a deep grinding sound; *Rowan* struck the breakwater.

At first light, the captain ordered Kelley, the only qualified diver aboard, over the side to take a closer look at the screws. Sure enough, one blade of the port propeller was bent three inches forward, the second was eighteen inches forward, and the third about thirty inches. The starboard propeller, rudder and port strut bearings, reduction gear and engine all checked out, but at speeds over fifteen knots, *Rowan* began to shimmy like a flapper. Until repairs could be carried out, we would have to run on only one engine.

I didn't know how lucky I was when *Rowan* hit that breakwater. With no yard facilities available in either Casablanca or Gibraltar, we would have to return to the Brooklyn Naval Shipyard to carry out repairs. Helen must have been praying for me again. By the end of the first week in April, we were part of a convoy making a return voyage stateside.

My days as a bachelor were about to end.

The Wedding

12 April 1943. When I got off the ship in Brooklyn, the first thing I did was to call Helen. After the preliminary I love yous, I asked her if she still wanted to get married. I hadn't seen her in almost two months and wanted to make sure she hadn't changed her mind. She hadn't. I was relieved and excited and nervous all at the same time.

3 May

Monday. 0800. As soon as my leave began, I was off the ship and into town to buy a wedding ring for Helen. Around 1030, I met her near the Bronx County Courthouse. We hugged for a few minutes then, hand in hand, headed up the long stairway to the license bureau and stood in the marriage license line. When our turn came, I stepped up to the window and said, "We want to get married." Helen slipped her arm through mine, smiling at the clerk.

The woman behind the desk hardly gave us a second glance. "Fill this out," she replied, handing us some papers, seemingly unimpressed by our announcement. We completed the forms,

The bride in blue

paid the $2 fee, collected the stamped forms and left. We were ready.

I took Helen back home by subway, picked up her luggage and walked back to the train. My mind was so preoccupied that I don't remember boarding the subway on my way downtown to the Taft Hotel where we would be staying for our three-day honeymoon. I arrived around 1400. When the peace and quiet of the room closed in around me, I stretched out on the bed and conked out. Suddenly, a knock at the door jarred me awake. I glanced at my watch - almost 1700. I opened the door and found Bob and Ernie standing there, grinning at me.

As soon as I cleared the cobwebs from my brain, I placed a long distance call to Macomb to talk to Mom. She was teary, but happy for me. "I hope you're making the right decision," she told me. Before she hung up she added, "I have faith in you."

The wedding was set for 1930 in the rectory of Our Lady of Refuge, just around the corner from Helen's house. By the time we got to the house at 1830, the wedding party was beginning to assemble. It was mostly Helen's family, including her sisters Kathleen and Bernie, and brother Joe. Her younger brother, James, was in Oklahoma in the Army. Cousins Nancy and Sheila Flynn, Mr. and Mrs. Quinn, Bob and Ernie rounded out our group. Bob, Ernie, Kathleen, Sheila, Nancy and I walked over to the rectory of the church, which was just a couple of blocks away.

1900. Joe drove Helen, Mr. & Mrs. Quinn and Bernie to the church in the Dodge. When Helen entered the door of the rectory, dressed in a light blue dress and hat with shoes to match, my heart skipped a beat. She was the most beautiful bride I have ever seen.

Father Foster greeted us and as he looked over the necessary papers, he took the time to talk with us and help us relax. Then he opened his book and the ceremony began. I don't remember much of it. Helen said that when I put the ring on her finger I pushed it on so hard, it hurt. I guess I wanted to be sure it would never come off. I do remember that when the ceremony was

Harvey, Helen & Lew

over, Ernie glanced at his watch and said, "It's 1937." At first no one was quite sure what he meant. "That's 7:37 p.m., civilian time," he offered as clarification.

After the ceremony, everyone went back to the house for a light wedding dinner. I had just gotten something to eat when Helen's father took me aside and started chatting with me. "Everything went well at the church, didn't it?" he said in a congenial way. I agreed with him but I was pretty sure that wasn't what he had in mind to tell me, so I kept my answer brief. I waited for him to go on.

The Newlyweds

"You know," he said, not disappointing me, "first impressions are the most lasting." When I stared at him blankly, he continued, "Take it easy on the drinking tonight." I caught his meaning. I took his advice and had nothing to drink except the champagne toast later that evening. I was glad to have had all my faculties for that most memorable of times.

It was time for us to depart. Helen hugged everyone and I shook a lot of hands. Then, Ernie, Bob, Bernie, Helen and I walked over to the subway station and proceeded to the Hotel Taft in downtown Manhattan. After I carried Helen over the threshold of our room, we opened a bottle of champagne Ernie had brought, drank a toast and departed for the Hotel Roosevelt where Guy Lombardo was playing. The music was soft and sweetly romantic. Helen and I were thinking how nice it would be to be alone but our wedding party would not hear of it.

At one point, Bob left the table and disappeared for a few minutes. When he came back, he had a big smile on his face. Then Guy Lombardo stepped up to the microphone and said, "Mr. and Mrs. Seeley just got married today. Let's bring them up to dance with a nice round of applause."

Helen and I were embarrassed under the glare of public notice, but there was no backing down. All the dancers cleared the floor and stood watching us, waiting for us to dance. The orchestra played *Let Me Call You Sweetheart* as the spotlight followed us. Thankfully, after a turn around the floor, other couples joined in and when the music stopped, they clapped and we went back to our table.

Helen and I were really ready to call it a night. Over the protests of the others, particularly Bob, we made our move to go back to the Taft. But the party didn't end there. They decided to come up to the room with us. Bob launched into one fond childhood memory after another. "Remember that time..." he again began. "Good night, fellows," Helen replied. We tried to herd them toward the door and just about the time we were sure we had them out, Ernie would pipe up with, "I want to tell you about the time...." It was clear they weren't going to take any gentle hints. Shoving didn't seem to have much effect, either.

It was sixteen-year-old Bernie who finally showed some sense. She hooked her arm in the arm of each of the others and said, "Come on! We're going to leave these people in peace!" Gratefully, we closed the door behind them. With only two and a half days left of our honeymoon, every moment was precious and we didn't want to share that time with anyone else.

Thursday. It would soon be time to report back to the ship. After a breakfast of toast and coffee, we had to make one of our first married-life decisions: either I could escort Helen back to the Bronx, or we could have a few more hours at the hotel. Spending the extra time together was the easy choice.

We stayed until 1030 and then went together as far as Sands Street Station. I walked with Helen toward the Bronx train and as she stepped on the escalator, she stumbled slightly. Even though she really didn't need my help, I was not close enough to catch her. I realized that this is how our life together probably would be. She would have to cope for herself. I couldn't be sure I'd be there when she needed me most. She turned toward me and smiled to let me know she was all right.

We waved to each other one more time. When the escalator carried her out of sight, I turned toward the Brooklyn train. Our partings had been difficult before, but this one was even more painful. Had we known what lay ahead, it might have been unbearable.

The Soft Underbelly

Returning to the ship after my honey-moon, I saw Bill Hagen near the gangway, looking sad and dejected. It turns out that he, too, was supposed to get married this week. He had called his girl, Trudy, to come out from Chicago. Trudy had made hurried arrangements and headed for New York but as luck and wartime travel would have it, she hadn't arrived. She would get there an hour after we shoved off. It would be a long time before their chance would come again. As I headed below to stow my gear, I said a silent prayer of gratitude that our wedding plans had gone so well.

Before we sailed, an old friend and crewmate, Bill Ward dropped by to say good-by. He was heading to radio school and would rejoin the ship in a few months. As I wished him well, I had no inkling of how long it would be before I saw him again.

A tall, lanky Texan named Floyd Worthington came aboard to fill Ward's shoes. None of us knew that Worthington had had a premonition of the future that had him near tears. Said a friend some time later, Floyd was convinced that if he sailed with the ship, he would not be coming home. In spite of his fears, he said nothing. He did what the rest of us did, what we had always done - his duty.

7 May

1500. Friday. Under the gathering clouds of a spring rain, *Rowan* and the other ships of DESRON 8 headed out to sea. The first destination was Norfolk, where we picked up convoy UFG-8A to North Africa. The crossing took us just under two weeks and on 23 May, we moored in Mers El Kabir, Algeria. This would be the staging area of the first full-scale assault on Italy.

For the next six weeks, the order of the day was drill, improve readiness, drill, prepare, and drill. We cruised the

Floyd Worthington

Mediterranean from Algeria to Gibraltar. Although submarine attacks were not common, air attacks were. The Luftwaffe, flying out of bases in Germany and Italy, kept us from getting bored.

15 June

We were patrolling off the coast of Gibraltar when Harvey noticed a speck on the horizon. He raised his binoculars to his eyes but at first, he couldn't tell if it was even moving. Soon, it came within range. His signalman's training for aircraft silhouette identification helped him recognize it as a twin-engine British Beau fighter. It was in big trouble.

The Beau fighter was loosing altitude fast and as it got closer, it was obvious that one of the wings was dangling. Harvey relayed the information to the bridge and the ship was brought about to intercept the plane. When it was still about three miles away from us, it crashed into the sea.

Rowan could approach no farther as we found ourselves on the edge of a known minefield. A lifeboat was lowered and the rescue team dispatched to pick up the survivors who by now, had managed to abandon the plane and get into their inflatable yellow dinghy. Harvey was in the rescue boat.

Carefully, the lifeboat picked its way through the dangerous waters. The greeting the *Rowan* crew received was surprising. When the coxswain signaled all stop, the rescuers could clearly hear the two fighter crewmen cussing and fussing, as Harvey described it. The co-pilot's diatribe didn't abate even when it was time for them to abandon the dinghy. "You dumb arse," he shouted at the pilot, "who told you you had to make such a bloody low pass! Showing off, were you? Who were you trying to impress? This will play well back home, won't it? I can see it now: 'Fighter Pilots Downed by Schooner Mast!' Dumb arse!"

Eventually, Harvey was able to piece the whole story together. The two Englishmen had been on a mission over Naples, strafing a German three-masted schooner. On the last run, the pilot had gotten carried away and had flown so close that he nipped the wing on one of the masts. With one wing dangling, he had tried to make it back to their base in North Africa. The fighter sank like a stone as soon as it hit the water. The two pilots had barely escaped with their lives. It was their good fortune that *Rowan* spotted them because they were a long way from home when their luck ran out. They were grateful for the rescue but the pilot was probably most grateful for being rescued from the incessant barrage coming from his co-pilot.

8 July

It was two months since I left my bride back in New York. We had since escorted a convoy to Malta, but had found anchorage difficult. Frequent air raids had littered the harbor with the masts of sunken ships. It looked like the graveyard of some kind of prehistoric beasts. Now naval activity along the North African coastline had reached an all-time high. American and British ships, troop transports, supply ships, oilers, landing craft and all types of support and escort vessels had gathered. On 12 July, we received orders to proceed north. The invasion of Italy was about to begin.

14 July

0915. We were in the third assault wave of Operation Husky. Off in the distance, cruisers were firing salvos at shore targets. Allied forces had amassed 3,200 ships, boats and landing craft, 4,000 aircraft and 250,000 troops in a fleet that stretched one mile wide and sixty miles long. This was to be even bigger than Casablanca as the Allies prepared to attack what Churchill had called "the soft underbelly of Europe." In the days to come, we would find that there was nothing soft about it.

We lay off the harbor at Gela as the ships of the troop and supply convoy we had escorted from Mers El Kabir circled into the protected anchorage outside the harbor. The Allied invasion was well underway and for the early arrivals, it had been tough going. The destroyer *Maddox* had been sunk in less than two minutes, the victim of a torpedo launched from a German plane. Enemy aircraft pounded the liberty ship *Robert Rowan*, loaded with ammunition. All hands abandoned ship and a short time later, she blew up in a spectacular ball of flame. But the U.S. Navy got in its licks. Destroyers *Shurbrick* and *Jeffers* joined the cruisers *Savannah* and *Boise* in pummeling the coastline with well-aimed salvos. Other destroyers fired on shore targets, including tanks and bridges, air and underwater targets.

15 July

Rowan's assignment was to patrol up and down the harbor area to keep it clear of U-boats and mines, and to provide anti-aircraft cover and rescue when needed. Darkness fell after 2100, and with it came the deadly German night fighters.

Jilcott was standing lookout watch when he saw the German fighters engage an Allied plane. He couldn't see what had happened but the result of the engagement was clear enough. Through his binoculars, he could see what appeared to be a bright orange flare heading directly toward us. He passed the word to the bridge.

"Hard to port!" the captain ordered. At the helm Icenogle turned the wheel sharply to take us out of harm's way. Ahead of us, the remnants of a Royal South African Air Force B-24 splashed into the sea. It burst into flames on impact and exploded, scattering oil and fire in a wide circle around it.

Ford ordered away the rescue party to look for survivors and Harvey was the signalman assigned to the rescue boat. The burning wreckage sank and the night returned to pitch black. With mines just a few feet below the surface and visibility less than five feet ahead of them, their mission was both difficult and dangerous. Unless they proceeded very slowly, they ran the risk of accidentally overrunning the survivors.

Suddenly, one of the *Rowan* men called for quiet, certain he had heard a voice. They cut engines. There it was again. "Help me!" a voice pleaded through the darkness. It was off the port quarter. The whaleboat turned and inched forward.

"Where are you?" Harvey shouted.

"Here I am. Help me, please." Again, the whaleboat corrected course. After several painstakingly slow minutes, Harvey spotted the survivor, bobbing up and down in the water. He was clutching the body of another man in his arms.

The whaleboat came alongside and Harvey leaned over to haul the conscious man aboard. The flyer let go of his mate and when he did, the other slipped below the waves. Harvey grabbed the survivor and pulled him up over the gunwale. "Careful, matie," said the flyer calmly. "Me leg's been blown off."

Harvey was sure the man was in shock and didn't know what he was taking about. It was too dark to see anything so he carefully ran his hands down the flyer's leg. The thigh was fine. The knee was fine. The calf was.... Harvey stopped cold when his hand wrapped around a jutting piece of splintered bone. The pilot was correct. The flesh had been completely blown away.

With a nervous laugh, the flyer said, "20-mm shell got me just as we were going down. Don't know how I managed to bail out. When I hit the water," he winced as he took a deep breath, "I had to kick the leg away. That's how I knew it went. I really don't feel anything."

The *Rowan* team then went after the second flyer, who was floating face down in the water just a few feet away. Harvey reached over the side and wrapped his arms around the man's waist. It was like sinking his hands into a bowl of jelly.

"When we were hit," the South African explained, "we had to bail out. Too low for parachutes. Couldn't jump. Too low for that." He paused for a deep, labored breath, and said, "Must have broke every bone in his body when he hit the water."

Harvey made it back aboard the ship before he let go of the dinner I had prepared that evening. By some miracle, the survivor didn't bleed to death while waiting for rescue. He lived to return home to South Africa, but his fighting days were over.

Anthony Barrale

22 July

We reached Tunis where we were dispatched from the invasion area around the tip of Sicily to open up Palermo. Once there, *Rowan*, along with *Wainwright*, *Mayrant*, *Rhind*, and *Trippe* would take up the duty of defending the newly taken Italian city. Our job was to give fire support, patrol for subs and provide escort service.

25 July

1215. As I was cleaning up from the dinner meal, I noticed we were slowing down and I looked out of the porthole to see what was going on. Lookouts had spotted a small sailing craft about four miles off Cape San Vito, Sicily. *Rowan* was dispatched to corral the vessel, which we did easily.

A whaleboat was lowered with an armed boarding party. Harvey was among them, as was redheaded, blue-eyed

Radioman Second Class Anthony Barrale. The latter was included in the party because, despite his appearance more typical of an Irishman, his parents had come from a small town about ten miles from Palermo, called Belmonte Mezzano. He understood Italian and spoke it fluently. Lt. John Wyatt, in command of the whaleboat, told Barrale to keep silent and give no indication that he understood Italian.

Mr. Wyatt's precaution proved invaluable. Aboard the sailboat were five men, each one dressed in civilian khaki clothing. Their pants legs and shirtsleeves were rolled up, giving them the appearance of fishermen. According to Harvey, when the *Rowan* crew boarded, it wasn't fish they smelled, but a rat. Something about these men just didn't add up. Meanwhile, Barrale kept his mouth shut and listened.

Through elaborate hand gestures and loud, slow speech, the five men tried to convey that they were just poor ordinary men trying to eke out a living in a harsh world. Harvey looked down at their feet. If they had been fishermen as they claimed, wouldn't their feet be suntanned and leathery? The feet that Harvey observed were snowy white. So were their forearms. Their hands were smooth.

The five men were taken aboard the whaleboat and their sailboat scuttled. As the boarding party made its way back to the *Rowan*, Barrale sat close to the Italians, passively listening. His face betrayed no comprehension. Sure enough, the man who had been the spokesman began to chat conversationally in Italian with the others. He said, "They don't know who we are. Just stick to the story about being fishermen. They won't keep us. Then we can rejoin our unit." Barrale grinned to himself. "Gotcha," he thought.

Once aboard the *Rowan*, Barrale reported to Lt. Wyatt what he had overheard. Four of the Italians were lined up on deck. The fifth, the one who was clearly in charge, was brought into the wardroom. In correct Italian, Barrale introduced himself to the officer and told him he and his men were under arrest.

With all pretense gone, the officer replied in perfect English, "I see I am not as clever as I believed, after all." He introduced himself as a lieutenant colonel in the Italian army. His men got caught away from their unit and they were trying to get to Naples so they could rejoin it.

When the interrogation was over, the colonel asked if he would be allowed to send a message to his wife. Lt. Wyatt looked a little puzzled. U.S. Naval ships didn't usually send messages to enemy territory. Nevertheless, he said, "I'll see what we can do. What's her address?"

"She's at her brother's house. He's a butcher in Brooklyn." Everyone looked at him in surprise. "Brooklyn," the colonel repeated, "New York. USA." The silence that greeted his news demanded more explanation. "I too was a butcher in New York. When the war began, I returned to Italy to fight for my country but I left my wife in America. Italy was too dangerous. I like Americans, but I love Mussolini." he explained. "The Germans, I have no use for." As soon as we arrived in Palermo, the prisoners were turned over to the U.S. Army.

While we were in Palermo, Barrale went ashore for a few hours. His family had emigrated from the area and he wanted to see the ancestral home first hand. He and three other men from the *Rowan* stopped into a store that sold wine from very large casks. Intrigued, he asked the storekeeper about the vintage. The local man asked him, "How do you speak such good Italian? And with a local accent, at that?"

Barrale replied, "My father, Frank Barrale, comes from Belmonte Mezzano."

When the shopkeeper heard the father's name, he embraced the American sailor like a long-lost relative which, it turned out, he was! "Hey, everyone!" he shouted, running out to the street, "this boy is Frank Barrale's son!" He went back to Tony and said, "I'm Romano. I'm your cousin! A distant cousin. But still, a cousin."

Barrale knew his family would be very pleased to know he had run into a relative. "Do you think it would be possible for me to get in touch with the rest of my family?"

"Oh, sure," Romano said cheerfully. They made arrangements to meet the next morning down at the dock. Tony wanted to give some gifts to his relatives, things like soap and a few staples that were in short supply in the war torn area. That night during a Luftwaffe bombing raid, *Rowan* received orders to head out to sea. We never returned. All the gifts that Barrale had carefully packed to give to his newfound family remained aboard the ship until they found their final resting-place at the bottom of the Mediterranean.

When Tony went home some months later, he told the story to his family, but they had already received a letter from an uncle in Palermo. He had gone down to the dock the next morning and waited in vain for the ship to return. He wasn't sure what to think. Was his American nephew angry with him, he asked in the letter, for being on the "wrong side" of the war? It was a long time before Barrale could resolve the mystery for his uncle.

26 July

The Mediterranean was heating up. The Nazis were not willing to concede Italy without a fight. They launched wave after wave of air attacks, and one of those nearly took us out. Just before 0900, *Rowan* and *Mayrant* were patrolling the mouth of the Gulf of Palermo not far from the coastal headlands that thrust out into the sea. Like sentries walking a picket line, the two ships cruised back and forth, crossing each other at midpoint.

0931. *Mayrant's* radar picked up a blip and before anyone could make an identification, three Junker 88s swooped low around the headlands. In no time, they were on us. *Rowan* was too close for them to release their bombs but *Mayrant*, which was heading away from them, was in perfect range. The captain ordered us to open fire with the anti-aircraft guns just as the first Junker was delivering its stick of three or four bombs. These dropped on the *Mayrant's* starboard side at a distance of less than 150 yards.

Harvey saw *Mayrant* begin evasive maneuvers - speed increased to twenty-five knots and the rudder put over to full right - but a second Junker closed fast. Attacking from the port quarter, it dropped two bombs about five hundred yards ahead. *Mayrant's* guns fired at the lead target off the port bow as the third plane made its run and dropped a stick of four bombs that straddled the ship.

"*Mayrant's* taken a close hit - about five feet off the port beam," Harvey reported to the captain. A second landed about forty yards off the starboard beam. The concussion split open seams on both sides of the destroyer. *Mayrant* was accelerating and turning hard when the explosions erupted. "She's listing badly sir."

Aboard *Mayrant*, nearly every man, including one officer named Franklin D. Roosevelt, Jr., son of the President, was thrown to the deck or up against bulkheads. All main and auxiliary steam power was lost and she lay dead in the water. Her forward engine room and aft fireroom were completely flooded. Emergency generators kicked on but electrical demand soon overloaded the system and all power was lost.

Through his binoculars, Harvey watched the wounded ship. Suddenly, he saw a most peculiar sight; guns, ammunition, gear, and everything but the kitchen sink went flying over the side. It appeared that *Mayrant*'s captain, Commander Walker, wasn't about to abandon his ship. He ordered everything that wasn't nailed down jettisoned in order to keep his ship afloat. It worked. We stayed on station to offer assistance and protection until she was rescued by a couple of minecraft, the *Skill* and the *Strive*.

Mayrant was towed into port, waist deep in the water. Thanks to "fine seamanship and invaluable assistance" from the *Strive*, *Mayrant*'s captain reported, the destroyer survived. We aboard the *Rowan* were particularly happy our squadron mate was still afloat. Had we been a hundred or so yards farther along, we could have been hit. Once again, DD 405 dodged the bullet, or in this case, the bomb.

27 July

Rowan was ordered to Lake Bizerte on the northern tip of Tunisia to refuel. This area was less ravaged by war and swimming parties were organized. The water was clear and refreshing and that was all the encouragement I needed to dive in. Like many of my shipmates, I wore my inflatable life belt and practiced unclipping it from around my waist, inflating it, and securing it around me again. I had no premonition of the future. The activity just gave me something to do while I swam.

This respite from the war lasted only one day. We heard air raid sirens going off ashore and moments later radar reported incoming aircraft. A squadron of German fighter planes swooped low and straddled us with bombs. Our luck held and, again, we dodged the bullet.

30 July

Palermo. Instead of anchoring outside the harbor, we were moored inside, close to town. No liberty was granted but just being moored was a treat. It gave us a much-appreciated break from the constant rolling of the ship.

U.S. soldiers were everywhere. Occasionally from our mooring, I could look ashore and see a group of German prisoners being herded along. U.S. Army trucks and jeeps were by far the most common vehicles, but an occasional tank rumbled by. All that commotion made me glad that my transportation and bed were in the same place.

Air attacks were a nightly event. If there's an air raid while you're underway, you have some small comfort in knowing you're a moving target. Tied to the mooring, you're a sitting duck. To make it more difficult for the enemy pilots to sight in on us, smoke pots were set out along the pier and lighted at the approach of enemy aircraft. But the Germans still took their shots. On one raid, a small patrol craft moored just ahead of us took a hit. Everyone aboard was killed, including an army officer who, tired of cold chow, had come aboard the night before to get a good hot meal. It was his last.

It wasn't unusual for Army personnel to come calling on the Navy in search of decent food. One day while we were in Palermo, two soldiers from General Patton's division came into the galley and struck up a friendly conversation with Bob and me. They told us about their experiences and hardships, and about the souvenirs they had found. The last subject was designed to pique our interest. When they saw they had our attention, they changed the subject to food.

"C-rations are really starting to get me down," said the first soldier.

"Yeah," I agreed. "They're pretty awful."

"You know what I'd like to have?" he went on with a description that bordered on passion. "I'd like to have a thick stack of pancakes. Thick, hot, tender, the kind you can sink your fork into." He had my mouth watering. His partner looked a little glassy-eyed, too. "Boy," he concluded, "that would be great."

"Pancakes are my favorite, too," I nodded.

189

"Do you suppose," the soldier began and then hesitated. He started again, "Do you suppose I could talk you out of enough pancake mix to serve, say, two hundred? Just enough for the guys in my outfit?"

I scratched my head. "Two hundred, you say?" I thought about how much I hated C-rations and how much I loved pancakes. And after all, we were on the same side. "We don't have any ready-made mix," I replied at last, "but I tell you what. If you come back this afternoon, I'll see what we can do."

The two soldiers warmly shook my hand and Bob's. "You don't know what this means to us," they said. With a friendly wave, they departed.

For the next hour or so, Bob and I set about mixing up two hundred portions of dry ingredients - flour, powdered eggs, sugar, dry milk, salt and baking powder. All they would have to add was water and a little elbow grease to mix it all together. We rationed out sugar to make syrup and butter to top it all off. Shortly after dinner was over, the two soldiers returned and accepted the provisions and directions gratefully. I don't think they could have been happier if I had just told them the war was over. With profound thanks, they shouldered their treasure and left.

The next afternoon, I was in the galley and to my surprise, the soldiers were back again. This time they had something for Bob and me. "We heard that you fellows don't get ashore too often, so you don't get much chance to collect souvenirs." Opening up a package that contained two Italian rifles, one for Bob, one for me, the first soldier said, "The pancakes were a big hit and the fellows said they would like you to have these as a token of our appreciation."

I was pleased that our efforts were recognized and delighted to have the weapons. As the soldier had indicated, we were not in a position to pick up things like rifles. Even if we could get to shore, our officers were constantly trying to impress upon us the dangers of looking for such things. Many an American, they reminded us, had been killed or wounded by booby traps baited with souvenirs.

The rifles, which had been taken from Italian soldiers who had surrendered, had not been cared for and corrosion had taken its toll to the point that they would never be used as weapons again. Bob and I disassembled weapons and for several days, occupied ourselves by trying to remove the rust. We hounded the gunner's mates for advice and materials for getting them into condition so they could be preserved. When we were finally satisfied that they were as good as we could get them, we covered them in heavy coats of oil and grease and wrapped them carefully in cloth.

We just had to figure out where to store them until we could get back to the States. They wouldn't pass muster in an inspection. We decided to stow them in a peak tank in the after part of the ship. With infinite patience and effort, we removed the thirty-some bolts that held the cover in place, and slipped the rifles down into the tank. It was an ideal hiding place. As far as I know, that is where they remain to this day.

As July turned into August, a new push began in the war. As part of Task Group 88, we moved along the north coast of Sicily in support of Patton's Seventh Army. There were many areas along Patton's route where the retreating Germans set up roadblocks to stall his drive. Our job was to pound Nazi shore gun emplacements to soften them up as their foot soldiers traveled from Palermo to Meson. We were also called upon to escort LSMs carrying landing parties ashore behind German lines. The Axis forces countered with frequent and vicious night air raids.

4 August

We had just completed a bombardment run somewhere along the coast when we came under attack by a flight of four Messerschmidts. They were upon us so suddenly, I had not been able to reach my general quarters station before the attack began. Just as I was reaching the #2 upper handling room, the ship was starting into a hard turn to port. I looked out ahead of me and a German bomb exploded off the port bow. Adrenaline hit me like a locomotive. I dropped to the deck and covered the back of my neck with my hands. The hit was so close that sprays of water cascaded over me. A few feet to my left, the duty gun was already firing, the concussion of it roaring like thunder in my ears.

My knees shook as I crawled to my feet and pulled open the handling room hatch. With trembling hands, I donned the sound-powered phones and reported, "Number two upper handling room, manned and ready." It was comforting to have the hatch dogged down behind me. In less than a minute, our gun commenced firing.

I could hear reports coming in over the headphones. The fire control officer, Lt. (jg) Brown, directed us to concentrate our fire on the plane that had just dropped its bomb. From somewhere in the after part of the ship came a shout over the headphones, "Control, Control! There's another plane coming in on our port quarter!"

Lt. Brown's voice came back calmly, "F___ 'em. Wait till I get this one."

The second incoming plane dropped its payload but Ford ordered quick evasive maneuvers and the projectile missed us by a comfortable margin. Lt. Brown's cool concentration paid off. The five-inch battery belched out smoke and fire and brought down the target in a ball of yellow flame.

9 August

We were screening a landing force and giving fire support to Patton's drive. It had temporarily stalled at a bridge, which the Germans had wired with explosives. The Krauts were hoping to cross it and blow it up, preventing the American forces from pursuing. *Rowan*'s orders were to fire on the retreating Germans while they were still on the American side of the river. The bridge was blown that day, all right, but the German's didn't do it. General Fries, Commander of the 29th Panzer Grenadiers, credited a cruiser. Rear Admiral Samuel Eliot Morison in *United States Navy in W.W.II*, Volume IX, credited the destroyer *Plunkett*. Both were wrong.

We had been engaged in shore bombardment for several hours when we received a "check fire" order. A short time later, the word came down to unload the guns through the barrel, which meant that the loads would be fired off rather than risk withdrawing the charges. All four of our guns were still loaded. Because the firecontrolman had noticed a problem with sighting, he decided to line up on the bridge to test his aim. On his order, all four guns unleashed a salvo. We had not been ordered to destroy the bridge; it was just a convenient target.

Normally, it will take fire control two or three tries to hit something at that range but on our first salvo, we scored a direct hit. With the added help of the demolition charges set by the Germans, the bridge blew sky high. There wasn't enough left of that span to make a decent toothpick. I wonder who was more surprised, the Germans or our fire control director.

As a result of that lucky shot, the German retreat was cut off while the Nazis were still on the U.S. side. They were forced to wade across the river, which they had mined. With the Americans bearing down on them, they had to clear the river quickly. This delay forced a long traffic jam of stalled German vehicles and war machines. At that moment, the American landing force hit the beach. According to one source, the result was "confusion and great difficulties." The landing force killed two hundred fifty, captured one hundred, disabled four tanks and took a good number of vehicles.

12 August

There was an unmistakable air of confidence among the men of the *Rowan*. We had been forged into a battle-tested team, strong in the face of adversity and ready to handle anything the enemy had to throw at us. Almost anything.

As I celebrated my twenty-fifth birthday, and Bob his twenty-second, I never suspected that in less than a month, most of that team would be dead.

Salerno

3 September. I had been married four months and had spent less than three full days with my bride. I didn't do much celebrating because, first, my wife was half way around the world and, second, there was a war on and I was in the middle of it.

Since late August, *Rowan* had been operating in and around Oran. There, a combined U.S. and British attack force had begun amassing in preparation for the invasion of the Italian mainland. Task Group 81.6, including destroyers *Wainwright, Rowan, Trippe, Rhind, Plunkett, Niblack, Benson, Cleaves, Mayo, Knight, Cole, Bernadou, Dallas, Woolsey, Bristol, Edison, Ludlow* and *Nicholson*, was to escort troop transports and capital ships.

During this time, Torpedoman Jack Goodpaster and Machinist's Mate Boyce M. Bradley, were transferred off, and a few new men, including Tony George, a fireman first class, and Lt. (jg) John Fietz, came aboard. Bill Ward, who was due back from radio school, had not arrived. Travel during the war was unreliable and if you missed your connection, you had to wait for the next one. He hoped to rejoin the ship when we returned to North Africa.

With personnel changing almost every time we came into port, it was important to check the Watch Quarter and Station Bill, a large organization sheet displaying the duties of each man in emergency and watch conditions. It was posted outside the mess hall.

'S' Division, including cooks and laundrymen, had been reassigned to the magazine for general quarters. The magazines were below the waterline and I didn't much care for that duty. The compartments were cramped and hot, and being down there was like being locked away in a dungeon. You couldn't see what was going on, and the only contact with the rest of the ship was through the sound powered phones. My station had always been in one of the upper handling rooms on the main deck. With two years' experience in that position, I was more comfortable and familiar with those duties. While neither Bob nor I greeted the new assignments with much enthusiasm, we made no comment. We just did what we were told.

Lt. John Fietz

The reassignments were an attempt to improve efficiency, getting personnel to battle stations when general quarters was sounded. It was another of Captain Ford's innovations, and though he was still not very popular among the crew, his sometimes ruthless demands had turned the men of the *Rowan* into one of the finest fighting crews in the Navy.

That accomplishment was all the more remarkable considering that the crew was made up of young men in their late teens or early twenties who probably would have been more at home plowing fields or driving taxis. *Rowan*'s crew were men of courage and determination who faced challenge at times with apprehension or even fear, but always without hesitation.

1 September

Mers El Kabir. We stopped to take on fuel and provisions. This would be our last chance for a little rest and relaxation before we returned to the war zone. Liberty started at noon and expired at 1600. Small communities like this North African town could not support a wholesale invasion of sailors. To maintain good relation with the local people, liberty parties were restricted to twenty-five men from each ship. Moreover, because of the danger of air attacks, ships in port had to be manned at all times, ready to get underway at a moment's notice. In spite of precautions, sometimes sailing orders came in and a ship had to take off leaving crewmen behind.

3 September

1500. *Rhind*, which was tied up alongside *Rowan*, received orders to investigate the report of a submarine just outside the harbor at Oran. Without advance notice, she weighed anchor and was off. When her liberty parties came back an hour later, they found they were stranded. The twenty-five sailors were dispersed among the rest of the ships of DESRON 8 for transportation back to their ship. Six of them were assigned to *Rowan*, including Joseph Chaszar, Roy Lane, Antonio Nieto, Richard Snyders, John Eckstein and John Richardson.

That evening, the task force got its orders to move out. The destroyers formed a screen around the invasion force and at a speed of ten knots, proceeded northeast, arriving off the coast of Salerno on 8 September. The escort's first task was to provide cover for troop landings. In no time, the German and Italian air forces set about lodging their protests with the Allies. Their planes commenced a heavy air attack.

I was on duty in the galley when the first incoming fighters were spotted. General quarters was sounded and there was no time to do anything but turn off the heat under anything cooking and race to my battle station in the #2 magazine. I undogged the hatch, which was always secured for watertight integrity while at sea, except when duty personnel were entering or leaving. I slipped through the narrow opening, dropped down into my position and as soon as the rest of the magazine crew arrived, dogged down the hatch. I settled the telephone set over my ears and called in, "#2 magazine, manned and ready."

The ship accelerated and turned from port to starboard and back again in evasive maneuvers. I could only guess what was going on topside. We passed so many rounds, I was sure we were spitting back as much lead as was being dropped on us. The attack ended, and all clear was given. Even before I could return to the galley, another incoming wave was reported and we were back at stations again.

When we finally secured from general quarters, I went back to the galley to salvage what I could of supper. With so many interruptions, it was useless to try making regular meals. Spam sandwiches topped the list of menu items. No one complained. They were just glad to eat, no matter what it was.

8 September

Late in the evening, Ernie Harvey came down from the bridge to tell me that the Italians had surrendered. Before long, word of the surrender had reached virtually everyone aboard, and each man had his own interpretation of what it meant. Some said we'd be heading back to New York in a few days. Others heard it would be Boston. Still others spoke grimly of German determination to fight to the last. Harvey had just conveyed the facts without commentary.

When my brother and I discussed the surrender, we came to one conclusion: No matter which rumor was correct, we would keep right on doing what we had been doing for the past two-and-a-half years - getting meals out, standing watches and not getting enough rest. The word, nevertheless, was a great morale booster. We all knew the war was not over, but we were a whole lot closer than we were before. The enemy had been pushed back a little farther and we were going to try to keep them going all the way back to Germany.

9 September

We moved along an eight-mile stretch of shore from the south bank of the Sele River to Agropoli, screening the invasion force. Sometimes we were called upon to provide shore bombardment and to defend constantly against air attacks. Our fire support was apparently effective, for Admiral Davidson, who commanded our group, received a message from General Lange of the Fifth Army.

It read:

"Thank God for the fire of the Navy's ships. Probably could not have stuck it out at Blue and Yellow Beaches. Brave fellows. Please tell them so."

Nightfall brought a new wave of action. To better see their targets, the enemy dropped illuminating flares during those bombing raids. As they slowly fell to earth, they illuminated the sky like the noonday sun. It was a most terrifying experience to have one of those flares burst overhead. As long as the sky remained lit, those in the flare's wash held their breath, fearing they would be the next targets.

When the night air attack began, the gunnery officer ordered us to use flashless powder. The flash generated by the smokeless powder made it too easy for the enemy to sight in on our position at night. A round of smokeless powder was passed in error to the #2 gun, and fired. I was at my station in the #2 magazine when the incident occurred. The gunnery officer was furious. His response to that mistake saved my life and doomed another man. He called over the headphone, "Who's in charge of the #2 magazine?"

I replied immediately, "Seeley, sir."

"Seeley," he said tersely, "come up here and take over the #2 upper handling room."

"Aye, sir," I said to acknowledge his order. I didn't know what had happened or who was responsible. While I was not unhappy about returning to the upper handling room, I didn't give it much thought one way or another. I headed for my new general quarters station up on the main deck.

10 September

0500. The battle raged on through the night and by dawn, all hands were weary. Finally, we secured from general quarters and watch condition II was set. Half the crew stayed at quarters, while the other half either went about their regular duties or caught up on some much-needed rest. I looked for Bob to see how he was doing but he was already in his bunk, fast asleep. He would be on duty in the galley in a few hours, so I didn't wake him.

With a sigh, I crawled into my bunk. It felt good to stretch out and close my eyes. I knew I wouldn't have much time to relax because at 0800, I would have to report to my watch station. While I slept, *Rowan* continued to patrol the coast of Salerno without incident.

That evening, the action started again at 2000, when flares were dropped overhead from high altitude bombers. General quarters sounded and I ran for the #2 upper handling room just as the first bombs rained down around us. The concussion of nearby explosions ripped through the night. *Rowan* dodged, maneuvered, and changed speed, trying to run an unpredictable course.

This was by far the hottest action we had ever been in, and I'm not ashamed to say I was scared. You can't dig a foxhole in a steel deck. There's no place to hide when a bomb goes off a few feet away from you. I couldn't see much out of the handling room powder scuttle but I could hear plenty. Those explosions were much too close for comfort.

We received orders to escort transport ships carrying wounded out of the combat zone. German planes overhead were making life miserable and to protect the transports, the destroyers of our squadron circled around them blowing dense smoke from our stacks to obscure visibility. One by one, the transports got underway, many of them slipping anchor rather than waiting to reel in the chains. As soon as they were moving, we came about and shepherded them toward the mouth of Salerno Bay.

The entrance to the bay had been blocked by mines but just before the invasion, Allied mine sweepers had cleared a path about one hundred fifty feet wide. Egress was slow; we couldn't make much more than five or six knots as we threaded the needle through the narrow passage. Thankfully, the Germans showed little interest in the departing convoy. As we cleared the breakwater, they broke off their attack and turned back toward the Italian coast. We proceeded without further harassment from the air.

2240. Once clear of the bay, the convoy fanned out in standard formation. *Rowan* took up her station about 4,000 yards off the convoy's starboard bow. Cruising at ten knots, we turned southwest toward North Africa. With general quarters secured and watch condition III set, the battle-weary crew stood down. The night was calm as *Rowan* glided through the sea.

Life slipped back into routine. Harvey had the eight to midnight watch on the signal bridge. Bob was in the galley baking bread. Bud Desch crawled into his bunk and fell asleep instantly. I was still too wound up to sleep, so I grabbed a book and headed aft to the #4 handling room, my favorite nighttime reading spot. There was always a light on there and I was isolated from interruptions. For once, I welcomed the monotonous routine of escort duty. I had had all the excitement I could handle.

Although I was not conscious of it, I knew my safety and well being was in the hands of my shipmates. I had complete confidence in those on watch. I was equally confident in my ship. *Rowan* had come through the worst of battles in fine form. I couldn't imagine a situation that her agility and speed was not equal to. *Rowan* wasn't just some hunk of cold metal. She had a personality all her own. There was no other ship like her. I belonged to her and she to me. The constant throb of the screws was familiar and comforting. *Rowan* was safe. *Rowan* was home.

I read for a while, then went topside to catch some fresh air. *Rowan* pushed back the sea, and as we made our way toward Oran, I started thinking about my recent marriage and three-day honeymoon. I couldn't wait to get back to New York. I lost myself in those sweet memories.

I doubt I would have enjoyed them as much had I known of the danger that lay unseen just a few thousand yards off our starboard beam.

E-Boats Attack

10 September. 2345. The twelve-to-four watch was coming on to relieve. Bob Hill and gun captain Pappy Cole took over the duty in the #2 five-inch gun mount. Jim Gagnon had the sonar watch. Jim Riley, Bob Abbott and Frank Attinger were on the steaming watch in the forward fireroom. Wayne Easterling, who was not on duty, was catching a nap. Throughout the ship, bleary-eyed sailors who hadn't gotten enough sleep were taking over from bleary-eyed sailors who hadn't gotten any at all.

In the Radio Shack, Worthington, Henry Huguenin, Ethan Loe, Harris Rivers and George Rose were changing the watch in the interior room, where messages were received and decoded. Barrale was in the exterior transmitting room.

In the pilothouse, Icenogle took over at the helm. Harvey was filling in his relief, Jilcott, lingering on the bridge to shoot the breeze. The door to the radar/sonar room was open and the steady ping-ping of the sonar, added to the customary sounds of the ship, was reassuring.

11 September

0015. At the sonar screen, Jim Gagnon picked up the chilling hydrophone effect of a torpedo heading toward us. "Torpedo!" he called out. "Twelve degrees off the starboard bow." It missed us by less than one hundred feet.

Jilcott had also recognized the sound from the sonar. "Torpedo," he shouted.

The officer of the deck responded immediately. "Hard right rudder. Increase speed to fifteen knots." *Rowan* turned north to run down the torpedo track in search of the enemy ship that had fired the projectile.

Harvey jabbed the general quarters alarm switch and the blaring burp, burp, burp of the alarm brought everyone to his feet, racing for battle stations.

A moment later, Captain Ford appeared on the bridge and took charge of the action.

Down in his bunk, Bud Desch struggled back to life when the alarm cracked through his consciousness. He had been asleep for only an hour, just long enough to be completely out of it. Through his mental fog, he reached instinctively for his shoes and jumped from his bunk. Wiping the sleep from his eyes, he headed for his battle station on sonar. Gagnon, whom he relieved, raced to his general quarters station in the #2 upper handling room.

Easterling was on his feet before he was awake. As he raced up the starboard side toward the director, he wondered what was going on. He joined Chief DePriest, Hunter, Fox and Hennessy, and reported his station manned and ready.

Bob Hill had spotted the approaching torpedo from where he had been sitting in the doorway of the #2 gun mount. He jumped up and turned to the gun captain, shouting, "Torpedo!"

Pappy Cole, who was wearing the telephone headset, had heard the report from the bridge. "They've already got it up there." A second later, the alarm went off.

Regulations were that anyone on gun watch must remain in place until relieved, but the #2 loader on watch in the #2 gun mount ran to his battle station before his relief arrived. Hill was left by himself, to do double duty. He hoped the rest of the crew would show up quickly.

Kelley had been sitting on the hatch leading to the engine room, talking with the off-going watch. At the sound of the alarm, he raced forward through the galley passageway to his battle station in the damage control party. He had recently been reassigned to this position from the depth charges when he was advanced to machinist mate first class.

Abbott was relieved by Herbert Retallack, and headed up to the starboard side 20-mm gun on the deck house, just aft of the stack. By the time he got there, Ben Murphy and Willis Collier were already manning the gun. Abbott strapped himself into the shoulder mounts and reported his gun manned and ready.

My brother ran to the #1 magazine, crawled inside and when the last man was in, dogged down the hatch, sealing in himself and the others. I ran to my station in the #2 upper handling room. Just as I finished my report, I felt *Rowan* heel over hard as we turned north to run down the torpedo track.

Radar did not pick up a surface target and it was presumed that a submarine had fired the torpedo. In preparation for the attack, Captain Ford ordered depth charges to be armed and the bridge telephone talker, Torpedoman Walter Garrigus, passed the word to set the charges for shallow barrage.

Sonar sweeps continued trying to locate the suspected submarine. At a speed of fifteen knots, we should overtake a U-boat within a matter of minutes. By now, we were quite a distance from the convoy, still no target had been acquired, either visually or by instrument. Something had fired that torpedo, but had it been a sub? If so, why couldn't it be located? Had the U-boat submerged and slipped under our keel, and was it now heading back toward the slow-moving troop transports that carried the wounded back from the Salerno landing?

"Three surface targets, 5,000 yards dead ahead," radar reported.

Harvey glanced into the radar room and saw three blips traveling northbound in a "V" formation.

"Increase speed to twenty knots," Ford ordered. We were not closing on the targets. "Twenty-five knots." The targets were still moving away from us. "Twenty-seven knots."

Down in the engine room, Jim Riley was wondering what was going on as he cut in all boilers in response to the captain's orders. Oil poured into the firesides, building the two boilers to superheat. *Rowan* would be ready to crank out even more speed in a matter of a few more minutes. He and the black gang would see to that.

On the bridge, Captain Ford stood in the darkness, listening to the reports coming from radar. "Inform Commander Task Group 81.6 that a torpedo crossed our bow and we are investigating the possibility of E-boats."

"Range 4,900 yards and closing," radar reported.

"Bring the forward guns to bear," Ford ordered. Fire control sighted in. The windows of the bridge were lowered in preparation for firing.

"4,800 yards and closing."

"Open fire." The guns roared out.

"Request permission to set depth charges on safe," Garrigus asked. This request was a precautionary measure and was the prudent thing to do, as there was no submarine threat.

"Range increasing to 5,200 yards," radar called at the same time. The captain did not respond to Garrigus' request.

Garrigus tried again. "Request permission to set depth charges on safe." The five-inch guns roared, drowning out his request for a second time. The captain did not respond. On his own initiative, Garrigus ordered the charges set on safe. They had been set to detonate at thirty feet. He followed up on this action until he obtained a confirmation report that all charges had been reset. Within the hour, his foresight and initiative would save many lives.

Up on the director, Gerry Hunter was the pointer and Willard Masters, the trainer. They were peering through the range finder, a large telescope with cross hairs in the eyepiece. Each of them had similar eyepieces and working as a team, they would crank the director around and up or down until the crosshairs were on the target. They would lock in. Hunter would close the firing key and the guns would fire. During this night action, fire control range finding was guided by radar. When two pips or lights on the screen matched, Hunter fired. Through the optics, he watched the shells scream toward their target, like fireballs racing through space. The lead target was hit dead on and disappeared from the radar screen.

The two remaining targets separated and proceeded on diverging courses, but their direction was right back at us. Word was received that another destroyer had been dispatched from the convoy to back us up but they were as much as half an hour behind.

"Full right rudder," Ford ordered. "Increase speed to thirty-two knots." Our course would bring us back toward the convoy and the second destroyer, which would improve our odds in this fight.

Four minutes passed. "Contact 2800 yards off the port quarter," radar called.

"Open fire with all guns."

"One and Two cannot be brought to bear," the director reported.

"Range 2500 and closing."

"Commence firing with Three and Four," Ford countered. The guns blazed to life. "Hard to left. I want all four guns on him."

"Range 2200 and closing. 2000 and closing."

This was torpedo range. Being broadside to them left our flank fully vulnerable. "Full right rudder," Ford called out, trying to bring the E-boat astern, giving him less of a target.

Icenogle pulled hard on the wheel and *Rowan* heeled into the turn. He looked up at the bulkhead clock. 0130.

Harvey leaned out over the signal bag on the port side of the bridge, trying to get a visual sighting through his binoculars.

"1400 yards. 1300 yards."

"Torpedo wake!" the lookout shouted.

Survival and Rescue

*R*owan was still swinging hard to starboard with the full right rudder and had completed about thirty degrees of the turn when she was struck in the #3 magazine. Two almost simultaneous explosions ripped through the ship. The first one was the torpedo tearing a hole through the hull. The second started in the #3 magazine where hundreds of rounds of five-inch ammunition detonated. As the fireball expanded, it set off thousands of rounds of 40-mm and 20-mm ammunition sitting at the topside guns.

Harvey, his eyes glued to his binoculars, searched for the wake of the torpedo. In the split second between the first explosion and the second, he lowered his glasses to look aft, certain a gun had blown up from a hang fire. The second explosion roared out, flinging debris in every direction. Shrapnel and a warm, soft mass brushed across his face. A heavy object struck him on the battle helmet, flinging him, barely conscious, to the deck.

Something was searing his neck. Ears ringing from the concussion, he was confused and disoriented. Images of his life flashed into his mind. He reacted instantly, shouting out loud, "I'm too young to die!" Shaking his head to clear it, he muttered, "I've got to get to my feet." But the deck was not where it was supposed to be. Phone lines fouled around his feet and body. He couldn't see anything and he groped around until he touched a ladder on the side of the pilothouse. Struggling to free himself from the entanglements, he pulled himself upright. He heard a roar that sounded like a waterfall and suddenly realized that the ship was nearly under water. Seconds later, his feet were wet.

In the pilothouse, glass shattered and crashed across the deck. Bob Icenogle was thrown, stunned and bleeding, from his position at the helm and landed on top of one of the officers. He lay there for a second, dazed and hardly breathing. The officer must have believed him already dead as he shoved the motionless body aside in his own effort to escape. Icenogle shook his head and tried to get the world back in some kind of order. He tried to return to his duty at the wheel, but the deck was in the wrong place. Where was the horizon? Just as he was trying to sort things out, the Mediterranean came pouring through the bridge.

At the sound of the explosion, Desch, in the sonar room, leaped backward over his chair. From where he was crouching, he could look aft out the doorway. Debris and pieces of metal were flying past. As he stood up, he saw Kelley running aft. Cautiously, Desch eased out to the wing of the bridge, trying to stay upright on the ever-shifting deck, debating whether the ship would stay afloat. The last thing he wanted to do was abandon ship unnecessarily. Within seconds, his decision was made for him. As the bow began to rise, water roared in around him.

As the sea reached the gunwale of the bridge, he dove into the water head first, swimming away from the undertow as hard as he could. He turned back to see if he had made it but inches from his head, the starboard end of the bridge was coming down right on top of him. A strange feeling of euphoria came over him. He was transformed from a scene of sheer terror into an incredible world of soft, billowing light. There was no sound, no people, no voices, no water, no body, no weight. He felt total peace and pleasant thoughts of childhood drifted through his mind. In that moment, he realized that he was dying, giving up without a fight. Angry that he could allow himself to die without regard to the anguish he would cause his mother and his pregnant wife, he willed himself to return.

In an instant, he was back to reality, surrounded by the black Mediterranean night. Alone. The only sounds he could hear were his own movements in the water. He wondered if he were the only one alive. To conserve his strength, he kicked off his shoes and trousers for fear they might lug him down. He kept his shirt as protection from the sun in case they were not rescued right away. A sea bag floated by about a hundred feet away and he swam over and grabbed it. Then he spotted a raft. Clutching the sea bag to his chest with one arm, he used the other arm to paddle toward the life raft.

Captain Ford had been standing behind Icenogle, conning the ship when the explosion hit. He was slammed down on his back to the deck of the pilothouse. Hardly able to believe what had happened, he struggled to his feet and worked his way to the door on the port side to see what was going on. He knew immediately that the ship was dead. His men were already jumping overboard. With his left hand on the hinge side of the doorway, he stood watching with one foot in the pilothouse and one on the wing of the bridge, determined to wait until everyone was away so he could do the same. As the ship started to sink, the rushing water slammed the door shut with terrific force, amputating three fingers of his left hand and pinning his foot. Trapped, he was being dragged down with the ship. Suffering excruciating pain and barely conscious, there was little he could do but resign himself to what seemed certain death.

Up in the director, Masters was hurled on top of Hunter and killed instantly. Hunter pushed the trainer off and crawled out a small door above his head. The ship was already at such a steep angle, he could barely maintain his hold on the director. As *Rowan* rolled over, he slid off into the sea. The turbulence of the water twisted and turned him, pulling him under. He calmed his rising panic and suddenly when he was about ten feet under, an escaping air bubble carried him up to the surface. Fearing that the danger had not yet passed, he began to swim for all he was worth to get a safe distance away. He turned around just in time to see *Rowan* go under.

The explosion propelled Easterling forward, slamming his head against the bulkhead in the director, cutting a deep gash near the temple. Blood gushed down the side of his face. Terror gripped him as he crawled toward the hatchway. He looked down at the rising water and prayed, "Help me, God. I can't swim!" At that, a feeling of peace came over him and he knew it would be all right. As the water swirled around him, he reached out and a life raft bumped up under his arm.

Barrale in the Radio Shack had been thrown to the floor. He clawed his way to his feet and lurched for the door. He turned back toward the black interior transmitting room and shouted as loud as he could, "Abandon ship! Abandon ship!" Rupert McCall and David Barry escaped ahead of him. But Barrale could wait no longer for the other men. The Mediterranean was swirling around his ankles. With one more glance over his shoulder, he made his escape. The sea poured through the open hatch, pinning all the other radiomen inside.

Roy Danielsen, the oil king, had no assigned general quarters station and when the torpedo was sighted, he had gone forward to the #1 fireroom to be available in case he was needed. When he heard the explosion, he climbed the ladder and got to the hatch just before the water reached that point. He stepped out into the sea and swam away as hard as he could, and fought the suction caused by the sinking ship.

To Jim Riley, also in the #1 fireroom, the explosion sounded like a huge glass building exploding. Then everything became silent. No guns firing. No screws turning. Not even the usual sound of water rushing against the hull. The lights were out. It was like hell in the hot, silent, dark world below decks. Instinctively, he snapped on his flashlight to check out the engine gauges. The readings seemed impossible. The boiler water gauge read empty. He was sure there was a hole in the side of the ship. As if to confirm his conclusion, he felt the ship roll to starboard, then back to port. He knew he had to get topside before the water came in through the starboard hatch.

With no time to spare, he raced to the ladder where he found Frank Attinger clinging to the handrail, frozen with fear. Pushing past him, Riley shouted at him, "Abandon ship, buddy. Let's get out of here!" Attinger didn't move. Riley was already past him and didn't look back. When he reached the top, he found the hatch cover already open and just as he got to the top rung of the ladder, water began pouring down on him. He was sure he was a dead duck. Suddenly, air pressure escaping from the fireroom shot him clear of the hatch and deposited him unscathed into the sea. As soon as he was clear, he turned around to see first the bridge, then the #2 gun mount, #1 gun mount and finally, the bow slip backward beneath the waves.

William Laughlin was in the #1 upper handling room just aft of the chief's quarters, one deck below the main deck. As soon as *Rowan* was struck, he knew he had to abandon ship. With the deep tilt astern, he fell more than walked, back toward the ladder leading up to officer's country. He crawled along the ladder that was, by now, horizontal instead of vertical. The pitch of the deck deepened until the bow pointed straight up. He rolled down the officer's passageway into the water, which was now flooding the passageway of the ship's office. Laughlin took a deep gulp of air and swam underwater to the exit door. Trying to keep calm, he forced the door open. He emerged onto the deck, which was now some twenty feet below the surface.

No one knows for certain what happened to Kelley after Desch spotted him going aft. Without a thought to his own safety, he had dived into the inferno, no doubt trying to help the men trapped amid the twisted wreckage of the after part of the ship. He always gave his all, but this was one case where courage was not enough. Willis Doyle Kelley was never seen again.

The torpedo hit just aft of the engine room, rupturing steam lines with devastating consequences for anyone down there. No one had a chance to escape. Those who were not killed outright were probably scalded to death by the escaping steam or trapped beneath parts of the ship torn loose by the explosion.

There was only one survivor of the after part of the ship: Bob Abbott, back on the 20-mm gun. Immediately after the ship was hit, he found himself in water up to his knees. By some miracle, he had been blown, gun and all, off the ship. But the danger was far from over. He was still strapped in and sinking like a stone. He hardly had a chance to take a deep breath before going under.

Fighting against time and the urge to breathe, he fumbled with the straps. Finally, he freed himself and popped to the surface, gasping for air. The fuel oil and smoke from the explosion hung heavily around him, making breathing difficult. Exhausted from the struggle, he tried to blow up his lifebelt but found that he could not. It had been punctured in the explosion. He looked around. The ship was gone. Off to his left, he saw a life raft. Too dazed to comprehend what had happened to him, he swam over to the raft to hang on. He looked in vain for his buddy, Paul Cash.

After Hill dove into the water, he was caught in an eddy that sucked him downward as the ship sank. More surprised than afraid, he remained calm. A few feet under, the suction suddenly released him and he floated to the surface. He turned around and saw the last of *Rowan* as she slipped out of sight. He unhooked his life belt and blew it up. As he kicked off his shoes, he looked around to assess his situation.

"Hey!" he heard someone nearby shouting, "who are you?" It was Richard Hennessy. "Help me," he said. "I can't swim." In one arm, he held a piece of debris that was keeping him afloat. In the other, he was holding onto Ensign John Richardson, one of the passengers from the *Rhind*, who was injured.

Hill quickly swam over to him and together they maneuvered the officer over to the raft, which was already full of injured men. Another young officer, who was already on the raft, gave up his place to Richardson. He volunteered to swim over to another raft, "to see how they were doing," he quipped. He returned a short time later saying, "That raft has all the 'wheels.' I was out-ranked."

When the ship was hit, John Merker, the sight setter in the #2 gun mount literally stepped out of the gun enclosure and fell into the sea. The undertow pulled him down amid a rain of debris. He opened his eyes as he struggled against the downward pull and saw two bodies trapped in the whirlpool above him. He couldn't tell whether he was going up or down and it seemed like an eternity before he reached the surface. He choked on the fuel oil-sea water cocktail awaiting him as he gasped for air. Then he noticed that most of his clothing was missing. His life belt was ripped and useless. A powder can floated by and he grabbed it for support. He looked around and spotted the life raft. When he got to the now overloaded raft, the men hanging off the side moved over and made room for him. "Anybody seen Moose?" he asked. #2 shell loader Warren "Moose" Huffman was missing.

As *Rowan* went down, Captain Ford was dragged down some twenty to thirty feet, caught by his foot. He was prepared to die, but when the ship rolled to port and the water pressure equalized, he was able to push the door open. As it swung away, he was miraculously catapulted to the surface. He sucked in a grateful lungful of air, then began to fumble with his life belt with fingers that were no longer there. Dazed and in tremendous pain, he was spotted by a sailor floating by on water wings made from a passing mattress.

The sailor kicked his way over to Ford and pulled him close so he could hang on. "Hey!" he shouted to the other survivors. "Over here! I have the captain."

Lt. Glenn was nearby tending to an unconscious sailor. "I have Burke here. Take the captain over to the raft," he directed.

The sailor carefully towed Ford over to Dr. Stoddard, who examined him. The captain's injuries were serious, but there was nothing that could be done for him except to get him out of the water. Carefully, the men lifted him onto the raft and tried to make him as comfortable as possible.

Harvey, entangled in wires, was dragged down maybe twenty or more feet. Through no effort of his own, he was freed and shot to the surface, gulping for air. But instead of air, he swallowed a mixture of seawater and fuel oil that his body instantly rejected. He heaved up large quantities of the bitter concoction. Injured and nauseated, he stripped off his jacket and binoculars, and treaded water. He couldn't see anything but nearby, he heard Lt. Glenn's voice calling to him. "You all right?" the officer asked him.

"I think so," Harvey answered, squinting to make out shapes or light of any kind, "but I can't see anything. I must have oil in my eyes."

"Can you inflate your vest?" Glenn asked.

"No, sir. It must be punctured."

"Well, hang on, sailor. I can't help you right now. This man is unconscious. His life belt has a hole in it and my kapok life jacket wouldn't support all three of us."

"I'll be okay, sir," Harvey told him," even though he didn't feel very confident of that. "Just point me in the right direction."

"There's a powder can a few feet in front of you."

Harvey groped until his hands closed around the casing.

"The raft is a few yards farther on," Glenn told him. "Can you swim?"

"Yes, sir."

"All right. Follow the sound of the voices." When Harvey was

Norm Crowder

on his way, Glenn felt for Burke's pulse. There was none. Others were still alive. He made a difficult decision and let the body of the dead man go.

Harvey took his bearings and began to paddle toward the sounds. As he approached the raft, Norm Crowder spotted him and pulled him in the rest of the way.

Doctor Stoddard asked him, "Are you injured?"

When Harvey answered affirmatively, a place was made for him on the raft. He sat there for a few minutes, too frightened of what he might find to investigate his injuries. Finally, he got up enough nerve to feel his neck. He was sure it was slit from ear to ear. Carefully, he brought his right hand around the left side of his neck. Although badly abraded by the chinstrap of his battle helmet, it was in one piece. He inched his fingers along a little farther and, to his relief, he discovered his head was still firmly attached. The salt and oil were making the abrasion sting like crazy. If only he could get the oil out of his eyes. They didn't hurt but it was annoying, not being able to see.

Crowder hung on to the side of the raft, looking around to see if he could render assistance. Thirty feet from the raft, he spotted someone floating by. He swam out and returned a few minutes later, towing a sailor back with him. The man was unconscious. "Who is it?" someone asked him.

"It's Burke," Crowder replied, spitting seawater out of his mouth as he struggled to support his weight and Burke's.

Dr. Stoddard tended to him immediately and discovered that SM2c James Burke was already dead. "He's gone, Norm," the doctor said. "There's no more room on the raft. You have to let him go."

"No!" Crowder insisted. "I'm not letting him go! I'm okay. I'll hold on to him." He looped a rope from the raft around his arm and kept a firm grip on the dead man.

When the *Bristol* arrived to pick us up, Crowder was still holding onto Burke's body. "Throw me a line," he called to the rescuers. The heaving line landed just a few feet from the raft and Crowder glided over to grab it. He fastened the line around Burke's waist and said, "Okay. Hoist him up." With Burke's body taken care of, Crowder swam to the cargo net and climbed aboard. He was the last one to be picked up. *Bristol* was underway even before he reached the deck. Because of Crowder's effort, Burke was listed as killed in action instead of missing. That deed of kindness undoubtedly saved one family from the torment of wondering about the fate of their loved one.

Aboard the *Bristol*, survivors were shepherded into the mess hall where they could be counted, the injured tended to under good lighting, and the officers could make a casualty report. Men wandered around trying to find their buddies. Some wept openly. Easterling, Hennessy and Harvey sat on a table, numb and dazed. A photographer came over and snapped a couple of pictures of them, one of which would wind up in newspapers back home all across the country.

Bristol hovered around the area of the sinking until the sun rose. As daylight filled the sky, lookouts scanned the horizon for more survivors. I kept the vigil with them, hoping that by some miracle, Bob would be found. Around 1000, something was spotted in the water and *Bristol* came alongside to retrieve it. I leaned over the side to get a closer look. It was the headless, legless torso of a sailor. His name was stenciled across his dungarees. It wasn't Bob. I felt both relieved and profoundly sad.

Shortly after dinner, the survivors who were physically able; gathered on the quarterdeck for a burial service. I looked around the group. Some wore bandages to cover wounds. Others were uninjured. Most were without shoes or socks, wearing ill-fitting clothes donated by men from the *Bristol*. Among them were Crowder, Hill, Hunter, Egan, McCardie, Barry, Gray and Abbott. Officers Wyatt, Hirschhorn, Brown, Highness, and Era stood together. The solemn faces of all those gathered scarcely revealed the true extent of their loss.

Lt. Glenn, who had taken over for the injured Captain Ford, called us to attention and led the brief service. I have no memory of his words. I was too drained from grief and sleeplessness for them to register. The only thing I recall clearly is hearing the soft sounds of *Bristol* moving through the water at a speed of about ten knots. Next to the port lifeline lay the bodies of Marl J. Cloninger, WT1c, William Fightmaster, S1c, and James F. Burke, SM2c. They were sewn into weighted canvas bags and laid out on flag-draped boards. A salute of three rifle shots was fired as the boards were tipped up, and the bodies of our shipmates were committed to the sea.

When the service ended, *Bristol* increased speed to twenty knots and set a course southwest toward Algeria.

It was the first stop on our long journey home.

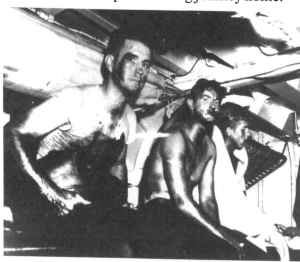

Easterling, Hennessy, Harvey aboard *Bristol*

Long Journey Home

12 September. After my long, sleepless night, I found my way to the mess hall for breakfast. Breakfast revived me somewhat, but prepared me little for the most difficult duty I had ever had to perform - writing to Mom and Dad. Censorship prevented me from saying anything about Bob or the ship, but I wanted to assure them I was all right and give them something to cling to in their anguish.

Fortunately, help was available. After breakfast, the officers of the *Rowan* gathered us in the mess hall and instructed us in how to get word home to our loved ones. Lt. Glenn told us to note the day and time so that our families would know we were alive the day after the sinking. "Try to say things they will regard as unusual but meaningless to anyone else, to call attention to a hidden meaning." In his simple words he showed great respect for our grief, grief I'm certain he too, was feeling.

I picked up a couple of "V-mail" forms, one for my folks and one for Helen, chose a pen from the supply provided, and found an empty table away from the other survivors to sit down to write. Around me, my shipmates were hunched over their work but for a long time, I just sat staring at the blank page. There were so many things I couldn't say because of censorship. How to begin?

I pondered over my task until it occurred to me to start the letter differently. Instead of the usual "Dear Folks", I would use a more formal greeting. I wrote:

September 12, 1943
  Dear Mother and Dad:
  Today is Sunday, Sept. 12 and I would certainly like to be attending church with you today, but the fortunes of war prevent that as you know, and it prevents so many other things. But we are getting hardened to it so that we can now take all the trials and hardships and heartaches in our stride for we realize we are in this fight to take what comes. If we cannot attend church as we used to, or get little or no leave so we can see those we love, or even if we should die in battle, we know it's for a good and honorable cause and we who are left must forget and carry on for those who depend on us.
  I know you worry about us, but we worry about you, too. It is important that we know you are well. I know you feel that if one of you should pass on you would not expect us to quit fighting just as we would expect you to. Courage is needed.
  I will close and pray I will see you soon.
  Love, Lewis

When I was finished, I tossed the pen down. Would they understand? And how would I tell my new wife? What could I say to her that she would consider unusual?

Just then, a yeoman came through the galley to inform us there would be Sunday service on the fantail at 1200. A light went on in my head. I picked up my pen and wrote, *"It's Sunday, September 12. Don't forget to go to church and say a prayer for me."* Telling Helen to go to church was like reminding the sun to come up in the morning but I had a feeling she would understand. I gave no specific information, but I let my love for her spill from my pen onto the paper. As I mailed the letter, I realized that while I was writing to her, the heaviness in my heart had lifted momentarily. It was almost as if I had been with her.

I had no way of knowing the agony of uncertainty she had endured until 18 September when my letter reached her. Later she would tell me about how she heard the news of the sinking, nearly twenty-four hours after the ship went down. Her sister, Bernie, met her when she got off work and the two of them went to the 9:15 showing of *On Borrowed Time*. They arrived home around 11:00 and a short time later, her father got home from work. Pop, as he was called, went into the front room to listen to the late news on the radio. Helen, Bernie and Anne went into the kitchen to have a cup of tea. Helen was just stirring milk into the strong brew when Pop came in, all excited.

"Helen, what's the name of the ship your husband's on?"

"*Rowan*," she replied. An unexplainable fear gripped her heart.

"Ro-anne?" her father repeated back to her.

"No, Pop. It's pronounced *Rowan*. Why?"

"It's been sunk," he said flatly.

Helen let go of the spoon in her right hand, feeling the blood drain away from her face. "What? Are you sure?"

"The captain on the ship is Lieutenant Commander Ford."

Helen knew Pop might have remembered the name of the ship but it was very unlikely he would have remembered the captain's rank. After all, Ford was never referred to by any title other than 'captain.' Whatever Pop had heard, Helen was certain it was about my ship. The shock left her speechless.

Anne said firmly, "I know how to find out what's going on." She went to the telephone and called the radio station Pop had been listening to. She asked to them to repeat the story. They confirmed it. There was no doubt.

Helen didn't know what to think. Was I dead? Was I injured? How could it be true? Why wasn't she notified as next of kin? Maybe the Navy Department hadn't yet registered the change after our marriage. Throughout a sleepless night, she wondered and worried and prayed.

The next day, Sunday, the phone began to ring early. Each time it did, she hoped it would be news about me. Instead it was someone who had heard the news on the radio and wanted to know if it was my ship. Around mid-morning, her Aunt Margaret called and said she had seen a photo in the newspaper and one of the men in it looked like Ernie Harvey, whom she had met when he visited their home. "There are three or four fellows in the shot. I can see someone else in the picture but you can't see his face - only his arm. Maybe it's Lew," she offered hopefully.

Struggling to control a rising sense of hope for fear she might be wrong, Helen called the office of the news service credited with the photo. She identified herself as the wife of one of the ship's crew. She asked to see the original, maybe there was more that had been cropped for the paper. The wire service told her she could have the photo but when she got it, there was nothing more she could learn. All she could do was go home and wait.

The phone continued to ring as more friends saw the photo in the paper. Every time it rang, people in the Quinn house would jump, scared to answer, yet eager to find out what the caller had to say. A family friend who was home on leave from the Army said it was just like a scene from a movie.

The tension was depressing. Everyone walked around Helen as if they were visiting a corpse in a funeral parlor. Finally she had enough. "I'm going to work," she declared. As a telephone operator, she would be near a phone at all times and besides, she needed something to keep her mind occupied.

Helen did her best to focus on her work. She told no one of the sinking. After a few hours, a friend who knew Helen had recently married, came over and asked cheerfully, "How's the old man?" Helen's eyes filled with tears. "Gees, what did I say?" her friend asked, puzzled by the reaction.

When Helen could finally control herself, she said, "His ship was sunk."

"Is he all right?"

"I don't know. There's no word yet."

News of the tragedy spread quickly among the telephone operators. Soon a compassionate chief operator came by and asked Helen if she wanted to go home and wait for word. Another person she didn't even know came by and offered to contact the Red Cross on her behalf. Everyone was thoughtful and willing to do anything for her. Helen insisted she was okay. "I came to work to be away from people asking me questions. I just want to do my job."

Her cousin Sheila, a long distance operator, put in a call to my mother to see if she had any further word but she had heard nothing. The only information she had was the telegram concerning Bob. There was no word about me.

Several long, tense, painful days passed before my cryptic letter arrived. When it did, she opened it with trembling hands. She read it several times, confused by its content. "I don't know what he's saying, reminding me to go to church. I can't make it out. I don't understand!" But then she caught on. She checked the date-September 12 - the day after the sinking. That's when she finally knew for certain that I was alive. She went to church that day, even though it wasn't Sunday. She had a lot to be thankful for.

When Helen told me her story, I was saddened that she had to agonize so long without word. But her story made me think of the families of all those men who were listed as "missing in action" for a year before they were declared dead. For them, the wondering was far from over. When the telegram came on the day after the anniversary of the sinking, they would have to go through the sorrow all over again.

13 September

Aboard the *Bristol*, I tried to pick up the pieces. It was difficult because all that remained of my old life were the clothes on my back. I had nothing to give me a sense of purpose and meaning. Still, my will to live was strong and I would not permit myself to wallow in sorrow. I had to survive, to get home to my wife and family. I desperately needed something to do.

As I aimlessly wandered around the ship, I passed the galley, where the aroma of coffee brewing greeted me. It was strangely soothing. It meant routine and order. Without a second thought, I went to the cook on duty and asked if he could use some help. With so many extra mouths to feed, he put me to work immediately. For me, it was like righting a table in a house that has been flattened by a tornado. It was therapy, a way to keep from going insane. The harder I worked, the better I felt.

16 September

Bristol arrived in Oran and the survivors were transferred to NOB Oran Tent City #4, a SeaBee camp, to await transportation stateside. It was one of those instant population centers spawned by military necessity. Neatly aligned along arbitrary streets of parched earth, it was a collection of Quonset huts large enough to house about fifty men each. Tent City was a hot, dusty, gloomy place that was about as inviting as a prisoner of war camp. For the time being, it was home.

We were the first survivors this location had to accommodate. Facilities were primitive, supplies almost non-existent and no one seemed to know what to do with us or what services, beyond food and shelter, we were entitled to. Our pay records were lost when the ship went down and with our official records in Boston, we couldn't draw any money. That meant we couldn't get any clothing.

Norm Crowder, *Rowan's* chief storekeeper, went nose-to-nose with a young disbursing officer, a ninety-day wonder, who didn't want to let loose of any money without some kind of individual pay record. With the determination of a bulldog, Crowder kept at him. He poured through the Navy Regulation and Bureau of Supplies Account Manual until he found the section that gave the officer the authorization to pay us. Very reluctantly, the officer paid $100 to each enlisted man and $200 to the officers.

Crowder's next chore was to get us some clothing. Ten days after the sinking, I was still limping around in a pair of paper slippers that came in the Red Cross package and my dungarees still smelled of fuel oil. Getting us outfitted took Crowder all the way to the commanding officer of the base. He cut through red tape and indifference and we soon had whites, dungarees, socks, and much-needed shoes. Although I don't think I told him so at the time, I was grateful to Crowder for all his efforts in our behalf.

With my basic needs satisfied, I sat down to write home.

September 21, 1943

Dear Mother and Dad:

I am now attached to a naval shore station, somewhere in North Africa. I am well. I am not, nor have been in any hospital. Do not worry about me. I am waiting transportation to U.S. Upon my arrival there, I am expecting leave. I do not know how much, but

enough. I hope that I will be able to come home to see
you.
   Until then, take good care of yourselves. I will see you
as soon as possible.
   Lewis

As I mailed the letter, I started feeling restless. With nothing to do, I feared I might sink back into that dark emotional hole I was trying so hard to escape. Working had helped me back on the *Bristol* and so when a call was put out for volunteers to accompany the permanent shore patrol in and around Oran, I jumped at the chance. I was sure that doing anything was better than doing nothing. I didn't know what I was in for.

My partner was a tough and savvy former New York City police officer. Although he had been on duty in Oran for only a few weeks, he knew his beat. Our duty was not to arrest the men in uniform but to try to keep them out of trouble. I think he got a kick out of watching my reaction as we patrolled through the red light district most frequented by servicemen. We chased soldiers and sailors out of some of the most disgusting, filthy, rat-infested hovels I had ever seen.

Two weeks of this duty was enough for me and fortunately, we got word that our transportation had been arranged out of Algiers, about 150 miles away. I had no regrets about leaving either my buddy, or my beat, behind.

We would make the trip from Oran to Algiers by train. The crew was to ship out the following day by passenger train but our baggage, which consisted mostly of our personal belongings, was to be sent ahead by freight car. I had seen the passenger trains, rickety old French 40 and 8 cars, and knew there was very little difference between them and the baggage cars, except the former were covered and therefore slightly more comfortable. When the call went out for five volunteers to guard the baggage, I stepped forward right away. We were given a rifle and enough C-rations for a week, and stationed on top of the open freight cars.

Back in the States, a 150-mile train trip might take five or six hours, even under the worst conditions. But this was Algeria and there was a war on. Travel time was counted in days, not hours. The sea bags had a tarpaulin thrown across them, which we were told we could use as a shelter. As the journey began, the train would stop for no apparent reason and sit on the tracks, sometimes for hours. The five of us guards learned to take advantage of these unscheduled stops, making small fires alongside the tracks over which we could heat the C-rations to make them a little more palatable.

Once, while I was heating a can of stew, I had a feeling I was being watched. I looked up over my shoulder quickly and saw a row of ragged Arab children standing on top of the embankment staring at us. The other guards noticed them too, and we decided to share some of our food with them. But the children would not approach us. They just stood there silently watching us, statue-like and silent, until our train moved out.

The day passed into night and the sunset lit the west in brilliant colors. The new moon offered no relief from the pitch-blackness of the night that fell across the land and only the twinkling stars broke the monotony of the sky. The steady clakety-clack of the wheels rolling down the track soothed me. I found a comfortable spot among the sea bags, pulled the tarp over me and fell into a deep, dreamless sleep.

Suddenly, a jerking motion and the slam of stressed metal jolted me awake early the next morning. Confused by the unfamiliar surroundings, I was nearly on my feet ready to head for my battle station when I realized where I was. What I had heard was the sound of the train trying to climb a long, steep grade. The locomotive was having trouble pulling the cars up the hill. It would get only so far, run out of steam and retreat down the hill to make a second run at it. And a third.

On the fourth run, the locomotive took off, wheels screaming against the track. The jolt uncoupled a section of cars about three cars ahead of ours. I sat bolt upright. The locomotive continued going forward but we were slipping backward. Looking down the hill behind us, I saw that the downgrade ran for several miles. We were on a runaway train, picking up speed by the second!

Behind us, a brakeman jumped off the caboose and as the car ahead of him rolled past, he jumped aboard it and began to tighten the handwheel that set the brake. Then, he jumped off that car and waited for the next car to come past him to repeat the action. His efforts didn't seem to have much effect as we were still picking up speed.

My heart pounded against my chest. I had just escaped a sinking ship and I wasn't about to be killed by an overturned freight train. The other guards must have been thinking the same thing because the five of us abandoned ship, or train, if you wish. We stood by the tracks and watched as the cars rolled back down the hill for a good three miles before they finally came to a halt. The five of us trudged back down to our car and waited for the locomotive to return for us.

Now familiar with the routine of hurry up and wait, once back to our car, we broke out the C-rations and settled down for a meal and another long wait while the necessary repairs were carried out. The sun was well past the mid-heaven when we were loaded back aboard and the train backed several more miles down the hill. Then, with the throttle full open, the engineer raced us forward. Three days and three nights later, we made it to Algiers.

When we reached our destination, our officers were anxiously awaiting us. Their train had passed ours en route and arrived a full day ahead of us. The ship we were to travel on, the *Athlone Castle*, had been scheduled to depart four hours earlier and was being held up for us. As soon as the last man and sea bags were aboard, the gangway was hauled in. Had we moved any slower, they would have clipped our heels in their haste to get underway. At last, we were homeward bound.

The *Athlone Castle* was a British passenger liner converted into a troop transport when the war began. It was by far the most deluxe ship I had ever been on. Ten times the number we had aboard could have been easily accommodated. After the hair-raising adventure we had getting from Oran to Algiers, it was a relief to have so much space, no duties to perform, and a solid deck under foot. At a speed of twenty-five knots, we took off unescorted and traveled in a straight line to New York.

9 October

The third anniversary of the date I entered the Navy. It was also the day we arrived in New York.

As we steamed up the river to our docking location in New York harbor, I stood on deck under a brilliant blue fall sky and soaked in the beauty of the skyline. When the *Athlone Castle* tied up a short time later, I was anxious to touch American soil again. In my haste to go ashore, I left my life belt on my bunk. It was my last memento of the USS *Rowan*.

Had I known where I was heading, I might not have been in such a hurry. The survivors were transferred to the infamous Pier 92, a place that made boot camp seem like a pleasure resort. The regimentation was so strict that we felt more like we were prisoners of war than casualties of war. Only one man was treated with special respect. It was Joseph O'Conner. His father had died about the time of the sinking and his papers were processed quickly so he could go home on a hardship leave. Seeing him go only added to my sense of loneliness. I wanted badly to be with my loved ones.

As soon as I could, I called Helen to let her know I was in. She wanted to come down to see me right away but I was concerned for her safety. The neighborhood was rundown and seedy and the last thing I wanted was for my beautiful young wife to walk through the gauntlet of idle sailors, who might have been too long at sea. Her brother Joe came to the rescue and escorted her down to the dock.

When I saw her approaching, I knew I was finally home. I couldn't wait to get my arms around her; we had a lot of time to catch up on. But we had no privacy and being with her was almost worse than being without her. After we hugged and kissed I pushed her away from me for fear of losing control. She didn't understand and for a short time, actually wondered whether I still loved her. I tried to reassure her, but we would have to wait until I was released from Pier 92 to celebrate my homecoming.

The next day, I got liberty and made a beeline for the Bronx, but when I arrived, my heart sank; Helen was at the dentist. The family fussed over me and did their best to keep me company but it was clear that the only company I was looking for was Helen's. When she finally arrived, I opened the door for her and said, "Fine thing! After all this time and you're not here when I get home."

Helen threw her arms around me and fired back a snappy reply. "Fine thing! You walk in on me and didn't even let me know you were coming."

Everyone gathered around me and wanted to know all about what had happened. But as I sat there in the comfortable familiarity of Helen's home, my emotional restraint weakened. I could feel the pain growing inside me, demanding release. I needed to be with Helen - alone. I whispered to her, "I have to talk to you." She nodded and led me up to her room.

As soon as we closed the door behind us, I wrapped myself in the comfort of her arms and surrendered to the sorrow welling up in me. I laid my head on her shoulder and sobbed as I never had before. She held me close and wept with me for what seemed a very long time. When the pain at last subsided, I dried my eyes and whispered, "I needed that. I've been waiting for over a month to let loose and cry."

Helen comforted and soothed me with her gentle words. At last, I felt ready to be with the family again. As I went into the bathroom to wash my face, she went downstairs and asked everyone to please not ask me anything about the ship. If I volunteered the information, that would be okay but please don't probe. Everyone was terrific. When I came downstairs, they were warm and friendly but not too inquisitive.

I would not be able to spend much time at home until I was released from Pier 92. That time seemed to drag on forever but it was only a couple of weeks. When the day came for each of us to go our separate ways, Norm Crowder, who had done so much for us survivors in Tent City, had to do some haggling with yet another disbursing officer. The negotiations continued until the officer finally agreed to let Crowder vouch that each survivor was who he said he was and that he was due the pay he was due.

22 October

Monday. 0800. The men of the *Rowan* stood in line, and waited in turn to be officially recognized. When my turn came, I gratefully took my pay and headed out the door. At that moment, I did not know I would never again see most of those men with whom I had shared such an important part of my life. But I didn't care. I couldn't think in terms of 'never again.' I was still trying to make it one day at a time. Even if I had known it, I doubt I would have done anything differently. I had had enough of sorrow and separation. Saying good bye would have reopened my fresh wounds and that was something I was not willing to endure.

I stepped out into the bright sunshine and did not look back. I wanted nothing more than to forget the past and dedicate myself to building the future. I was fortunate to have Helen there to help me. She was my anchor, my stabilizer, the only one in whom I could confide. No one could have done more to help me bind my invisible wounds. A few months after my return, she gave me something that helped me heal more than anything else could have - she told me we were going to have a baby.

23 June 1944

My first daughter, Mary Elizabeth, was born.

At that time, Captain Harrison was at Norfolk, and I went to see him. I told him about the sinking and we cried together. When I was about to leave, he asked if there was anything else he could do for me. I joked, "How about some more leave."

The next day, I received my papers authorizing my leave. It seems I was entitled to two and a half days for every month I was overseas. Captain Harrison saw to it I got every single day of it. I was assigned temporary duty in the base galley at Norfolk. One of the regular cooks there kept complaining that he had been in the Navy for three years and hadn't been to sea. He was afraid the war would be over before he saw any action. I had had all the action I ever cared to have but I knew it was just a matter of time before I was shipped out.

The thought of going back to sea left me cold. I remembered how easy it had been back in boot camp for Bob and me to get on the same ship, and I wondered out loud whether it would be as easy for the cook to make his dreams come true. He jumped at the chance. We got the go-ahead and made the swap. I don't know what happened to him but I got eighteen months of shore duty. By the time I got my next assignment to sea, the war was over.

As the years passed, I thought less and less about the *Rowan*, except on those occasions when I would awaken from a nightmare. Eventually, even they became only rare occurrences. Every now and then, I'd run into one of my former shipmates. We'd shoot the breeze for a while, but I never felt any pull to get together with them again. The memory of the *Rowan* faded into the distance. It was simply a chapter in my life, one whose last page I was glad to turn.

Retirement changed that. With so much free time on my hands, I began to remember - bits and pieces, at first. But I was ready for more. Now, I needed to find my shipmates.

Rowan's crew, September 1941

Reunion

I t took two years of detective work but with a lot of help from Harvey, who was now known as Chris, and Ted Smith, I had tracked down a number of the survivors. Each of them had a few addresses of former shipmates, and an ad placed in the *VFW Legion Magazine* and the *Navy Times* netted us several more. By the end of August 1985, it looked like we might have enough of a group to make a decent party.

After so many years, I didn't know what to expect. There was the possibility that we would call a reunion and no one would show up. But we were determined to try. It was as if an invisible force was pulling us together again. I don't know what we expected to learn or find in each other's company, but nearly every man we contacted had the same story - after four decades, each felt the need to see his old shipmates again.

Jack Burgess, a plank owner (one of the crew when the ship was put into commission), volunteered to host the reunion at the Fort Magruder Inn in Williamsburg, Virginia. He planned a few excursions, including one to historic Williamsburg and another to the Norfolk Naval Base. Everything was set.

233

8 September 1985

Helen and I arrived on a hot, humid morning. Weather forecasters promised record-breaking heat for this time of year, not a very encouraging prospect, considering the outdoor events we had planned. After so many years in food service, I fretted over the details. Old habits are hard to break. But that was just a familiar way for me to distract my mind from what was really bothering me. I was actually more anxious about seeing my shipmates again.

Gratefully, we entered the coolness of the hotel lobby. As I went up to the front desk to register, I realized that an older fellow standing nearby was staring at me. He wore a Stetson hat, plaid shirt, bolo tie, Levi's and black boots. When I looked in his direction, he spoke to me.

"You're Seeley, aren't you?"

I was taken off guard. "That's right. I'm Lew Seeley."

"I thought it was you!" he said chuckling, extending his right hand to shake mine. "I'm Clay. Malcolm Clay. I was seaman first when she went down."

Although I didn't remember Clay, the way he recognized me made me feel that everything was going to work out just fine. I didn't know at the time that he had overheard me give my name to the hotel clerk. It was probably better that I didn't know. Not knowing helped set the stage for hopeful expectation.

The reunion started out slowly as new arrivals came in one by one. Many of the men didn't even know each other on the ship. Meeting forty years later, having had nothing in common then and even less in common now, put a strain on topics of conversation. Some talked about the trials of old age, or recent operations, or grandchildren. I was beginning to think the meeting with Clay was a fluke.

Then, Allen Neal spotted Bob Icenogle and a noisy, tearful reunion ensued. Ted Smith and Bill Ward sat together and started tapping out the old radio codes they used and their laughter echoed through the room. Finally, someone pulled out a photo of the crew taken in September of '41. All of us gathered around it, adjusting bifocals to get a clear look at the images now yellowed with time.

"Were you aboard when we went to Hawaii?"

"No. I came on in Philadelphia. August '41."

"What was the name of that ship that hit us in the fog?" someone asked.

"I believe it was *Mayrant*," another offered.

"Where were you when she was sunk?"

"I wasn't aboard. I went to the *Buck* first. Then the *Bristol*."

"Weren't they sunk?"

"Yeah. I had a way with ships."

The room started to heat up, but not from the weather. We were finally getting what we had all come to find. The years dropped away and we were once again as we had been a lifetime ago.

Tuesday, 10 September

2355. The captain had arrived early and it was as if he couldn't get enough of being with his men. Stern and unyielding four decades earlier, now at 83, he was just one of the men, drinking like a sailor on liberty. The only problem was that some of the men still harbored resentments toward him. He may have been aware of their feelings but he paid no attention to them. He was here to have a good time and nothing would stand in his way.

Midnight came and went, and a few of them men remained in the hospitality suite, unwilling to break off the conversation. One of them was the captain. Mrs. Ford, who had already retired for the evening, came back down looking for her husband. She went up to him and said quietly, "Bob, do you have any idea what time it is? You're no spring chicken, you know. You should be in bed."

He took her hand and smiled, "I'll be along when I'm finished, Edith. This is something I have to do," he said. She surrendered to his wishes and went back to the room.

Ford got up a little unsteadily and poured himself another drink. When he sat down again, he said to all of us, but to no one in particular, "I know some of you still think I'm a son-of-a-bitch." He looked around at the men. All eyes were on him. His eyes narrowed and he was the captain again. "I did what I had to do. When I came aboard, the ship was a mess. It was dirty. And the crew wasn't fit for combat."

"There was nothing wrong with the *Rowan*," one of the men said tersely. "We would have been fine if you hadn't hounded us all the time."

"I just wanted to get us all home in one piece."

"It didn't work out that way, did it?" another commented with biting sarcasm.

Ford's eyes, once so steely blue, were now clouded with age. "I did the best I could," he said softly. His eyes filled with tears. He paused, trying to compose himself. He took a ragged breath and said, "If only I could have gotten information faster. If I had ordered the turn a second earlier...." He bowed his head and rubbed the stub of his left hand.

Bill Ward spoke quietly, almost as if he were talking to himself. "I don't think it would have made any difference. Even if we had had the latest radar and sonar equipment and instant access to the information, the Germans would still have gotten us. That was just the way it was." He thought for a second, then added, "It wasn't you that sunk the ship, Captain. It was the war. It was just the war."

Later that night, when Ford finally retired, he woke his wife. He had had too much to drink and his words were a little slurred, but there was no mistaking his joy as he told her, "Edith, they don't think I'm such a son-of-a-bitch after all." He slept better that night than he had in years.

Survivors of the sinking and former crew of the *Rowan* at the 1986 reunion. Back row: George Curry, E. W. "Al" Smith, Newton Marler, Steve Kess, Bob Alderman, Leroy Byxbe, Albert Hornby; Middle row: Malcolm Clay, Harold McCardie, Norm Crowder, Bill Ward, Bill Hagen, Jack Goodpaster, Clifford Haynes; Front row: Jack Burgess, Chris Harvey, Walter Garrigus, Lew Seeley, Bob Icenogle, Allen Neal.

11 September

2000. We gathered at a banquet to commemorate our dead comrades and celebrate all the men of the *Rowan*. Chris Harvey got up to address the group. He said many things, but one phrase stayed with me. "The great fellowship of the reunion," he said, "has cured many things."

His words got to my heart. While I hadn't completely forgiven myself for living when my brother and so many of my friends did not, I was making progress. I still had the nightmares. Ever since the sinking, when the day was quiet or in the stillness of the night, I would imagine I heard Bob's bugle call. The sound was so agonized that I would instantly block it out, unable to stand the pain.

I looked around the room at the faces of my shipmates and realized that something had changed inside me. I was among the only people who knew what I had been through without a single word of explanation needed. The ship was our common bond. In renewing that bond, each of us was finding strength, acceptance and forgiveness.

As I sat in the company of my shipmates, I started to think. Maybe the nightmares were Bob's way of guiding me, trying to get me together with the people who could understand and help me. Maybe the cry of pain and torment I heard all these years was not his, but mine. Maybe he was there *to help me*. Through those images of the past, he was urging me to remember, not for his sake, but for mine.

A feeling of lightness and warmth came over me. And then I knew that the time had come for the dead to sleep, not in their moment of agony, but in the warmth of love and brotherhood shared and remembered and never forgotten. This realization was both a gift from my brother and my greatest tribute to him.

Just then, I thought I heard Bob's bugle call. No longer a cry of anguish, it was a pure and simple, familiar refrain. As it played in my mind, I softly sang the words:

All is well
Safely rest
God is nigh.

Epilogue

I did not begin this journey into the past to help others. I did it to help myself. And so, the reunion was an unexpected bonus. The fact that it happened at all was amazing, but to find so many of my former shipmates after so many years was nothing short of a miracle.

I have tried over and over again to capture in words the images and the impact of the reunion, and have never come close. How do you put into words what it's like to have the fragments of your life come together? Or to find answers to questions you had long ago given up finding? Nothing I wrote ever did justice to the experience.

There are some treasured memories that stand out. One in particular, happened some years later when Micki Pulos and Elexandra Walker, the sisters of Tony George, came to the reunion. They wanted to know how their brother died. We sat at the same table at the banquet and over dinner, Micki told me how she had heard about her brother's death. She was only a girl at the time but after nearly fifty years, that moment was still as fresh and clear in her memory as it was the day it happened. Without warning, tears welled up in her eyes. "Excuse me," she said abruptly and hurried from the room. When she came back a few minutes later, she had composed herself. "I'm so sorry," she said. "I'm embarrassed."

"There's no need to be." I told her, because I knew just how she felt. I had been there often enough, myself. "You're among friends here. We've all done our share of crying. I don't feel ashamed to cry any more."

I had come a long way from the nightmares that had started me on my journey to rediscover my past. The story still makes me cry, but ghosts no longer haunt my dreams.

Since that time, there have been more reunions. For a while, it seemed we were finding new members each time we met. Age and health have caught up with a lot of them. Mr. Wyatt died after the first reunion. The captain died a short time later. When I got word that Fred Quinn, who came aboard with me in 1940, died, it was like a chapter ending in my own life.

For a while, I learned of each passing with a sense of loss. But in time, that was replaced with a sense of gratitude. At least I had a chance to get reacquainted with the crew and when they died, to send a note of sympathy to the relatives. Before this project, I missed many opportunities. For example, my oldest daughter lived near Richard Hennessy but we never knew it until after he passed away. Captain Harrison was mayor of Coronado while we lived in San Diego, but he died before I found out about him.

I spent many years trying to forget about the events and people who were so much a part of my youth, but I have come to appreciate how much they contributed to making me the person I am. In retrospect, I believe it's better to remember, even if it does mean facing pain and sadness. I can only say how grateful I am for all those who came to be part of the reunions, from the first to the last. They have helped me realize that my life is complete and whole. In spite of its pain and sorrows, or maybe because of them, it has been a good life, one that I am glad to have lived.

Twenty-nine officers and men attended the first *Rowan* reunion in Williamsburg on September 9-13, 1985. Eighteen of them were survivors. Some have been at every reunion since then. Others came only once. We've lost a few along the way, and found others. Each and every one of them contributed to this story - my story, their story, history.

Lorraine's Post Script

On August 12, 1999, Dad turned 81. Shortly after midnight on the morning of August 13, he quietly passed away. Mom was at his side when he breathed his last.

My father never thought of his life as remarkable. I don't think I did, either, until I took the time to record his story. As a result of my efforts, I have come to appreciate him for his courage, honesty, dedication and commitment.

By way of follow up, here's a little about some of the survivors and former crew:

Bob Abbott Both of his ears were ruptured when the ship was sunk, but with the help of hearing aids, was able live a full, rich life. He worked on an almond ranch, where he was head of maintenance.

Tony Barrale Before he left the Navy, he became a chief. He sold insurance after the war.

Malcolm Clay Always a cowboy at heart, when he left the Navy, he put an oar over his shoulder and went inland until people started asking him what that thing was. He put down roots in Meade, Kansas, where he became a rancher.

Norm Crowder stayed in the Navy and retired as a Lieutenant Commander.

Bud Desch went back to Pennsylvania after the war. Because of poor health, he was never able to go to any of the reunions, but he and Dad spent some time together.

Roy Danielsen He was the son of a merchant marine, but got out of the Navy after the War and returned to California.

Wayne Easterling After the sinking, he went into a state of deep depression. When he finally hit about a low as he could go, the Light of God got through to him. He realized that he had lived for a reason. He dedicated the rest of his live to the One who had saved him on September 11, 1943. He became a minister.

Robert S. Ford stayed in the Navy and retired as Rear Admiral. He moved to California, where he remained until his death.

Jim Gagnon got a degree in Hospital Management. He worked for the Veterans Administration for many years. He attended the DESRON 8 reunion in Bloomington, Indiana in 1984, but died before the first Rowan reunion.

Walter "Gus" Garrigus stayed in the Navy. Although he was recommended for a medal for his actions that saved the lives of seventy men, he was never officially recognized for his service. In spite of this oversight by the Navy and Congress, Garrigus remains a hero in the eyes of his shipmates.

Bill Hagen finally married Trudy. After leaving the Navy, he moved to Chicago where he worked for the Northwestern Railroad and later worked for the Teamsters as a local truck driver in Chicago. After retiring, he and Trudy moved to Florida.

Ernie "Chris" Harvey During his convalescence in Philadelphia, he met and married his nurse. When he returned to Georgia, he attended Emroy Law School. Since he had been blinded, Vivian read his law books to him, and he memorized them. When he graduated, Emroy offered a degree to Vivian, as well, but she refused. "One lawyer in the family is enough!" she stated. Chris remained in practice in Decatur for more than 40 years.

Richard Hennessy worked for the Evanston, Illinois, Fire Department where he was loved and respected for his dedication and generosity of spirit. He died in 1968.

Fred Hirschhorn returned to Connecticut after the war and became an investment banker.

Gerry Hunter returned to his native Pennsylvania after the war. He was at the DESRON 8 reunion in 1984, and went to many reunions after that.

Bob Icenogle had a silk screening business in the Chicago area. He was a great supporter of the reunions.

John Jilcott once served as mayor of a town in Colorado. He moved to Wyoming, but when his health declined, he moved back to Colorado. Because of poor health, he was never able to attend a reunion.

Steve Kess never even told his wife about his experiences aboard the *Rowan*. Fortunately, he kept his diary that served as a basis for much of what appears in this book.

Shifty Lanou was promoted to ensign right before the *Rowan* went down. Later he went to another destroyer and served in the Pacific theater. He died of a heart attack in 1946.

William Laughlin was in the construction business after the war. He died shortly after the 1988 reunion.

Harold McCardie became a printer in Kansas City. Later, he moved to Colorado. He was a great supporter of the reunions.

John Merker went to Illinois and became an engineer after the war.

Allen Neal worked in construction in California after the war. He returned to his native Kentucky and became a farmer and later, a professional auctioneer. Before his health failed, he went to every reunion and brought his wife, children and grandchildren with him.

Rudy Paez was never found, but at a reunion of the next generation *Rowan* (DD 782), someone said that Paez had come aboard to work on the new ship's radar system.

Howard Rea originally from New Jersey, was an attorney in the Denver area. He died before the first reunion.

Jim Riley was a railroad engineer in Wisconsin.

LeRoy Tefft died before the first reunion.

Richard Uliano retired from the Navy shortly after the war. He died at the age of 92.

John Wyatt stayed in the Navy. When he retired, he returned to North Carolina where he founded a Naval Reserve unit.

Of the former crew who contributed to the book,

Bob Alderman a Plank Owner, was in the Black Gang aboard the *Rowan*. After he got out of the Navy, he moved to Norfolk

Jack Burgess Water Tender. He was transferred off the *Rowan* in February 1943, and went to the *Burns* (DD 588). He stayed in the Navy and retired as a chief.

George Curry Seaman 1c when he left the *Rowan*, he spent time in the Shore Patrol. When he got out of the Navy, he went to Columbus, Ohio and served as police officer for thirty years.

Jack Goodpaster Torpedoeman, owned a bar in Aurora, Indiana. After the first reunion, he wanted to find his old buddy, Allen Neal. He had heard about an auctioneer by that name and on the chance that it might be the same one, went to Kentucky to see if he could find him. He stood in the back and watched, until he was convinced he had the right man. He went up to Neal, and said, "Do you know me?" It took Neal a few seconds to figure it out, but their reunion was joyful and tearful. Jack died on August 20th, a week after Dad died.

Beverly R. Harrison retired as admiral. He became mayor of Coronado, California. He died in 1968.

Clifford Haynes Signalman, later Quartermaster, stayed in the Navy and served aboard submarines for more than 20 years.

Albert Hornby a Plank Owner, was a radioman aboard the *Rowan*. After the War, he moved to California.

Newt Marler Torpedoeman, originally from Alabama, stayed in the Navy and later became an officer. He was aboard a destroyer that was sunk during the invasion of Normandy. He retired in New Orleans.

Helen J. Seeley was a career Navy wife until 1968, whe Dad retired from active duty. She and my father were married for 56 years when Dad died in August 1999. But her story is the topic for a new book!

Al Smith Radioman, originally from Montana, after the War, he went to work in the aerospace industry in California.

Hugh O. Smith Plank Owner, his son, Robert, found me via the internet. The senior Smith said reading the book helped him find out what happened to his former shipmates and gave him a lot of peace.

Ted Smith Radioman, stayed in the Navy and became a Warrant Officer.

Bill Ward Radioman, worked with the railroad after the war. He and his wife attended nearly all the reunions until Eileen, his wife of many years, died.

The families of Lewis Ferguson, John Fietz, Tony George, Floyd Worthington, John Johnides, Willis Doyle Kelley, Jim Gagnon, and Joseph La Borde contributed photos and anecdotes. It is my fervent hope that I have paid to each of those men the honor they so richly deserve.

INDEX

E

EASTERLING, Wayne H., S2c, v, 203, 204, 211, 217, 241
ECKSTEIN, John R.*, S1c, v, 197
EGAN, James I., SoM3c, v, 218
ELLIS, Homer H. Jr., TM3c, ii
ENGLEHUTT, Walter L., MM2c, ii
ERICSSON, Warren C., S1c, ii
ERNST, Raymond, CMM(AA), ii
ESTABROOK, Albert E., CPhM(PA), ii, 103, 121

F

FAHNESTALK, Harvey C., 2c, ii
Fairfield City (Freighter), 136
Fedala, North Africa, 154, 155
FERGUSON
    Azra H., CMM, ii, 97
    Lewis H., EM3, ii, 244
FIETZ, John E., LT(jg), ii, 195, 244
Fifth Army, 199
FIGHTMASTER, William H., S1c, ii, 218
FLYNN
    Nancy, 175
    Sheila, 175, 222
FORD, Edith, 235
FORD, Robert S., LCDR, v, 3, 52, 149, 150, 156, 162, 166, 168, 169, 183, 192, 196, 204, 206, 207, 208, 211, 215, 218, 235, 236, 241
FOX, William H., FC(M)1c, ii, 204
FRENCH, Clayton F., S1c, ii
FRETWELL, Billy C., TM1c, ii
FURLOW, Talmage R., EM2c, ii

G

GAGNON, James S., SoM2c, v, 2, 203, 204, 241, 244
galley, 31, 33, 34, 35, 36, 42, 43, 44, 45, 49, 50, 51, 52, 59, 60, 70, 73, 75, 76, 77, 80, 84, 86, 89, 96, 100, 111, 113, 114, 121, 135, 140, 141, 152, 160, 171, 189, 190, 197, 198, 200, 201, 206, 220, 223, 230
GARRIGUS, Walter F., TM2c, v, 206, 207, 241
Gela, 182
GELINA, Jose, St1c, ii
GEORGE, Tony G., F1c, ii, 195, 239, 244
Germans, 3, 4, 55, 70, 76, 79, 91, 92, 95, 97, 109, 115, 116, 117, 120, 122, 130, 131, 134, 135, 136, 137, 140, 143, 144, 153, 154, 156, 181, 182, 186, 188, 189, 191, 192, 193, 197, 198, 200, 201, 236
GIALOMBARDO, John, S2c, ii
Gibraltar, 9, 153, 172, 180
GLENN, Everett M., LT, v, 142, 143, 144, 146, 215, 218, 219
GOLDMAN, John L., EM2c, ii, 97, 139
GOODPASTER, John T. "Jack", 119, 142, 144, 145, 195, 243

GRAY, Festus P., S1c, v
GREEN, John J., LT(jg), ii
GRONEK, Alexander F., Cox, ii
GRUEHL, George R., SoM2c, ii
GRUEL, Clifford L., WT2c, ii
Grumman, 55, 61
GUESS, Delbert E., MoMM2c, ii
GUNNOE, Willie, S2c, ii
GUTHRIE, Harry O., S2c, iii

H

H.M.S. *Athlone Castle* (British Transport), 227
H.M.S. *Dutchess (British Destroyer)*, 104
H.M.S. *Fury* (British Destroyer), 130
H.M.S. *Kent* (British Destroyer), 104
H.M.S. *Keppel* (British Destroyer), 130
H.M.S. *Leamington* (British Destroyer), 130
H.M.S. *Ledbury* (British Destroyer), 130
H.M.S. *London* (British Cruiser), 130
H.M.S. *Norfolk* (British Cruiser), 130
H.M.S. *Offa* (British Destroyer), 130
H.M.S. *Wilton* (British Destroyer), 130
HAGEN, William H., S1c, v, 2, 179, 242
HAGGERTY, Edward J., Y2c, v
HAINES, Martin L., ENS, v
HAMER, John C., S1c, iii
HANNA, Frederick K. Jr., F2c, iii
HARDEE, Wilber J., S2c, iii
HARKEY, Robert J., S2c, iii
HARRELL, Eugene, F2c, iii
HARRISON, Beverley R., LCDR, 27, 40, 71, 75, 83, 86, 88, 92, 93, 94, 115, 116, 117, 118, 119, 120, 122, 132, 134, 142, 143, 144, 145, 146, 149, 150, 166, 169, 240, 243
HARRISON, Hosla C. Jr., S1c, iii
HARRISON, Jack H., 111
HARTER, James W., MM2c, iii
Hartlebury (British Merchantman), 136
HARVEY, Ernest C. Jr., SM2c, v, vi, vii, viii, 3, 5, 74, 75, 81, 82, 83, 89, 102, 111, 112, 114, 116, 117, 118, 122, 123, 124, 126, 128, 140, 142, 143, 150, 156, 161, 174, 177, 180, 181, 183, 184, 185, 187, 188, 198, 201, 203, 204, 206, 208, 209, 215, 216, 217, 221, 233, 238, 242
HATCHELL, Clarence, SC2c, 33, 34, 43, 44, 80
Hawaii, 49, 50, 51, 52, 53, 54, 63, 65, 70, 94, 95, 100, 234
HAYNES, Clifford, SM3c, 243
HEDGES, Marion F., MM2c, iii
HEFFERNAN, J.B., CAPT., USN, 153
HEGLIN, "Muscles", 117
Heinkel, 132, 133, 134
HENNESSY, Richard J., S1c, v, 204, 214, 217, 240, 242
HENRY, Ned, S1c, v
HILL, Robert B., S1c, v, 46, 203, 204, 205, 214, 218

Photo Notes

Figure-Credit (Contributed by….)
Cover--Crew of the USS Rowan, September 1941. US Navy Photo (L.E. Seeley) Cover design by John Conforti, MagicImage Productions, Inc.

● Francis Kirwin "Bob" Seeley (L. E. Seeley)

● L. E. Seeley (L.E. Seeley)

● Fred Quinn (Fred Quinn)

● USS *Rowan* US Navy Photo (L.E. Seeley).

● Lt. Cmdr. Beverly R. Harrison (Pam McGeachy)

● USS *Rowan* US Navy photo (L.E. Seeley)

● John Johnides (George Johnides)

● Goon Alderman, Ernie Karbowski & Steve Kess (Steve Kess)

● Roy Danielsen in Hawaii (Roy Danielsen)

● Lt. John Wyatt (Gretchen Wyatt)

● Violet Seeley (L.E. Seeley)

● Seeley family (L.E. Seeley)

● James R. Lankford and Robert F. Abbott (Bob Abbott)

● Ernie Harvey (E. C. Harvey)

● Bury, Bxybe, Hagen, and friend (Bill Hagen)

● William Mihans (William Mihans)

● "Davey Jones" (Ted Smith)

● USS *Rowan* US Navy Photo (L.E. Seeley)

● B.H. "Bud" Desch (Bud Desch)

● Willis Doyle Kelley (Orville and Arlene Kelley)

● USS *Rowan* U.S. Navy photo (L.E. Seeley)

● "Muscles" Heglin and Gerry Hunter (Hunter)

● Ted Smith (Ted Smith)

● Jack Goodpaster (Jack Goodpaster)

- Helen J. Quinn (L.E. Seeley)

- Quinn Clan- (L.E. Seeley)

- Heinkel A.P. photo (L.E. Seeley) Note: We could not find the organization that took the photo. Survivors weren't sure whom the photographer represented. We contacted UPI and AP and neither claimed it. The newspapers that ran the photo couldn't help us, either. We regret that, in spite of our best efforts, we are unable to properly credit this photo.

- Robert S. Ford (Robert S. Ford)

- Eileen and Bill Ward (W.R. Ward)

- The Bride (L.E. Seeley)

- Harvey, Helen & Lew Seeley (L. E. Seeley)

- The Newlyweds (L.E. Seeley)

- Floyd Worthington (Lyman Worthington)

- Tony Barrale (Anthony Barrale)

- Lt. John Fietz (Robert Fietz)

- Norman Crowder (Norm Crowder)

- Easterling, Hennessy, Harvey - Press Association (E. C. Harvey) Note: We could not find the organization that took the photo. Survivors weren't sure whom the photographer represented. We contacted UPI and AP and neither claimed it. The newspapers that ran the photo couldn't help us, either. We regret that, in spite of our best efforts, we are unable to properly credit this photo.

- *Rowan*'s Crew US Navy Photo. (L.E. Seeley)

- Shipmates Reunion (L.E. Seeley)

Resources

Donahue, Joseph A., <u>Tin Cans and Other Ships</u>. North Quincy,
MA: The Christopher Publishing House, 1979.

Roscoe, Theodore. <u>United States Destroyer Operations in
World War II.</u> Annapolis, MD: Naval Institute Press,
Tenth printing, 1988.

Roscoe, Theodore. <u>United States Destroyer Operations in
World War II.</u> Annapolis, MD: The United States Naval
Institute, 1953.

Morison, Samuel Eliot, <u>United States Navy in World War II,
Vol. IX</u>, Annapolis, MD: The United States Naval
Institute, 1956.

Action Diary of the USS *Rowan*.

Diary of Francis Kirwin Seeley.

Diary of Stephen F. Kess.

Interviews with survivors, former crew, and family members.

Intuition and dreams